Bigotry, Football and Scotland

Edited by John Flint and John Kelly

EDINBURGH
University Press

© editorial matter and organisation John Flint and John Kelly, 2013
© in the individual contributions is retained by the authors

Edinburgh University Press Ltd
22 George Square, Edinburgh EH8 9LF
www.euppublishing.com

Typeset in 10/12pt Goudy Old Style by,
Servis Filmsetting Ltd, Stockport, Cheshire, and
printed and bound in Great Britain by
CPI Group (UK) Ltd, Croydon CR0 4YY

A CIP record for this book is available from the British Library

ISBN 978 0 7486 7036 9 (hardback)
ISBN 978 0 7486 7037 6 (paperback)
ISBN 978 0 7486 7038 3 (webready PDF)
ISBN 978 0 7486 7039 0 (epub)

The right of the contributors to be identified as authors of this work has been
asserted in accordance with the Copyright, Designs and Patents Act 1988.

Contents

Neglected Perspectives: Class, Gender and Football Supporters

Conclusions

Acknowledgements

John Flint and John Kelly would like to thank John Watson at Edinburgh University Press for his enthusiastic support for the idea of this book and for all his assistance. We are also most grateful to Jenny Daly, Lisa Parr, Rebecca Mackenzie and Eddie Clark at Edinburgh University Press. We wish to thank Lord Jack McConnell of Glenscorrodale for his foreword and Kelly-Anne Thomas for her help in arranging this. We are grateful to Ian Brooke for his copy-editing and Zeb Korycinska for compiling the index. The book has undoubtedly been improved through the insightful expertise of the reviewers who commented on the proposal and the manuscript and we very much appreciated our academic colleagues who were willing to act as readers and referees.

Alasdair McKillop would like to thank Tom Gallagher, John D. C. Gow, Bill Murray and Graham Walker for reading and commenting on an earlier draft of his chapter and to express his gratitude to Dave Scott for discussing various issues.

Some of the material in one section of Chapter 3 was originally published in an article entitled 'Hibernian Football Club: The forgotten Irish?' in *Sport in Society*, 10: 3, 514–36. A longer version of Chapter 4 appeared in *Irish Historical Studies* in 2006, XXXV: 138, 200–19. We are grateful to the publishers for granting copyright permission to reproduce this material.

Contributors

Joseph M. Bradley is Senior Lecturer in the School of Sport at the University of Stirling. http://www.sports.stir.ac.uk/staff/Joe_Bradley.php

Joe Crawford is a researcher and teacher in the School of Applied Social Science at the University of Stirling.

Andrew Davies is Senior Lecturer in the Department of History at the University of Liverpool. http://www.liv.ac.uk/history/. He is the author of *City of Gangs: Glasgow and the Rise of the British Gangster*, to be published in June 2013.

Paul Davis is Lecturer in the Department of Sport and Exercise Sciences at the University of Sunderland.

John Flint is Professor of Town and Regional Planning in the Department of Town and Regional Planning at the University of Sheffield. http://www.sheffield.ac.uk/trp/staff/johnflint

Kay Goodall is Senior Lecturer in Law in the Stirling Law School at the University of Stirling. http://www.law.stir.ac.uk/staff/KayGoodall.php

Niall Hamilton-Smith is Lecturer in Criminology in the School of Applied Social Science at the University of Stirling. http://www.dass.stir.ac.uk/staff/Dr-Niall-HamiltonSmith/92

John Kelly is Lecturer in Sport and Recreation Business Management in the Institute for Sport, Physical Education and Health Sciences at the University of Edinburgh. http://www.ed.ac.uk/schools-departments/education/about-us/people/academic-staff?person_id=224&cw_xml=profile.php

David McArdle is Senior Lecturer in Law in the Stirling Law School at the University of Stirling. http://www.law.stir.ac.uk/staff/D.McArdle.php

Lord Jack McConnell of Glenscorrodale was First Minister of Scotland from 2001 to 2007. One of his government's priorities was addressing sectarianism in Scottish society, hosting a series of summits and launching a number of action plans and initiatives. He was made a life peer in 2010.

Alasdair McKillop is the co-founder of, and a writer for, The Rangers Standard website. http://www.therangersstandard.co.uk/index.php/about-us/our-writers

Patrick McVey is a retired IT manager of a UK Government department and a regular contributor to online Celtic blogs and forums.

Margaret Malloch is Senior Research Fellow in the Scottish Centre for Crime and Justice Research (http://www.sccjr.ac.uk/) at the University of Stirling. http://www.dass.stir.ac.uk/staff/Margaret-Malloch/41

Ryan Powell is Principal Research Fellow in the Centre for Regional Economic and Social Research at Sheffield Hallam University. http://www.shu.ac.uk/research/cresr/sp_ryan_powell.html

Irene A. Reid is Lecturer in the School of Sport at the University of Stirling. http://www.sports.stir.ac.uk/staff/irene-reid.php

Michael Rosie is Co-Director of the Institute of Governance at the University of Edinburgh. http://www.sps.ed.ac.uk/staff/sociology/rosie_michael

Stuart Waiton is Lecturer in Sociology and Criminology in the Department of Social and Health Sciences at the University of Abertay, Dundee. He is the founder of Take A Liberty (Scotland). https://portal.abertay.ac.uk/portal/page/portal/SHARED/s/S513892

Foreword

I can still remember the first time I was asked – in my first week at University – what school I had attended. It was only later that I discovered the significance of the question and started to encounter the Catholic–Protestant divide that was all too common in Scotland back then. Growing up in a small, rural community on the Isle of Arran, I was aware of differences but had never encountered the depth of hostility that had built up elsewhere over decades. It shocked me, and it was more than just football rivalry, more than just schools and more than just the West of Scotland.

Twenty-five years later, as First Minister, I had the opportunity to do something about it. For years Scotland's 'secret shame' had been swept under the carpet, but I felt our new Parliament could be a focal point for national leadership and change. Although most obvious at certain football matches, religious bigotry continued to exist in the home, at school and even sometimes in the workplace. But I believe that we showed the power of bringing together churches and faiths, football teams, education leaders, marching organisations, workplace and business representatives. We did drive deep change into organisations and set a positive example for future generations. I have no doubt that our summits and, in particular, the action plans that were agreed and then monitored, made a difference.

Ending bigotry requires consistent leadership and unity behind a balanced approach. But it is also important to study the history and existence of sectarianism to fully understand the causes and to deliver sustainable solutions. This collection of work helps inform this debate and keep these issues alive. It is a very welcome contribution to our national understanding and I congratulate all those involved.

If we learn the lessons of our past and we act with determination to change our future we can consign to the dustbin our history of religious hatred and sectarianism.

Lord Jack McConnell of Glenscorrodale
February 2013

Introduction

1 Football and Bigotry in Scotland

John Flint and John Kelly

Bigotry, *Football and Scotland* seeks to improve our understanding of Scottish football's relationship with what is commonly referred to as 'sectarianism'. It does this against the backdrop of the extraordinary events of recent football seasons in Scotland which have contributed to the passing of the Offensive Behaviour at Football and Threatening Communications (Scotland) Act 2012 on 14 December 2011. Although the Scottish Government had held two previous summits on sectarianism (in 2005 and 2006), the major catalyst for the implementation of the Offensive Behaviour Bill was the so-called 'shame game' between Celtic and Rangers, the two football clubs considered to be the major sectarian protagonists. This match, played on 2 March 2011, resulted in thirty-four fans being arrested inside the stadium, three Celtic players booked, seven Rangers players booked, three Rangers players sent off, managers Ally McCoist and Neil Lennon squaring up to one another at the final whistle and widespread public condemnation from politicians, journalists and football officials.

These events were far from isolated in a season that also witnessed a multitude of incidents considered by some to have sectarian undertones. These included a referee being exposed as having lied about a major decision made against Celtic, the assistant referee from the same match resigning and alleging internal Scottish Football Association (SFA) pressure to cover up the events, a subsequent referee strike, the SFA chief of referees resigning in the wake of emailing a joke about the Pope and child abuse, and perhaps most disturbingly a number of Celtic associates[1] (the manager, players, a lawyer and an MSP fan) being posted bullets and homemade devices meant to cause harm. Celtic manager Neil Lennon was physically attacked by a Hearts fan during a Hearts v. Celtic match, Rangers were found guilty of 'discriminatory chanting' and Celtic of 'illicit chanting'[2] by UEFA. Additionally, in 2012 Rangers entered administration and had its assets sold to a new company which then registered with the SFA, subsequently entering the Third Division as the old club was liquidated. While these latter events would seem to owe little to sectarianism, they too have become embroiled in it, with Rangers' chief executive Charles Green alleging that bigotry played a part in the decision to ensure Rangers' new club entered Division Three rather than the Scottish Premier League or Division One (see BBC 2012).

COMPETING DEFINITIONS

Producing a single collection on Scottish football and bigotry is, therefore, a much-needed but perilous endeavour. This is largely because few groups agree on the definition of the popular yet polysemous term sectarian/ism. What exactly does it mean, how is it evidenced or experienced and how may it be eradicated (if it is even deemed a problem needing to be eradicated)? The fallout from the circular debates created by such ambiguity is what motivates academics like ourselves to continue discussing it.

We believe there are two general positions that pervade debates about sectarianism in Scotland. There are those who deny there is any significant problem, viewing sectarianism as no longer existing in any meaningful way beyond football-related banter, while others argue sectarianism continues to blight Scottish life. This latter position consists of competing definitions, with two meanings of sectarianism being conflated to give misleading and confusing accounts. For instance, having an identity based on ethnic and religious elements is to have a sectarian identity. This type of non-bigoted sectarian identity is largely accepted in the UK for those descendants of Asian and Middle East groups. For example, to be a British Pakistani or British Jew is to have a sectarian identity but it need not – and usually does not – involve being bigoted or intolerant towards non-group members. These identities refer to groups of people who define themselves or are defined by others in part through their religion and ethnic origins. They encapsulate dual or even multiple identities. However, the second definition of sectarianism, which is often confusingly used interchangeably with the first, means exhibiting prejudice or bigotry towards others as a result of one's perception of the other's (real or imagined) religion and ethnicity (where the ethnicity has religious connotations).

In Scotland the discursive formation of sectarianism is used to indiscriminately describe anti-Catholic/Protestant prejudice *and* legitimate religious and ethnic identifiers, thus contributing to a crippling ambiguity around ethnic and religious bigotry in Scotland (Kelly 2011). This is why as editors we intentionally avoid using the word 'sectarian' in our book title, preferring bigotry instead. This demonstrates an interpretive assumption about sectarianism on our part – that the actual problem is not one of Irish/Ulster identification or expression but rather one of religious bigotry and ethnic intolerance (racism). Of course, this ethno-religious bigotry often emerges from prejudices against these respective sectarian identities. As readers will see, individual contributors use a variety of words ranging from 'bigotry' to 'religious prejudice' and 'offensive'. While these are appropriate words in particular contexts, we would urge readers to be aware of the contrasting conceptual phrases some contributors use and to ensure when reading that they maintain conceptual clarity about exactly what elements of sectarianism (if any) each author is particularly discussing.

For many in Scotland, overtly expressing Irish-Catholic or Ulster-British identities or having visible republican or loyalist sympathies are sufficient to be branded bigoted due to popular perceptions of 'sectarian'. The discursive formation adopted by influential sections of Scotland's media and political classes frames these identities as part of a cancerous tumour needing to be cured. Yet, such negative branding and pejorative criticism of group identities *per se* is itself dangerously close to being latently intolerant,[3] characterised as it is by an over-determined conception of national cohesion that demands homogeneous assimilation at the expense of inclusive integration, multiculturalism and difference.

Like racism and sexism, ethno-religious bigotry is grounded in relations of power and these hierarchies of power need to be acknowledged if sectarian relationships are to be understood, never mind 'fixed'. What is often missing in sectarian discourse is an analysis of ethnic *relations* rather than simply religious difference. Recognising these dangers, Finn (1990: 5–6) argues that, when used in Scotland, sectarianism 'avoids any identification of causality, neglects any analysis of social and political power within Scotland and implies equal culpability for prejudice between majority and minority communities'.

One would not analyse race relations in Britain by ignoring the history of colonialism and its residual legacy, yet this type of *retreat to the present*[4] occurs when analysing ethno-religious bigotry in Scotland. As Bradley (2006: 25) outlines:

> Having knowledge of Ireland's conquest, exploitation and domination by Britain is crucial to understanding the position of the Irish and their offspring within British society, particularly in Scotland ... Almost all the relevant political, popular and academic literature, including from the Scottish media industry and the developing anti-sectarian industry, do not acknowledge this colonisation in any relevant commentary.

Such contradictions, paradoxes and expressions are far from unique to Scotland, or Scottish sport (see Bradbury 2011; Madan 2000). Fletcher (2012: 623–4) demonstrates how sports fandom often consists of performative elements of cultural and political resistance. He shows that in cricket, sections of British Asian communities openly reject 'notions of "Englishness" (embodied through the England team) because of historical antagonisms', preferring to support their nation of descent:

> [I]t is within the context of resistance that British Asians are able to articulate an 'oppositional postcolonial sensibility', whereby the primary function of disavowing their association with the England team is to emphasise (where relevant) their sense of alienation from, and dissatisfaction with, certain aspects of British society.

A long-term historical sensitivity and international perspective are central to enabling even partial understanding of bigotry, football and Scotland, but so too is contextual sensitivity to more recent historical events. In Scotland sectarianism is often anchored in public and media discourse as a non-hierarchical dualism constituting *Protestant Rangers and Catholic Celtic* ('the bigot brothers'), thus stripping it of its central power dynamics. Equal culpability might be justified but the facts must be presented in their proper context for this to be authentically judged. For most of the twentieth century Rangers refused to knowingly sign Catholic players, only ceasing such practices in 1989[5] having never admitted it nor apologised for it. Celtic never operated an equivalent anti-Protestant policy. These contextual facts are vital, not in any attempt to unfairly single out Rangers or shame them into an embarrassing admission about an old regime. They are simply essential for any genuine attempt to understand the current relations for two related reasons.

First, there are some Rangers fans who question sectarianism's relevance in the modern day: '*That was years ago . . . what relevance has this now?*' Second, in relation to this growing abdication of (partial) culpability, some have questioned why historically few Scottish Catholics support Rangers or would wish to play for them when significantly more Protestants have felt able to be involved with Celtic at club and fan level.[6] Without historical context this could be interpreted as Catholics having a ghetto mentality that is absent among Protestants, particularly if the necessary context of Rangers' previous anti-Catholicism is overlooked. These important questions can only be answered with any degree of trustworthiness if we fully disclose the full contexts. For instance, it seems understandable if Catholics have had little empathy with or appetite for supporting Rangers given these contexts. It is reasonable to assume that most fans of both clubs are over the age of twenty-four and will therefore have lived during the period when Rangers refused to sign Catholics. Cultural shifts take time and it is plausible to connect this previous practice with continuing Catholic suspicion around Rangers in current times, not least given that anti-Catholicism remains part of Rangers fan culture.[7] That a high percentage of Catholics in the central belt prefer Celtic to Rangers is understandable given these and other contexts.

There is an undeniable and continual fascination with sectarianism beyond the offices of salivating newspaper editors, image-conscious football executives and specialist academics. A note of caution is required at this juncture. The academic world's enduring fascination with sectarianism is sometimes pejoratively viewed as the crusading campaigning of ignorant ivory towers dwellers detached from the 'real' world. Such inverse patronising misses two important points. First, academics are real people who live, work, socialise and, dare we admit, support football clubs in the same Scotland as 'real' people. If racism becomes a normal pathology in racist societies from which few escape its reach (Allport 1979), sectarianism's alleged effects are unlikely to escape academics any more than anyone else. Second, sectarianism debates are often matters of interpretation, related to particular historical, political and religious contexts. The nuances of such debates are seldom subject to universal laws such as those observed in the science laboratory. Social life does not permit such neat and objective facts to be observed, recorded and explained. Therefore, the latent philosophical (ontological and epistemological) positions adopted and promoted by many commentators justifies, nay demands, academic attention from social scientists.

As academics in this field we feel obligated to analyse bigotry and football given that they continue to permeate political, popular, media and academic discourse in Scotland, eliciting widespread disagreement about the meanings, causes, reach and effects of their relationship. What are the popular and officially endorsed ontological assumptions about sectarianism and how do these contrast with minority and unofficial assumptions? Does sectarian behaviour extend beyond religious bigotry to include ethnic and political allegiances and rivalries? For instance, is it sectarian to identify with Ireland or Ulster, to sing Irish rebel songs or Ulster loyalist songs and to fly the Irish Tricolour or Red Hand of Ulster? Even if these acts are sectarian, are they necessarily bigoted or are they mere expressions of culture that others may not understand or like? Is the expression of loyalism or republicanism constitutive of sectarianism or must it include explicit reference to religion? Is it sectarian to oppose one's football club placing the Earl Haig Poppy on the club shirt or is this a political issue? Even if one could define sectarianism to everyone's satisfaction, *how* does it manifest, how is it witnessed and experienced?

That is, what are our epistemological assumptions? For example, now that there are no apparent structural or institutional factors contributing to sectarianism (such as employment discrimination or religious inequality within higher education), does this mean that it has disappeared? Has an increasingly secular and inter-married Scotland decimated ethno-religious bigotry? Or is it now something more likely to be witnessed and expressed attitudinally and/or in discursive terms in more subtle ways than outright employment practices, inter-marriage statistics or church attendance might suggest? What will the police and courts deem to be religiously aggravated and is this the same as the now illegal act of being 'offensive'?

GOVERNING SECTARIANISM

'It is the tactics of government which make possible the continual definition and redefinition of what is within the competence of the state and what is not' (Foucault 1991: 103). Since 1999, there has been an intensive and sustained focus on governing sectarianism, epitomised by the Scottish Executive's (2006a) Action Plan on Sectarianism. This makes an explicit connection between Scottish football and sectarianism, arguing that 'Tackling sectarianism in football is central to creating [a] truly multi-cultural and multi-faith Scotland . . . based on mutual respect . . . and it is time to eradicate [sectarianism] from Scottish football' (Scottish Executive 2006b: 2).

Four key features of this governance may be identified. Firstly, there has been an attempt to enhance the evidence base. This has included reviews of existing evidence (Nicolson 2002; McAspurren 2005), studies by central and local government and civic organisations, including research on sectarianism in Glasgow (NFO 2003), the Orr Review of Marches and Parades (2005), the Nil By Mouth-sponsored examination of sectarianism online (O'Loan et al. 2005), the STUC and Scottish Government investigation of sectarianism in the workplace (Finn et al. 2008) and the recent study of Football Banning Orders (see Chapter 9). There have also been attempts to redefine Census categories on Christian religious denominations, to audit the scale and cost of parades and to establish the number and nature of religiously aggravated offences in Scotland.

Secondly, legislation has been deployed, including the introduction of religiously aggravated offences, Football Banning Orders, local government licensing enforcement (of public houses and street traders related to sectarian conduct and paramilitary paraphernalia) and fixed-penalty notices, culminating in the Offensive Behaviour at Football and Threatening Communications (Scotland) Act. A third feature of the contemporary governance of sectarianism has been a project of reducing the visibility of 'sectarian' conflict and realigning the spatial dimensions of sectarian behaviour, including the programme of shared campuses and school twinning schemes (Flint 2012) and initiatives by local authorities to reduce the presence of religious (primarily Loyal Order) parades. A fourth feature has been the use of surrogate regulators in which a range of institutions become embedded in the governance of sectarianism. The mechanisms for regulating conduct comprise educational campaigns delivered by central government ('Sectarianism: Don't Give it, Don't Take It' for schools, the One Scotland Anti-Sectarianism Award), cultural projects like the play *Singing I'm No A Billy He's A Tim*, and campaigns by charities such as Nil By Mouth and Football for All (the Kick Out Bigotry project), local authorities and football clubs (Sense Over Sectarianism), and the National Union of Students Scotland's 'Stamp Out Sectarianism'.

Football organisations have been central to these developments. The SFA's national licensing scheme requires professional clubs to develop anti-sectarianism policies, and individual clubs and supporters have introduced their own initiatives seeking to codify acceptable and unacceptable behaviour (Bhoys Against Bigotry, Follow With Pride, Pride Over Prejudice, Old Firm Alliance, True Hearts Against Bigotry). Beyond Scotland, UEFA has imposed sanctions on both Celtic and Rangers for the allegedly unacceptable conduct of their supporters relating to chants and banners. It is within these governing frameworks that current debates about bigotry and Scottish football occur.

SELF-REFLECTION, 'OBJECTIVITY' AND BALANCE

The government and governing bodies have thus become powerful arbiters of what is acceptable and unacceptable. Yet caution is required. Walker (2007: 90) raises an important point regarding cultural reflexivity, namely the hypocrisy of accepting one's own right to an identity/dual identity while rejecting the right of one's rival to theirs. He highlights the irony of those in Scotland who feel Irish but fail to recognise the rights of those in (Northern) Ireland who feel British.[8] This is indicative of a curious trait engulfing ethno-religious identities in Scotland. Some Rangers fans will sing loyalist songs, attend 'Sash Bashes' and celebrate their Ulster loyalist connections and some Celtic fans will sing republican songs, attend 'Rebel Nights' and celebrate their Irish connections, while both groups will deride the other for being 'sectarian' oblivious to any irony. But everyone – not just these rivals – must reflect on their position, identity, judgements and ethnocentric framing of 'good' and 'bad' identities and 'good' and 'bad' politics in sport.

Cultural reflexivity and academic sensitivity are therefore important for understanding fan behaviours and values, and this requires an understanding of the acts, symbols, songs and remembrance of all groups as well as one's own group, that is, to practise what sociologists sometimes call sympathetic introspection.

Table 1.1 Rangers and Celtic fans' contrasting views on songs

Songs Rangers fans sing	Rangers fans' views on songs	Celtic fans' views on songs
Famine Song	Mocking inauthentic 'Irishness' and highlighting disloyalty to Britain by British citizens	Anti-Irish racism by asking the Irish diaspora 'Why don't you go home?'
Billy Boys	Anti-Irish rebel (based on their interpretation of the use of 'Fenian')	Anti-Catholic (based on their interpretation of the use of 'Fenian')
Songs Celtic fans sing		
Boys of the Old Brigade	Support for IRA terrorists	Easter 1916 lament
Roll of Honour	Support for Provisional IRA terrorists	Support for Hunger Strikers fighting for Ireland's freedom

In accord with our own plea to be self-reflexive, we recognise this collection will inevitably give particular insights into 'sectarianism' that others might not give. However, in Scotland there is a common yet misguided belief when discussing sectarianism that some form of objectivity and balance can and must be achieved. Three points need to be briefly noted in this respect. First, in ideologically con-structed and contested arenas (in which 'sectarianism' exists in Scotland) nobody achieves what Pilger (2007) refers to as the 'nirvana of impartiality'. Furthermore, there is sometimes suspicion of the accounts given by those identified as Irish Catholics or Ulster Protestants fearing subjective and biased accounts. In debates on racism and sexism respectively, people of colour and women seldom get accused of being biased or told that they are unable to provide trustworthy or authentic accounts, and nor should Ulster-Protestants or Irish-Catholics (or their supporters) in discussions of sectarianism. On the contrary, in studies where identity and power are central constituents, like racism and sexism – yet curiously not sectarianism – there is a school of thought that argues that having a subject position gives one more authenticity to discuss the issue.

We take neither position. The extent to which the arguments in this collection are deferentially appreciated or vociferously challenged should be determined solely on the basis of their arguments, evidence and theories, and these are to be found on the following pages. Second, when dealing with bigotry, racism or any prejudice, social scientists have a moral obligation to be value-oriented and not seek pure (and ultimately unachievable) objectivity. In the introduction to Allport's (1979: x) study of prejudice, Kenneth Clarke criticised those studying unequal and unfair power relations while seeking such scientific detachment: 'It has again become fash-ionable for some well-publicised social scientists to retreat behind the protective pose of valueless, moral relativism, and mere quantification as the inviolable requirements of social science.'

Being opposed to bigotry (being value-oriented) is compatible with producing evidence-based accounts in trustworthy and authentic ways. Moral relativism like that rejected by Clarke can be detected in those who fail to distinguish between bigoted and non-bigoted derogatory football songs and those who do not even see a point in 'ranking such songs in a hierarchy of acceptability'[9] (Bruce 2010: 116). We argue such hierarchies and the accompanying analytical clarity to determine their nature – as bigoted or non-bigoted – are essential if we are to understand the nuances of ethno-religious bigotry in Scotland, especially now the new Bill has conflated 'offensive' and religious/ethnic hatred. The third point about objectivity and balance centres on dealing with the evidence. If the evidence proves to be uneven then as critical researchers we should not seek to artificially provide 'balance' by being imbalanced with the evidence in the misguided quest to be seen to be even-handed.[10] Let the evidence speak for itself and if it is more one-sided than balanced, let us question why, not manufacture false equity. This may of course involve claiming some evidence is stronger and more generalisable and does require some interpretation, selection and omission. The key is to justify one's evidence and the theoretical explanation given to explain it in its fullest and most accurate context possible.

ABOUT THIS BOOK

There is a considerable existing literature on bigotry and sectarianism in Scottish football and society and this existing work is extensively referred to by contributors as this volume builds on the important previous work of others. However, it is now thirteen years since the last major edited general academic collection on these issues was published (Devine 2000) and the events of recent seasons and the transformations in Scottish football that have occurred since Tom Devine's book demand new and further investigation. In developing our ideas, we hope that this book will:

- Provide contemporary academic analysis of the high-profile debates and controversies about bigotry, Scottish society and football. We believe that the academy has an important contribution to make through presenting the most recent empirical research evidence accompanied by trustworthy theories and in-depth knowledge.
- Offer a diverse range of approaches and perspectives, with contributions from criminology, cultural studies, ethnic and racial studies, gender studies, history, legal studies, philosophy, sociology, sports studies and urban studies. These varying disciplines are accompanied by differing football club, religious and political allegiances among the contributors and editors.
- Demonstrate how rigorous argument and debate (and there are clear and substantive disagreements among the contributors) can be undertaken in a positive framework where different viewpoints engage with, and try to learn from, each

other. This is a deliberate effort to avoid some of the hyperbole, caricature and entrenched positions which often dominate prominent discourse about bigotry and football in Scotland.

- Enable all of those interested in these issues to challenge and reflect upon their own understanding and position and to identify new issues that have, to date, been under-researched or under-debated. These include, for example, the geographical/club-based manifestations of sectarianism, the importance of gender and social class, the impact of new communication technologies and legislation, and broader arguments about rights, responsibilities, identities and freedom of expression.
- Enhance the engagement and interactions between various stakeholders, including academics and football supporters, in order to provide some voice for perspectives often overlooked or insufficiently listened to and to identify potential avenues for future work.

The book has been structured and presented in three broad sections, although there is considerable overlap between these. The first section attempts to facilitate a new understanding of the geographical, historical and social contexts that frame debates about bigotry and football in Scottish society. The second section presents debates about how sectarianism has been constructed and governed, with a particular emphasis on recent legislation and the role of the Scottish media. The third section highlights important dimensions and perspectives that are often neglected or understated in dominant discourses, including gender, social class and the viewpoints of football supporters themselves.

In Chapter 2, Michael Rosie begins by providing an overview of the events of the 2010–11 Scottish football season which both acted as the catalyst for the new legislation and framed the debates about bigotry within Scottish football and wider society. Rosie suggests that the available empirical evidence on hate crimes and perceptions and experiences of sectarianism need to be understood in framing our understanding of the realities of bigotry in Scotland. He then argues for the importance of moving beyond a narrow prism of the Old Firm, utilising the views of supporters of other Scottish clubs articulated through the growing use of online fora. Rosie concludes that, while clubs have taken significant action, addressing bigotry has, ultimately, to be a project for Scottish football itself – supporters, clubs and governing bodies – rather than being left to the domains of law and central government.

In Chapter 3, John Kelly challenges the geographical visualisation of sectarianism as being limited to manifestations in west central Scotland. Rather, he shows that, while supporters of Heart of Midlothian and Hibernian often portray sectarianism as an Old Firm problem, elements of what have been defined as 'sectarian' identities, images and conduct do feature within the support of the two Edinburgh clubs. Kelly argues that while a dominant construction of a non-sectarian identity is promoted by the clubs themselves and many of their supporters, there are also marginalised but legitimate expressions of ethnic, religious and political identities grounded in the particular histories of Hearts and Hibs that should be acknowledged rather than denied.

In Chapter 4, Andrew Davies reminds us that history provides many precedents and parallels for what we too often regard as specifically contemporary issues. Davies argues that, although the Old Firm was not the root cause of sectarianism in Glasgow, it did act as an incendiary spark for intensifying ethnic and religious divisions, rather than being a safety valve. Davies shows, through his study of brake clubs and the John Traquair case in the 1920s and 1930s, how there was a geographical and temporal geography to disorder, linked to stadia, public houses, transport corridors and match and parades days. For Davies, ethnic and religious affiliations could replace territorial gang rivalries during a period when both the manifestations of sectarianism and their policing and legal regulation were intensified.

In Chapter 5, Joseph M. Bradley also identifies the importance of historical perspectives, interpretations, narratives and identities within Scottish football and society, particularly for the supporters of Celtic and Rangers. He argues that these identities are expressed through cultures of music and song and expressions within public spaces, including those of Scottish football. Bradley suggests that Rangers' cultural attributes are, for many supporters, made meaningful through Protestant, Scottish, British, Ulster Scots and/or Royalist allegiances; while many Celtic supporters have accessed an alternative history and memory that challenges hegemonic understandings and beliefs and that Celtic in particular has provided an arena for the expression of an Irish-Catholic and political identity which has often faced hostility in wider Scottish society. Bradley concludes that these identities need to be properly understood rather than being superficially rejected or subjected to negative stereotyping.

In Chapter 6, John Flint and Ryan Powell define the contemporary governance of sectarianism as a form of civilising offensive, in which there are complex and ambiguous relations between modern state authorities and popular cultures. They show how the idea of a modern and enlightened Scotland rejecting religious bigotry is not new and how anti-sectarianism projects are inherently linked to the understandings of the economic, as well as social and cultural, requirements of a twenty-first-century nation. Flint and Powell argue that sectarianism is not merely about football-related disorder, but rather is part of wider attempts by different groups to secure a position in the physical and imagined spaces of contemporary Scotland, including through mechanisms of remembrance and commemoration.

In Chapter 7, Stuart Waiton investigates the apparent paradox of an invigorated political project to regulate and legislate against sectarian expression within football while the evidence suggests that sectarianism has declined significantly in Scottish society. Waiton critiques the 'anti-sectarian' industry and the new prominence of offence within relations between social and cultural groups, which he argues is disempowering and, ultimately, may even generate new forms of sectarian identity and sect-like behaviour. Waiton illustrates how the new legislation and new forms of communication are facilitating forms of asocial behaviour and undermining both strong connections between individuals and groups and the importance and legitimacy of genuine political debate and disagreements.

In Chapter 8, Paul Davis develops a contrasting argument to the previous chapter. Davis endorses The Offensive Behaviour and Threatening Communications

(Scotland) Act 2012 and constructs a philosophical case for football sectarianism being morally impermissible. While agreeing with some other contributors that sectarianism has declined significantly in Scotland, he suggests that this is precisely the reason why sectarianism in Scottish football should not be condoned, as to do so is to disrespect the very social practices of football itself. Davis concludes that, while there are moral imperatives for continuing to address sectarianism, the historical 'baggage' of Old Firm football supporters should also be treated with magnanimity.

In Chapter 9, Niall Hamilton-Smith and David McArdle assess the implementation of Football Banning Orders in Scotland and specifically their use to regulate sectarian behaviour at football matches. Based on a Scottish Government-funded study, Hamilton-Smith and McArdle identify significant weaknesses in the framing of the legislation and, in particular, the failure to sufficiently adapt English legislation focused on football hooliganism to the particularities of sectarian conduct in the arenas of Scottish football. Investigating specific cases in detail, they argue that there is a need to recognise more fully the complex relationship between media and political discourses and the interpretations of the law among club stewards, police officers and the judiciary.

In Chapter 10, Irene A. Reid utilises the lens of Scottish media coverage of Celtic manager Neil Lennon to argue that in contrast to its constructed national myth of tolerance, Scotland still has to adequately confront its national demon of intolerance to Irish ethnicity and religion, crystallising around discourses about Celtic FC. She shows how media representations that personalise, demonise and sensationalise coverage of these issues serve to deflect attention from a deeper malaise in Scottish society and politics and, in doing so, often protect the interests of the powerful. Reid suggests that a sociological imagination remains crucial to rectifying the limitations of dominant media representations of bigotry within Scottish football.

In Chapter 11, Kay Goodall and Margaret Malloch argue that advances in understandings of masculinity and the law in Scottish society need to be strengthened by a focus on the less visible impact that bigotry has on women in Scotland's communities. The chapter interrogates the new legal framework in Scotland and concepts such as public order, racism, religious prejudice, incitement to hatred and sectarianism. Goodall and Malloch then present key findings from their exploratory study of women's experiences and perceptions of sectarianism in contemporary Scottish society. They conclude that a gendered perspective is absent from current debates about the new legislation and that sectarian conduct, including gender-abuse dimensions, may sustain patriarchal and other unequal ethno-religious power structures rooted in control over public space.

In Chapter 12, Joe Crawford examines why anti-sectarianism has become such an issue for the SNP Government, culminating in the new legislation. He argues that offended elites epitomise the struggle to name the world, that is to impose a 'common sense' monopoly and 'legitimate' definition of sectarianism. Crawford also presents a case that the new legislation has wider political motives that are reflected in the interests being served by punitive paternalist powers to regulate sectarianism among the populations at the bottom end of the social class structure. He suggests that a neoliberal dominance is also evident in the lack of power of football supporters and the disparity between their interests and those running Scotland's most powerful football clubs and institutions who focus on market ideology and profiteering.

In Chapter 13, Patrick McVey reflects on his personal history and experiences as a Celtic supporter and argues that sectarianism has often been regarded by those running Rangers FC and other key stakeholders in the Scottish game as a mechanism for generating financial profits. McVey calls upon various actors to refute this false understanding and to ensure that sporting integrity and the progress of Scottish football is paramount. This necessitates assisting Rangers to address the remaining cultural elements of malevolent sectarianism and football supporters themselves being proactively organised to tackle the present crisis in our national sport.

In Chapter 14, Alasdair McKillop provides a much-needed Rangers supporter's account, which questions the terms in which the sectarianism debate is commonly framed. He explores Rangers' complex Protestant identity and, while being sympathetic to the legacy of tradition, suggests that twenty-first-century Rangers has an opportunity to shape a modern-day identity around more positive expressions of Protestantism than previously associated (fairly or unfairly) with Rangers for many years. McKillop highlights the tensions brought on by new media, especially message boards and fora, and how these can fuel further division, not least in the new vocabulary being developed between Third Division Rangers and the Premier League clubs.

NOTES

1. In addition to Celtic associates, a Glasgow branch of Irish Republican organisation Cairde na hEireann was sent a device meant to harm and the Edinburgh-based Catholic Cardinal O'Brien received a bullet in the post in the lead-up to the Papal visit to Scotland in 2010.

2. Rangers were punished for fans singing the Billy Boys and 'Fuck the Pope', and Celtic fans were punished for chanting 'Up the ra'. The fact that UEFA described Rangers' offence as 'discriminatory' and Celtic's as 'illicit' further illustrates the difficulty the authorities have in categorising these behaviours.

3. In England, this type of latent intolerance was exposed in 1990 when former Conservative cabinet member Norman Tebbit accused Britain's Asian diaspora communities of lacking loyalty by asking, 'Which side do they cheer for [at cricket]? Are you still harking back to where you came from or where you are?'

4. Sociologist Norbert Elias used this phrase to criticise those social theorists who overlooked the historical developments of society. He argued that to understand society fully we must understand its historical development over *la longue durée*.

5. Some claim this was Protestant exclusivism in a non-bigoted way and compare it to some of the Basque clubs' Basque-only policies. This is flawed on two counts. First, Rangers openly signed non-Protestants during this period (see Finn 1999). Second, while the Basque policy is still questionable to many, this is the policy of clubs who perceive their identity and nationhood to be submerged within a nation dominated by those hostile to their nationhood (irrespective of the accuracy of this or not), which does not apply to Rangers.

6. This is most clearly captured in the Celtic fans' choice of greatest-ever Celt, Protestant Jock Stein, being immortalised in statue form at the Celtic Park entrance.

7. For example, Rangers fan websites expose numerous threads and articles discussing

Catholicism and Catholics in negative terms. And some Rangers songs continue to include anti-Catholic and anti-Pope sentiments.

8. Walker's general point about groups acknowledging their rival's right to self-determine their own identity is correct. The example he uses, however, is more complex than he concedes. He notes the irony of those in Scotland who profess to be Irish yet perhaps lack sensitivity to those in Ireland who profess to be British. While the sentiments are correct, this conflates cultural and civic nationalism and their relationship with national identity. In other words, the British in the North of Ireland/Northern Ireland form part of what some consider an occupying nation within an island that is contested land. Scotland is not contested (in any comparable way) and the Irish in Scotland occupy no such parallel position. Of course, some within Scotland would still argue that large sections of those claiming to be Irish in Scotland support a united Ireland and therefore merit opposition based on this.

9. Bruce compares rival fans waving money at Liverpool fans to the Billy Boys and Famine Song.

10. Christine Grahame, the Justice Committee convener, was quite explicit about this quest for balance when asking about the proposed Bill. She said 'prosecutions under the 2003 Act will be more successful in relation to Rangers supporters singing – notwithstanding the point that the songs are not all sectarian – than Celtic supporters singing, behaving in a certain way or chanting, because that would not be deemed sectarian and would be more likely to be deemed political?' Panel member Professor Tom Devine responded, 'I do not understand your point', to which convener Grahame clarified by adding, 'My point is that it is not even' (p. 255 of Justice Committee official report, 13 September 2011).

REFERENCES

Allport, G. (1979), *The Nature of Prejudice*, London: Addison-Wesley.

BBC (2012), 'Rangers newco owner Charles Green makes bigotry claim over SPL rejection', 29 July 2012. Available at: http://www.bbc.co.uk/sport/0/football/19040706 (last accessed 2 December 2012).

Bradbury, S. (2011), 'From racial exclusions to new inclusions: Black and minority ethnic participation in football clubs in the East Midlands of England', *International Review for the Sociology of Sport*, 46: 1, 23–44.

Bradley, J. M. (2006), 'Difference and distinctiveness in Scottish football and society', in J. M. Bradley (ed.), *Celtic Minded 2: Essays on Celtic Football Culture and Identity*, Glendaruel: Argyll Publishing, pp. 11–64.

Bruce, S. (2010), '"No pope of Rome": football fans wearing false noses', in R. Esplin and G. Walker (eds), *Rangers Triumphs, Troubles, Traditions*, Ayr: Fort Publishing, pp. 115–23.

Devine, T. (ed.) (2000), *Scotland's Shame? Bigotry and Sectarianism in Modern Scotland*, Edinburgh: Mainstream.

Finn, G. P. T. (1990), 'Prejudice in the history of Irish Catholics in Scotland'. Paper presented at the 24th History Workshop Conference, Glasgow College of Technology/Glasgow Caledonian University.

Finn, G. P. T. (1999), 'Scottish myopia and global prejudices', *Sport in Society*, 2: 3, 54–99.

Finn, G. and Uygun, Y., with Johnson, A. (2008), *Sectarianism and the Workplace*, Glasgow: STUC and The Scottish Government.

Fletcher, T. (2012), '"Who do 'they' cheer for?" Cricket, diaspora, hybridity and divided loyalties amongst British Asians', *International Review for the Sociology of Sport*, 47: 5, 612–31.

Flint, J. (2012), 'Catholic Schools and Sectarianism in Scotland: Educational Places and the Production and Negotiation of Urban Space', *Policy Futures in Education*, 10: 5, 507–17.

Foucault, M. (1991), 'Governmentality', in G. Burchell (ed.), *The Foucault Effect: Studies in Governmentality*, Hemel Hempstead: Harvester Wheatsheaf, pp. 87–104.

Kelly, J. (2011), '"Sectarianism" and Scottish Football: Critical Reflections on Dominant Discourse and Press Commentary', *International Review for the Sociology of Sport*, 46: 4, 418–35.

McAspurren, L. (2005), *Religious Discrimination and Sectarianism in Scotland: A Brief Review of the Evidence 2002–2004*, Edinburgh: Scottish Executive.

Madan, M. (2000), '"It's not just cricket": World Series Cricket: Race, nation, and diasporic Indian identity', *Journal of Sport & Social Issues*, 24: 1, 24–35.

Nicolson, L. (2002), *Identification of Research on Sectarianism, Religious Hatred and Discrimination Within a Scottish Context. Briefing Paper*, Edinburgh: Scottish Executive.

NFO Research (2003), *Sectarianism in Glasgow*, Glasgow: Glasgow City Council.

O'Loan, S., Poulter, A. and McMenemy, D. (2005), *The Extent of Sectarianism On-Line*, Glasgow: Nil By Mouth.

Orr, J. (2005), *Review of Marches and Parades*, Edinburgh: Scottish Executive.

Pilger, J. (2007), 'Why they're afraid of Michael Moore', *Znet*, 17 October 2007. Available at: http://www.zmag.org/zspace/commentaries/3244 (last accessed 2 December 2012).

Scottish Executive (2006a), *Action Plan on Tackling Sectarianism in Scotland*, Edinburgh: Scottish Executive.

Scottish Executive (2006b), *Calling Full Time on Sectarianism*, Edinburgh: Scottish Executive.

Walker, G. (2007), 'The world of the Celtic-minded', in R. Esplin and G. Walker (eds), *It's Rangers for Me: New Perspectives on a Scottish Institution*, Ayr: Fort Publishing, pp. 75–93.

Rethinking Geographical,
Historical and Social Contexts

Outside the Hothouse: Perspectives Beyond the Old Firm

Michael Rosie

INTRODUCTION

This chapter considers the events of the 2010–11 football season from outwith the perspective of Celtic and Rangers, attempting to put 'sectarianism' in a broader context. It begins with an overview of the events in the first two-thirds of the season, culminating in a controversial Scottish Cup replay. Broader evidence for sectarianism is then examined which suggests that the public's perception – or indeed, fear – of sectarian conflict far outruns their actual experience of it. The views of non-Old Firm fans are then explored through the platform of a popular football discussion website. The chapter concludes that football clubs themselves – and in particular the Old Firm – could and should do more to reduce misbehaviour on and off the pitch.

THE 2010–11 SEASON

Observers of the first half of the 2010–11 Scottish Premier League (SPL) would have been forgiven for thinking that they were seeing the most petulant and disputatious season for many years. Increasingly heated and fractious exchanges between various spokespersons of the two dominant clubs, Celtic and Rangers, came as the latter maintained a modest but stubborn lead in the league table. After Celtic were denied a penalty in a match at Dundee United, serious questions were asked about the match official's explanation. It emerged that the referee had given an inaccurate, perhaps deceitful, version of the decision process to Celtic manager Neil Lennon. An assistant referee, who had been persuaded by the match referee to obscure the decision-making process, subsequently resigned, criticising the Scottish Football Association (SFA) and making claims of a bullying culture within Scottish refereeing. Unsurprisingly, Celtic insisted the match referee should resign. The picture was further muddied when it emerged that SFA Head of Referee Development, Hugh Dallas, had circulated a scurrilous e-mail image of the Pope (whether the e-mail was 'satirical' or 'sectarian' is a moot point). Trust was disintegrating, with multiple claims of impropriety and bias, victimisation and intimidation. This was not limited to ordinary supporters. At his club's annual meeting, Celtic chairman John Reid played to the gallery, warning of 'lies, conspiracies and cover-ups' against Celtic: 'We're not asking for special treatment, but neither will we be treated as less than anyone else. Those days are gone' (BBC 2010a). Such grandstanding – by a former Cabinet Minister – amplifies the claim by Bill Murray (1998: 154) that 'Celtic supporters have been obsessed throughout their history by the idea that the SFA and its referees are biased against them'.

Reid's insinuations came weeks after the referee of an Old Firm encounter had reportedly received death threats after awarding a penalty against Celtic (BBC 2010b). The fallout from the Tannadice debacle – for which the referee eventually resigned – and the ongoing e-mail scandal intensified pressure on referees facing the 'hothouse' of Old Firm rivalry. Here almost *every* game played by either team is a 'six pointer' and every decision 'for' one team (regardless of their opposition on the day) is seen as 'against' the other. To some degree the key battle lines and characters were all too familiar. Celtic and Hugh Dallas had history.

Old Firm tensions had risen as Rangers won nine titles between 1989 and 1997, equalling Celtic's 1966–74 record. Celtic halted Rangers' aspirations for a world record ten-in-a-row on the last day of the 1998 season. In May 1999 Dallas refereed a title-deciding Old Firm derby. In a frenzied match – which was won by Rangers 3–0 and which saw over 100 fans arrested – Dallas was injured by a coin thrown from the Celtic end and several attempts were made by Celtic supporters to confront Dallas on the pitch. That evening windows at Dallas's home were smashed by a Celtic-supporting neighbour (BBC 1999a; 1999b; 2000). Quite remarkably, Celtic responded by commissioning a behavioural psychologist to scrutinise the referee's 'body language'. Celtic subsequently claimed that 'the inescapable conclusion is [that] tension in the stands was created by certain gestures made by the referee'. Outwith the club there was strong feeling that Celtic should have been looking rather closer to home (Keevins 2000a; 2000b; Paul 2000).

Dallas was sacked over 'Popegate' but by November 2010 pressure on Scotland's referees led to near collapse in the operation of the game. With referees under unparalleled pressure with claims of 'bias' and 'conspiracy', and feeling inadequately supported by the football authorities, they voted to strike. Their decision came just days after Reid's allegations of 'lies, conspiracies and cover-ups'. Publicly referees noted only that their integrity had been subjected to 'incessant and adverse' questioning, leading to 'an unprecedented level of abuse and genuine concerns for [their] safety' (STV 2011). A recently retired senior referee, however, did not hesitate to single out the complaints from Celtic (BBC 2010c).

Yet things had only just begun. Celtic overtook Rangers over the festive period, including a 2–0 New Year win at Ibrox. With such a tight scramble for points, every single game became meaningful, every incident scrutinised and endlessly replayed, and tensions continued to rise. And it increasingly became personal. In January 2011, with Rangers slipping behind their rivals, it was reported that bullets had been sent to Celtic manager Neil Lennon. Lennon had become a key love/hate figure with little room allowed by Old Firm supporters for any shade of grey. Again Lennon has – and has suffered – 'history'. Lennon represented Northern Ireland with distinction until he signed for Celtic in December 2000. At his next international, in February 2001, he was abused by a section of the Belfast crowd. What riled these 'supporters' was not so much his religion – the previous seven years playing for Northern Ireland had passed without incident – but the fact that he now played for Celtic, a club associated with a particular version of Irishness. For the next international Lennon received widespread vocal support from the Windsor Park crowd, but prior to a game in August 2002 he received a death threat, ostensibly from a Loyalist paramilitary group. Lennon, understandably, retired from international football.

A victim of bigotry both in Northern Ireland and in Scotland, Lennon became a symbolic rallying point for Celtic fans, a clear example of anti-Catholicism and racism (see Reid 2008: 75 and this volume for a series of claims that Lennon has been victim to 'racist and sectarian narratives' within the Scottish press). For many Rangers fans Lennon epitomised all that they loathed – an Ulster Catholic, Republican in hue, promoting a sense of Celtic's victim-status. Lennon increasingly became, simultaneously, a folk devil and a folk saint, a cipher with no in between, simplified and dehumanised by *both* sides in the hothouse. A boyhood fan, player, captain and coach, there was no mistaking Lennon's commitment to Celtic: he has proved a passionate and capable young manager from his appointment in 2010. Lennon kicks every single ball from the touchline, just as he seldom shirked a tackle as a player. What is seen as being passionate and shooting from the hip, of course, may also be seen as being blinkered and unreasonable. Yet the hothouse, with an enthralled media cashing in on the recurrent headlines, seldom allows for nuance.

In early March 2011 Celtic defeated Rangers 1–0 in a highly fractious Scottish Cup replay. Three Rangers players were dismissed, there were repeated confrontations between players, coaches and officials, and thirty-four spectators were arrested. Rangers' El-Hadji Diouf was at the centre of controversy, at one point confronting Lennon in his technical area. Amid angry scenes at the final whistle, Diouf was red-carded. He then defied stewards and police by going towards the Rangers supporters behind their goal. If this was a tawdry scene, there was worse to come. As the backroom staff interacted with the customary handshakes, Lennon sportingly embraced Rangers assistant manager Ally McCoist, who made some sort of comment. Lennon responded furiously and was dragged away from the melee. The authorities had, apparently, seen enough. Stewart Regan, chief executive of the SFA, condemned 'the inflammatory and irresponsible behaviour' which had 'deeply embarrassed' Scottish football:

> We have already launched an investigation into all incidents that occurred and will do everything in our power to ensure there is no repeat. [. . .] The unedifying sight of two of the country's most recognisable and respected coaches engaged in an angry confrontation was not only unsavoury but exacerbated an already incendiary atmosphere inside the stadium and throughout the West of Scotland. The clubs have a duty of care to ensure that the image and integrity

of the game is upheld at all times. This was not adhered to last night. This week, Strathclyde Police reiterated their concerns over the heightening violence and public disorder around Old Firm derbies. It is incumbent on Rangers and Celtic to ensure a far more responsible level of behaviour. (Scottish Football Association 2011)

The same day First Minister Alex Salmond told the Scottish Parliament that a crisis summit with the clubs, SFA and Scottish Government had been requested by Strathclyde Police. Salmond insisted that 'the disgraceful scenes last night cannot be ignored' (Scottish Parliament 2011). The Old Firm replay of 2 March hardly exhausted the drama and hysteria of the 2010–11 football season. Indeed, as other chapters in this volume detail, it descended further with 'viable' explosive devices being sent to individuals employed by, or associated with, Celtic; Neil Lennon being attacked by a Hearts supporter at Tynecastle; and the league title going to Ibrox on the final day of the season. Here, though, it is instructive to dwell on the Cup replay and the summit that followed it. The focus will be on how the game and summit were seen by fans outwith the hothouse. Before doing so, however, stepping even further back from the Old Firm offers a very different view of conflict and sectarianism in contemporary Scotland.

SECTARIANISM THROUGH THE PRISM OF THE OLD FIRM

If the Old Firm rivalry represented a prism through which we might understand Scottish society, we would see a very worrying picture of tension, hatred and simmering violence. In fact, there is an all-too-common truism that assumes/claims that the rivalry represents broader and worrying divisions within Scottish society. Tom Gallagher (1985: 44) was correct to argue that 'The hate and hysteria on display at Old Firm matches does not tumble out of the social void', but there is danger in assuming that attitudes expressed on the terraces are straightforwardly imported from, or exported to, other areas of life.

This unreflective focus on football allowed one contributor to a Celtic-inspired collection to conclude that Scotland's sectarianism, more specifically anti-Catholicism, represented 'a problem perhaps every bit as bitter, poisonous and debilitating as that which infests Northern Ireland' (Donaldson 2004: 219). The attacks on Neil Lennon, according to one blogger, sprang from 'an ugly society that harbours and authorises a deep visceral hatred of Catholics in general and Irish Catholics in particular' (MacGiollabhain 2011). There was long an assumption that the Old Firm rivalry was a relatively 'safe' and manageable 'pressure valve' through which sectarian tensions could be channelled, pre-scheduled and largely symbolic, through song and tribalism rather than through riot and politics. Thus, the argument went, Liverpool and Belfast had communal riots and sectarian politics, Glasgow had the Old Firm. Such a view seems misplaced now that Liverpool's sectarianism is little more than a historical memory. As Tom Gallagher (1985: 46) argued, regarding the football as a 'safe channel' for sectarian tensions:

. . . is to see the Old Firm as a symptom, not a cause, of community disorder; in the past such a view may have had some validity but it is surely the wrong way of looking at today's situation. Disorders at Old Firm ties worsened in the 1960s and 1970s even as community relations improved in other important areas, so the hatred seems to have been a self-generating mechanism and not an outlet for other discontents.

A decade later, Simon Kuper (1994: 217–18), examining global football enmities, concluded that 'the Old Firm rivalry has outlived religious rivalry . . . and . . . has survived as a phenomenon because the fans enjoy it so much. They are not about to give up their ancient traditions just because they no longer believe in God.' Almost twenty years on, is the Old Firm rivalry, far from providing a safe conduit, in fact sectarianism's beating heart?

In support of such a – surprisingly heretical – view it seems highly suggestive that in a football season marked, at least from within the hothouse, by recurring complaints of bigoted conspiracy, that two events passed almost without comment. In September 2010, with the season underway, Benedict XI visited Scotland. Arriving in Edinburgh, he met the Queen before heading to Glasgow's Bellahouston Park. Here, remarkably, were two of the key symbolic characters in Old Firm mythology meeting cordially in Scotland. Just as remarkably, the Pope's visit sparked none of the controversy or fears of the 1982 visit of John Paul II. That event was prefigured by two years of campaigning by Orange groups, and there were real fears over the scale and mood of protests. In the event the 1982 protests proved small and poorly organised. In 2010 key grumblings sprang not from Orangeism but from secularists and there were no significant protests. The area set aside by Strathclyde Police to facilitate protests outside Bellahouston remained empty. Just as remarkable was the visit of the Queen to the Republic of Ireland in May 2011. Two days after the final round of SPL matches, the Queen laid a wreath in Dublin's Republican Garden of Remembrance, bowing her head in honour of those who had died in Ireland's struggle to free itself from British rule.

It seems difficult to reconcile the sectarian version of Scotland refracted through the Old Firm with that suggested through the highly successful Papal Visit and the remarkable – and largely unremarked within debates over Scotland's 'sectarian problem' – Royal Visit to Ireland. Yet the circle is easily squared: the sentiments and behaviour of the football terrace (or, indeed, the touchline) cannot be simplistically read off as 'emblematic' or 'representative' of Scottish society, culture or politics as a whole. It seems highly telling that accounts of sectarianism in Scotland are framed by, prompted by, and often limited to, accounts of rivalry and tension in football. Sporting tensions in the 1990s led to the composer James MacMillan's (2000: 15) claim that 'anti-Catholicism, even when it is not particularly malign, is as endemic as it is second nature', a claim that prompted an outpouring of debate and criticism. The centrality of football – or, rather, one particular rivalry within Scottish football – seems all the more significant when one considers that there are very few published accounts, popular or academic, on sectarianism within Scotland's politics, economic structure, employment, housing, social policy, resource allocation or constitutional debate. Indeed, what studies there are in these areas downplay the impact, or even refute the presence, of sectarianism (see, for example, Paterson 2000; Rosie 2004; Bruce et al. 2004; Paterson and Iannelli 2006; Raab and Holligan 2011).

A generation ago, Steve Bruce (1988: 151) argued that 'the relatively rare public displays of sectarian animosity are not the visible tip of a submerged mass of ice but are rather all that is left'. Since then the emerging empirical evidence has bolstered Bruce's claims about the 'sectarian iceberg'. Whatever the position in the past (on which evidence remains sketchy), it is now clear that in terms of key *life chances* – access to education, to jobs, to opportunities for social mobility – there are no significant, let alone systematic, differences between Protestants, Catholics and the irreligious. Indeed, in *life choices* – political values or choice of partners/spouses – there is very little evidence of sectarian preferences. The Census of 2001 revealed widespread religious inter-marriage and cohabiting partnerships (Scottish Executive 2005). Scotland's Protestants and Catholics think and act like each other, and indeed *love* and *live* with each other, rather more than the prism of football would suggest (see Waiton in this volume). Likewise, that prism tends to ignore those Scots who do not fit within the easy formula of Protestant *or* Catholic: in the 2010 Scottish Social Attitudes Survey, for example, by far the largest response to the question 'Do you belong to a religion?' was that of 'No religion' (48 per cent).

Recurrent scares over sectarianism have been driven by the Old Firm rivalry. Patrick Reilly (2000: 33) insisted that a focus on social structure and the labour market (regulated as it is by laws against discrimination) was irrelevant in the search for the 'cancer' of sectarianism:

> Crucially important though employment is, it is *not* the only thing that counts. And the trouble is that sectarianism does not disappear, but simply moves to other lodgings. That a cancer moves from lung to colon is not really a cause for celebration. It is pointless to look for discrimination where, by definition, it can no longer exist . . .

Reilly's argument had begun bullishly: 'To ask if there is anti-Catholicism in Scotland is like asking if there are Frenchmen in Paris.' It seems highly significant that once he concedes that sectarianism is no longer prevalent in the occupational lung, he turns to football to provide the colon. Indeed, what other candidates did he have?

SECTARIAN HATE CRIME AND EXPERIENCES OF SECTARIANISM

Concerns over sectarianism fed into the introduction of a 'religious aggravation' in the Criminal Justice (Scotland) Act 2003. For the better part of a decade, therefore, sectarian offences (among other hate crimes) have been monitored and liable to heavier sentencing. Examination of sectarian crime is illuminating, with the usual caveats that, as with other crimes, 'recorded' incidents will not exhaust the full and actual picture. Notably, religious hate crime is substantially and consistently lower – around one-seventh the frequency – than racist hate crime, and only somewhat more frequent than hate crimes based on (perceived) sexual orientation :

Table 2.1 Reported hate crimes in Scotland (number)

	Race	Religious	Sexual orientation	Transgender identity	Disability
2003–4	3,322	272			
2004–5	4,019	479			
2005–6	4,287	704			
2006–7	4,367	699			
2007–8	4,394	608			
2008–9	4,319	669			
2009–10	4,314	629			
2010–11	4,165	693	448	14	50
2011–12	4,518	897	652	16	68

Sources: Doyle 2006; Cavanagh and Morgan 2011

Official analyses of religious offences (Doyle 2006; Cavanagh and Morgan 2011) reveal consistent patterns: half of such offences (51 per cent in 2010–11) occurred in Glasgow, and most of the remainder (31 per cent) in the surrounding west of Scotland. Most offenders were young (61 per cent aged 30 or under), and almost all (95 per cent) male. Around two-thirds of the offences were described as alcohol-related.

Media attention here has headlined a supposedly disproportional victimisation of Scotland's Catholics (see, for example, BBC 2011a; Carrell 2006). A narrative around 'victims' and 'attacks' fuels the impression that sectarian crime in Scotland is violent and 'targeted' at Catholics. In fact, the figures suggest quite a different picture. Firstly, relatively few such offences are physical attacks – 6 per cent in 2010–11 related to an assault charge. The overwhelming majority (92 per cent in 2003; 81 per cent in 2004; and 73 per cent in 2010–11) related to a 'breach of the peace'. The lower figure for 'breach' in 2010–11 related to a new offence of 'threatening or abusive behaviour' from 2010 which accounted for 14 per cent of sectarian offences. Secondly, where an actual person was the 'target' of such behaviour, it was most likely to be a police officer (victims in 42 per cent of cases in 2010–11) or someone doing their job (11 per cent). In less than a quarter of cases (23 per cent) were 'members of the public' the targets of abuse – rather more (33 per cent) featured misbehaviour towards the 'community' at large.

In other words, the bulk of Scotland's recorded sectarian crime is conducted by young men, often drunk, in the west of Scotland (see Goodall and Malloch's chapter for a similar analysis). Offences are overwhelmingly anti-social and sometimes abusive and threatening. If anyone is 'targeted' it is police and other public service and retail workers. This is a dismal picture of urban incivility, a reminder that rather too many Scots – and particularly young men – drink too much, fail to behave themselves and when rebuked respond with foul-mouthed abuse. Depressing certainly, but less conducive to good headline-making than the *Sunday Mirror*'s (2004) spin: 'Catholics face Scots bigots hell'.

Official figures do indeed show that most sectarian crime is 'anti-Catholic' in nature. In 2010–11, 58 per cent of offences involved behaviour 'derogatory towards Roman Catholicism' while 37 per cent involved behaviour 'derogatory towards Protestantism'. Media reporting suggests Catholics being 'attacked' or targeted', but in fact no data is collected on the religious identity of the victim (where there are specific victims, rather than the world at large). Yet the seeming disparity in the figures has a less sinister explanation. Given the broad religious demography of the west of Scotland, it would require only that a roughly equal (and small) proportion of Catholics acted in anti-social and 'anti-Protestant' ways as Protestants acting in 'anti-Catholic' ways to produce a supposed 'disparity' in offences. To put this in simple terms: if in a town where there are twice as many Protestants than Catholics each community has a 0.01 per cent minority who behave in a religiously bigoted manner on an alcohol-fuelled Saturday night, then two thirds of sectarian offences would be 'anti-Catholic' in nature. That is not to say that in the real world Catholics and Protestants are indulging equally in sectarian hatred – we simply do not have the data to know – only that the underlying disparity in the numbers of Catholics and Protestants points towards a rather less frightening explanation than media coverage suggests.

The disjuncture between the football season and broader events, and the depressingly tawdry – rather than violent and widespread – nature of sectarian crime highlights a paradox. We all 'know' about religious bigotry, yet relatively few of us report having experienced it. Sectarianism appears to operate on two distinct levels. In terms of *perceptions*, sectarianism is seen as a widespread and fairly serious problem. But when people are asked whether they have *personally* experienced sectarianism, reports are – relatively speaking – infrequent. Sectarianism often seems to be something that happens to *somebody else*.

Here the findings of a study commissioned by Glasgow City Council (NFO Social Research 2003) are illuminating. The study, notably, received almost no media coverage and is little known outside academic and policy circles despite being made freely available to researchers. It strikingly illustrates a sharp disjuncture between how widespread Glaswegians felt different forms of 'sectarianism' were, and how rarely they claimed to have suffered them personally. Two-thirds of Glaswegians felt that sectarian violence and sectarian vandalism were 'very common' or 'quite common' in their city; over half felt the same about sectarian threats and sectarian intimidation/harassment. Smaller proportions felt that other forms of sectarianism were common.

Yet when these same respondents were asked whether *they* had experienced these things over the previous five years the numbers dropped very substantially indeed. For every *hundred* respondents who felt that sectarian violence was common in Glasgow, just *one* reported having suffered from it. We see a very similar pattern across all eight forms of sectarianism explored (Table 2.2).

This disjuncture between perceptions and experiences mirrors what we find in

Table 2.2 Perceptions and experience of sectarianism in Glasgow.

Form of sectarianism:	Perception (% believing 'very' or 'quite common')	Experience (% claiming to have suffered in past five years)
Sectarian violence	65	0.7
Vandalism	65	0.6
Threats	58	0.8
Intimidation or harassment	54	0.4
Employment discrimination	24	1.1
Different treatment by police	20	0.3
Different treatment by public services	15	0.2
Different treatment by council	13	0.5
Base	1,029	1,029

Sources: NFO Social Research (2003) and author's own analysis of dataset

the fear of crime. What makes people fear crime – even if the likelihood of being victims, particularly of violent crime, is very low – are the *discourses* around crime. Here media is a key player in constructing and sustaining public worry – and the fact that the Old Firm dominate back pages and sports bulletins means that their rivalry is a permanent feature of Scotland's news agenda, and 'sectarianism' becomes *familiar*, even to those who will never experience it. The Old Firm rivalry, therefore, is a highly partial and distorting lens through which to view Scotland. But it is also a major and everyday part of our news, and thus contributes to a widespread discourse about – and resultant worry over – sectarianism.

BEYOND THE OLD FIRM HOTHOUSE

But let us return to *that* season, and *that* Cup replay. Not all Scots are obsessed with football, and even among the obsessive not all are interested in Rangers or Celtic. But how did football fans outwith the Old Firm see the events of the fiery Cup replay and its aftermath? There are several mainstream media outlets through which we might monitor such views, not least phone-in radio shows and comments in print and online newspapers. Such outlets, however, may suffer from editorial selection: bearing in mind that the Old Firm 'sells', it is reasonable to assume that editors will prefer 'controversial' Old Firm-centred views to stimulate sensation and debate. Online newspaper comments are heavily moderated and prone to 'trolling' – indeed some outlets, such as the *Scotsman*, do not allow comments on Old Firm stories because of the levels of abuse posted. Here, then, I will examine an internet discussion forum run by football fans themselves. While abuse, trolling and impersonation are hardly unknown on such sites, they are generally free of editorial pre-selection.

The site examined here attracts fans from a wide range of clubs: *Pie and Bovril* (henceforth *P&B*) was set up in 2003 and currently has 21,500 active members (http://www.pieandbovril.com/). It hosts separate fora for the SPL, the three SFL divisions, and several other leagues. Notably it has a special forum which seeks to segregate Old Firm sniping: 'Rangers and Celtic fans can battle it out in here, safe in the knowledge that everyone else will steer well clear and leave them to it! If you must goad each other – please do it in here!' Non-Old Firm contributions to three specific threads will be examined:

'Rangers vs Celtic' – opened on 14 January 2011 to cover the original Cup tie. The thread is examined from 1 March when discussion of the replay commenced. The thread continued until 4 March and had 340 posts. http://www.pieandbovril.com/forum/index.php/topic/138178-rangers-vs-celtic/ (last accessed 31 August 2012).

'The Old Firm . . . Scotland's Shame' – opened on the late evening of 2 March 2011 immediately after the replay ended. The thread continued to 11 March and comprised 157 posts. http://www.pieandbovril.com/forum/index.php/topic/142028-the-old-firmscotlands-shame/ (last accessed 31 August 2012).

'Summit of decision-makers: sectarianism' – opened on 30 March 2011, several weeks after the summit meeting had been reported in Scotland's media. The thread continued until 31 March and contained fifty-three posts. http://www.pieandbovril.com/forum/index.php/topic/144069-summit-of-decision-makers/ (last accessed 31 August 2012).

The most cursory reading of *P&B* (as other football fora) demonstrates the widespread hostility that many football fans have towards the Old Firm, as well as a tendency to treat both clubs as a single entity. Most of the *Rangers vs Celtic* thread was taken up before the game by Old Firm fans, but other fans came to dominate as the game began to boil over. Throughout there were repeated references to dominant motifs in the criticism of both Glasgow clubs, most notably the comment by 'Richie' (a Motherwell fan) which poked fun at Celtic's reputation for 'paranoia' with the possibility that the tie might be decided by a penalty shoot-out: 'Let's hope it doesn't go to a shootout . . . Can you imagine the Celtic fans after Rangers are awarded 5 penalties?'

As the game progressed a key theme was disavowal of what fans were seeing on their television screens: it was seen as 'pathetic', 'embarrassing' and perversely entertaining (see Goodall and Malloch in this volume for a further discussion of the example of misogynist language evidenced in one of these posts). Views were often robust and earthy (minor editorial tidying has been undertaken with the views presented below, but profanities have been retained as in the original). Where specific blame was given, it tended to be towards the Rangers players in general and to Diouf and McCoist in particular. The key criticism of Lennon was for 'rising to the bait' of a deliberately provocative Rangers side:

yoda   What a complete and utter embarrassment some of these players are.
Ross County

utdtillidie   Embarrassing Scottish football for 110 years [. . .] Both teams should be thrown out the cup.
Ayr United

djchapsticks   Aside from Lennon being a prat and rising to McCoist's bait, I don't think Celtic did much wrong there. Rangers completely lost it, Diouf's show was one of the most pathetic things I've ever seen.
St.Mirren

Big River   That was laughable, disgusting and pathetic . . . but incredibly entertaining.
Motherwell

shedboy82   Car crash football, but very, very funny. It was a bit like watching two drunken, pockmarked, tracksuit-clad tarts tearing the peroxide from each other at bingo night. But not as sexually arousing, obviously.
Dundee United

In the immediate aftermath of the replay a thread was opened which identified both the clubs as, collectively, The Old Firm . . . Scotland's Shame. Just as with the 'in-game' thread, many posters focused on the on-field action and with similar conclusions. However, this thread also saw a number of posters reflect on issues around sectarian bigotry and whether and how it might be tackled. A very strong and clear view was that both Old Firm clubs and both sets of supporters were at fault. Just as clear was scepticism that Scotland's football authorities had the will or the wherewithal to address 'the same old story':

Unleash the Nade   And so it goes on, same old story, yet again. Two teams pumped up by their respective bigoted fans, ensuring the hatred and bile is carried forth in its usual 'traditional' manner [. . .] to top it all off, the respective 'leaders' square up like a couple of wee lassies [. . .] How totally embarrassing!
Hearts

steward17   Bigotry in Scotland puts bums on seats. The old firm mandarins and the SFA know this and god help anyone in Scottish football unwise enough to challenge this.
Scotland

Milo   Two Cheeks of the Same Arse [. . .] that's what the Old Firm have become.
Partick

As the thread wound down and media began to report the Old Firm Summit, little confidence was expressed in the effectiveness of the proposals:

The Scarf   These measures won't make fuck all difference. The only way to tackle the issue of [Old Firm] bawbaggery from both players and fans is to start introducing points deductions.
Inverness CT

The much-vaunted Old Firm Summit agreed six major points of action. Three focused on the police's role in managing fans (including 'greater enforcement of existing legislation to deal with sectarianism and drink-related offences'); another called for further study into the link between football matches and violent crime. The two remaining points related to the Old Firm. Firstly they committed 'to playing an enhanced role in a partnership approach to encourage responsible drinking'; secondly they agreed to reinforce the existing 'code of conduct for players and officials' (BBC 2011b). Notably, given that tensions had arisen from the misbehaviour of players and coaches on the park and on the touchline, the emphasis of the Summit was very much on misbehaving *fans*. One of the longer-term outcomes of the Summit, and the later tensions of the season, was the controversial Offensive Behaviour at Football and Threatening Communications (Scotland) Act 2012, which criminalised offensive chanting (including sectarian songs) at and around Scottish football matches.

For those on *P&B* the outcome of the summit seemed unimpressive and, perhaps, had missed the point. A key solution, posters on the Summit of decision-makers thread felt, should have come from within football itself:

FuzzyBear   Sectarianism has been a problem in this country for a hell of a lot of years and will be for a long time to come as the powers to be do not seem willing to do anything about it. The SFA/SPL have had numerous opportunities to come down hard on Celtic and Rangers but have done nothing.
Hamilton

Audioslave   [The SFA/SPL] should be focusing on how to quickly eradicate it from grounds with bans/fines to individuals and clubs – these things are in place but it seems no one has the bottle to actually carry it out.
Hearts

Pride of the Clyde   [. . .] hitting both clubs hard is the only thing that will make any difference and will then force them to address this problem.
Clyde

The summit, then, seemed – in its presentation at least – to deflect attention away from the Old Firm clubs themselves, and from the Scottish football authorities. In a joint press conference the chief executives of the two clubs argued that much of the coverage and debate around the Cup replay had been 'ill-informed'. Martin Bain of Rangers insisted that 'There are undoubtedly major issues for society in Scotland and with the best will in the world they cannot be blamed on a football club or cured by a football club' (BBC 2011c). For Celtic, Peter Lawwell argued:

While many of the issues surrounding the Celtic v. Rangers fixture have been blamed on the clubs, clearly there are a number of societal issues which need to be addressed. Celtic has and will continue to address these. How much more can the clubs do? We need help. The stigma always attaches itself to Celtic and Rangers. How much more can we physically do? (BBC 2011c)

Such claims received short shrift on *P&B*. **Ric**, a St Mirren fan, argued that 'Sectarianism is a practice generally indulged in by the fans of the [Old Firm]. Perhaps the clubs would like to take the lead on this rather than trying to shamefully blame society as a whole. Just a thought.'

CONCLUSIONS

How much more *could* the Old Firm do to combat the 'societal' evil of sectarianism? First of all, it is essential that credit is given where credit is due: both clubs contribute financially to and participate in anti-bigotry initiatives such as Glasgow City Council's *Sense Over Sectarianism* programme and have repeatedly asked their fans to refrain from bigoted singing and other sectarian behaviour. A BBC Scotland documentary at the heart of the troubled season revealed that Rangers had issued bans to over 500 fans across seven years for singing sectarian songs (BBC 2011d). Undoubtedly the regularity of sectarian and other offensive chanting at Parkhead and Ibrox has diminished. In part this is due to the steep rise in the number of season ticket holders at both clubs – such fans are easy to track at home games and are sensitive to losing their seats through misbehaviour. The travelling support of both clubs has proved rather more difficult to wean from their 'party' tunes. However, alongside such (undoubtedly valuable) efforts, both clubs have also pandered to the more 'tribal' instincts of their followers and have a tendency to circle the wagons when criticised. Murray argued in the 1980s that 'While arrogance stands as one of the features of the Rangers club and its supporters, paranoia belongs peculiarly to Celtic' (1984: 104). There may be some truth in this but from the outside it is easy to detect *both* features in *both* clubs alongside a heightened sense of defensiveness.

If Scotland's leading clubs are serious about their responsibilities around bigotry – and there is substantial evidence that they are – then it should not be beyond their capacities or influence to instigate heightened penalties for misbehaviour on and off the park. While UEFA has begun to investigate and punish clubs (including both of the Old Firm) for offensive fan behaviour at European games, the Scottish footballing authorities have felt hamstrung by the lack of clear guidance and powers in their Articles and Regulations. The onus, and the responsibility, has thus passed to the police and the Crown Office to apprehend and prosecute miscreants in the football stands – no easy matter when faced with several thousand fans. Here the Old Firm could take the lead and make a difference. It is surely time for the *clubs* themselves – all Scottish clubs – to equip the football authorities with the powers and the mechanisms to punish clubs for the misbehaviour of the supporters. The clubs, after all, *are* football. When clubs begin to lose valuable league points because their fans sing racist obscenities, or glorify terrorism, or indulge in sectarian abuse, or throw missiles, the minds of decent football supporters will be focused on the misbehaviour around them and we will see change. If we are to move beyond the claim that 'bigotry puts bums on seats' then radical and bold leadership by both sides of the Old Firm is essential.

REFERENCES

BBC (1999a), 'Rangers make history out of chaos', 3 May 1999, http://news.bbc.co.uk/1/hi/sport/football/scottish_premier/334094.stm (last accessed 31 August 2012).

BBC (1999b), 'Old Firm violence inquiry begins', 3 May 1999, http://news.bbc.co.uk/1/hi/sport/football/scottish_premier/334291.stm (last accessed 31 August 2012).

BBC (2000), 'Fan smashed referee's windows', 4 September 2000, http://news.bbc.co.uk/1/hi/scotland/910175.stm (last accessed 31 August 2012).

BBC (2010a), 'Celtic call for referee Dougie McDonald's resignation', 18 November 2010, http://news.bbc.co.uk/sport1/hi/football/teams/c/celtic/9206945.stm (last accessed 31 August 2012).

BBC (2010b), 'Old Firm referee Willie Collum receives threats', 26 October 2010, http://news.bbc.co.uk/sport1/hi/football/scot_prem/9128308.stm (last accessed 31 August 2012).

BBC (2010c), 'Scottish referees vote for strike action', 21 November 2010, http://news.bbc.co.uk/sport1/hi/football/scot_prem/9214212.stm (last accessed 31 August 2012).

BBC (2011a), 'Most Scottish religious hate crimes "target Catholics"', 18 November 2011, http://www.bbc.co.uk/news/uk-scotland-glasgow-west-15790225 (last accessed 31 August 2012).

BBC (2011b), 'Old Firm unite over anti-bigotry plan after summit', 8 March 2011, http://www.bbc.co.uk/news/uk-scotland-glasgow-west-12670175 (last accessed 31 August 2012).

BBC (2011c), 'Old Firm reaction ill-informed, say chief executives', 8 March 2011, http://news.bbc.co.uk/sport1/hi/football/scot_prem/9419199.stm (last accessed 31 August 2012).

BBC (2011d), 'The century-old problem plaguing Scottish football', 18 May 2011, http://www.bbc.co.uk/news/uk-scotland-13438080 (last accessed 31 August 2012).

Bruce, S. (1988), 'Sectarianism in Scotland: A Contemporary Assessment and Explanation', in D. McCrone and A. Brown (eds), *The Scottish Government Yearbook*, Edinburgh: Unit for the Study of Government in Scotland, pp. 150–65.

Bruce, S., Glendinning, T., Paterson, I. and Rosie, M. (2004), *Sectarianism in Scotland*, Edinburgh: Edinburgh University Press.

Carrell, S. (2006), 'Catholics bear brunt of Scottish sectarian abuse', *The Guardian*, 28 November 2011, http://www.guardian.co.uk/uk/2006/nov/28/religion.catholicism (last accessed 5 September 2012).

Cavanagh, B. and Morgan, A. (2011), *Religiously Aggravated Offending in Scotland 2010–11*, Edinburgh: Scottish Government Social Research.

Donaldson, A. (2004), 'An identity worth having', in J. Bradley (ed.), *Celtic Minded: Essays on religion, politics, social identity . . . and football*, Glendaruel: Argyll Publishing, pp. 218–26.

Doyle, K. (2006), *Use of Section 74 of the Criminal Justice (Scotland) Act 2003 – Religiously Aggravated Reported Crime: An 18 Month Review*, Edinburgh: Scottish Executive Social Research.

Gallagher, T. (1985), 'Soccer: the real opium of the people?', *Innes Review*, 36: 1, 44–7.

Keevins, H. (2000a), 'You've been framed; Celts use video of Old Firm shame game to nail ref', *Sunday Mail*, 30 January 2000.

Keevins, H. (2000b), 'Bonkers! Celts stars accused in dossier by mind doc', *Sunday Mail*, 6 February 2000.

Kuper, S. (1994), *Football Against the Enemy*, London: Phoenix.

MacGiollabhain, P. (2011), 'Attack on Neil Lennon at Tynecastle', 11 May 2011, http://www.philmacgiollabhain.ie/attack-on-neil-lennon-at-tynecastle/ (last accessed 31 August 2012).

MacMillan, J. (2000), 'Scotland's Shame', in T. Devine (ed.), *Scotland's Shame? Bigotry and Sectarianism in Modern Scotland*, Edinburgh: Mainstream, pp. 13–24.

Murray, B. (1984), *The Old Firm: Sectarianism, Sport and Society in Scotland*, Edinburgh: John Donald.

Murray, B. (1998), *The Old Firm in the New Age*, Edinburgh: Mainstream.

NFO Social Research (2003), *Sectarianism in Glasgow – Final Report*, Glasgow: Glasgow City Council.

Paterson, L. (2000), 'The social class of Catholics in Scotland', *Journal of the Royal Statistical Society (A)*, 163: 3, 363–79.

Paterson, L. and Iannelli, C. (2006), 'Religion, social mobility and education in Scotland', *British Journal of Sociology*, 57: 3, 353–77.

Paul, I. (2000), 'Dallas seeks SFA advice', *The Herald*, 31 January 2000.

Pie and Bovril, www.pieandbovril.com (last accessed 31 August 2012).

Raab, G. and Holligan, C. (2011), 'Sectarianism: myth or social reality? Inter-sectarian partnerships in Scotland, evidence from the Scottish Longitudinal Study', *Ethnic and Racial Studies*, iFirst Article, DOI:10.1080/01419870.2011.607506.

Reid, I. (2008). '"An outsider in our midst": narratives of Neil Lennon, soccer and ethno-religious bigotry in the Scottish press', *Sport & Society*, 9: 1, 64–80.

Reilly, P. (2000), 'Kicking with the Left Foot: Being Catholic in Scotland', in T. Devine (ed.), *Scotland's Shame? Bigotry and Sectarianism in Modern Scotland*, Edinburgh: Mainstream, pp. 29–40.

Rosie, M. (2004), *The Sectarian Myth in Scotland: Of Bitter Memory and Bigotry*, Basingstoke: Palgrave.

Scottish Executive (2005), *Analysis of Religion in the 2001 Census*, Scottish Executive National Statistics.

Scottish Football Association (2011), 'Chief Executive condemns Old Firm chaos', 3 March 2011, http://www.scottishfa.co.uk/scottish_fa_news.cfm?page=2550&newsCategoryID=36&newsID=7351 (last accessed 31 August 2012).

Scottish Parliament (2011), *First Minister's Question Time, Official Report*, 3 March 2011.

STV (2011), 'Scottish referees' body explains reasons for strike action', 22 November 2011, http://sport.stv.tv/football/clubs/aberdeen/211019-scottish-referees-chief-defends-strike-action/ (last accessed 31 August 2012).

Sunday Mirror (2004), 'Catholics face Scots bigots hell', 28 November 2004.

3 Is Football Bigotry Confined to the West of Scotland? The Heart of Midlothian and Hibernian Rivalry

John Kelly

INTRODUCTION

Such is the contested nature of ethno-religious bigotry in Scottish football, some will question the very inclusion of a chapter on Heart of Midlothian (Hearts) and Hibernian (Hibs) in a collection like this. Yet there has been some perception that Hearts and Hibs form an 'Edinburgh Old Firm' (see Kowalski 2004). Hognestad (1997) claims some fans of both clubs use sectarian songs and symbols in constructing their imagined identities. While it may be an exaggeration to suggest that the Edinburgh clubs and their fans are a mini Old Firm, equally it would be naive to omit the two capital city clubs from a study of bigotry, football and Scotland. Like their Glasgow counterparts, the Edinburgh clubs' identities have had varying degrees of 'sectarian' associations throughout their respective histories. This is unsurprising given that both clubs emerged in a rapidly changing Edinburgh experiencing significant Irish migration to the city. As good sociologists know, we should avoid the temptation to *retreat to the present*, overlooking crucial historical antecedents for fear of providing inadequately partial accounts (see also the chapters by Bradley, Davies and Flint and Powell).

This chapter, therefore, begins by providing a brief historical overview of both clubs' respective formative years, illustrating how an original Edinburgh camaraderie evolved into local rivalry. Drawing on a number of interviews with fans, it then outlines a selection of current views from the fans of both clubs, including the fans' perceptions of their own club and of their major relationship with their significant 'Other', their rival. This reveals how each club has residual elements of their respective histories impacting on their modern identity. But it also reveals the centrality of Edinburgh as a place in the imagined communities of both clubs. The chapter concludes with a discussion of some modern examples of alleged sectarianism surrounding the Edinburgh clubs and argues that the contrasting approaches Hearts and Hibs fans have in embracing their respective pasts reveals broader insights into common perceptions surrounding 'sectarianism' in Scotland beyond Edinburgh football fans.

THE FORMATIVE YEARS OF THE EDINBURGH CLUBS

The founding of Hearts is officially recorded as 1874, but evidence suggests they were formed in the autumn of 1873 at Washing Green Court in the Canongate area of Edinburgh (Mackie 1959; Alexander 2003). There is further ambiguity surrounding the origins of the club name, with the official accounts claiming it took its name from the Royal Mile dance hall frequented by its founders, while Alexander (2003) claims that Heart of Midlothian was chosen in honour of Walter Scott's 1818 novel of the same name.[1] The distinction is negligible as both would presumably have been named after the Tolbooth. Hearts joined the Scottish league in 1875 and quickly became established as a major club, winning their first trophy in 1878 against Hibs in the final of the Edinburgh FA Cup. Hearts, perhaps more than any other club, encapsulates a dual British-Scottish identity that has developed since their early days and their associations with McCrae's Battalion (the 16th Royal Scots British Army battalion):

> Kaiser Bill he came marching o'er Belgium and France
> To challenge the Empire with warlike advance.
> But the bravest of Hearts volunteered for the fray
> And threw in their lot with old Geordie McCrae!
> Come pack up your footballs and scarves of maroon.
> Leave all your sweethearts in Auld Reekie toon.
> Fall in wi' the lads for they're off and away
> To take on the bold Hun with old Geordie McCrae!
>
> (cited in Alexander 2003: 134–5)

On 25 November 1914, during the initial stages of the First World War when joining up was still voluntary, eleven Hearts players enlisted in McCrae's Battalion after a certain amount of pleading from the Hearts board of directors to 'remove the slur on the professional game' (Alexander 2003: 74). Following the successful plea for players, the club extended their official request to their supporters:

The Board of Directors of Heart of Midlothian Football Club hereby make a strong appeal to their supporters to join Sir George McCrae's Battalion . . . The players have shown the way and it is now up to the other sections named to complete the requisite number . . . Heart of Midlothian applicants are requested to state when enlisting that they wish to be included in the Hearts Company. Now then, young men, as you have followed the old club through adverse and pleasant times, through sunshine and rain, roll up in your hundreds for King and Country, for right and freedom. (cited in Alexander 2003: 81–2)

This official club call to arms for King and Country was an immediate success during a period marked by widespread castigation of the ever-increasing professional football for its alleged malevolent influence on the nation's youth (Alexander 2003). Allowing us insight into the hegemonic influences of the day, contemporary newspapers carried the following appeal:

> I say to the young men in this ancient capital and free country: *You are Strong; Be Willing!* . . . If only you will come forward in sufficient numbers you can stop the war. All cannot go, but if your home ties permit, and you shirk your obvious duty, you may escape a hero's death, but you will go through your life feeling mean. (cited in Alexander 2003: 76, original emphasis)

McCrae's Battalion itself had footballing and 'sectarian' antecedents, being formed out of the remnants of the Third Edinburgh Rifle Volunteers (3rd ERV) whose football team, established in 1874, became the first Edinburgh club. Led by John Hope, a Protestant who campaigned in favour of temperance and anti-Catholicism, the instantly successful 3rd ERV club's membership was confined to members of the corps who were 'specially selected Protestants, chosen on the basis of their "good character", as defined by dual commitment to No-Popery and abstension' (Finn 1994: 98).

The connection between the club and McCrae's was cemented further in 1919 when the club issued complementary season tickets to around one hundred survivors of McCrae's Battalion, with the front cover inscription: 'These men went to fight for King and Country . . . they are welcomed back to Tynecastle' (cited in Alexander 2003: 268).

In more recent times this has continued with the club, helped by fan contributions, erecting a war memorial to the 'Heart of Midlothian fallen', which was unveiled at Haymarket (see the chapter by Flint and Powell for further discussion). Additionally, the club organised the annual Armistice Day ceremony up until the 1960s when they began leaving it to the Salvation Army. These links to McCrae's Battalion and the events of the First World War were rekindled by the release of the compact disc single 'Hearts of Glory', which was officially advertised and endorsed by Hearts FC in the spring of 2004. Proceeds from sales went towards the memorial fund.

Hearts' rivals Hibs were formed in 1875[2] by members of the St Mary's Street branch of the Catholic Young Men's Society (CYMS) under the chairmanship of Irish-born Canon Hannan (Finn 1994; Lugton 1999).[3] Their formation was inextricably linked to the mass immigration of Irish Catholics to Edinburgh during the nineteenth century. On arriving in Edinburgh, many Irish settled in the slums of the Cowgate area of the Old Town, and gradually developed their own 'Little Ireland' (Lugton 1999). Little Ireland and the Port of Leith rapidly became associated with the Irish migrants. Shortly after the opening of Little Ireland's first Catholic church in 1835, 16,000 of Edinburgh's 133,000 population were Irish and by 1848 Leith's population included almost 2,000 Irish (ibid.). By the mid-nineteenth century 30 per cent of the Old Town population were Irish-born, with 25,000 in Little Ireland. Although at the time of the club's formation the Catholic Irish represented less than 10 per cent of Edinburgh's population, they were a significant minority who had developed their own sub-culture, becoming, as Lugton (1999: 18) suggests, 'Hibernicis ipsis Hiberniores: "more Irish than the Irish".'

Hibs were the first prominent 'Irish club' in Scotland, and initially their players had to be practising Catholics (Lugton 1999). The club's first secretary, Mal Byrne, drew up the rules of the new club on a document carrying the Harp and motto 'Erin-go-bragh' (Irish Gaelic for 'Ireland forever': Mackay 1986). Lugton (1999) records that Hibernian was chosen in honour of the 'Ancient Order of the Hibernians', which had been absorbed into the CYMS. Hibs quickly became established as a major Edinburgh club, with rapid success ensuing. This success probably contributed to the club's problematic relationship with other Scottish clubs and associations in its formative years. Both the local Edinburgh FA and the newly formed Scottish FA refused to allow Hibs entry to their associations (Mackay 1986; Finn 1994; Lugton 1999). Furthermore, the Edinburgh FA issued instructions to its existing members to refrain from playing any matches against Hibs (Lugton 1999). Demonstrating an early example of comradeship to its eventual rivals, Hearts agreed to play Hibs on Christmas Day 1875 (Lugton 1999). Throughout the 1880s there was widespread debate regarding whether Hibs' Scottish-born players should represent Scotland or Ireland. Mackay (1986: 4) quotes a contemporary account taken from the Scottish Football Annual. Referring to the SFA, it states: 'That body, thus early displaying a spirit which has all along marked their dealings with the Hibernians, *refused them admission*. "The Association was formed for Scotchmen" said they in effect' (original emphasis).

Finn (1994) suggests that part of the reason for Hibs' early league membership refusals can be attributed to opposition from the Edinburgh FA, probably as a direct result of the influence of the powerful (and original) Edinburgh football club, the 3rd ERV. Finn (1994: 91), who illustrates the anti-Catholic culture associated with the 3rd ERV, describes this opposition as revealing 'the extent to which religion, nationalism, militarism, politics and anti-Catholicism had a potent influence on Scottish football'. Mackay (1986: 4) records how, in 1876, it was only after a petition was signed on its behalf by all the prominent players in Edinburgh that 'Hibs were reluctantly admitted into the SFA'.

Notably, until 2005 when the club began serialising Lugton's three-book collection, the official Hibs website explanation of the club's formation stated 'our club was founded by Irish-born football enthusiasts [but] Hibernian immediately became fully integrated into the Edinburgh community'. Not only was there no reference to Catholicism – exclusively Catholic players in the early days, or Canon Hannan's and the CYMS's involvement – but the early difficulties encountered by the club in attempting to join the Edinburgh and Scottish football associations had been historically revised. The result was that both Catholic associations (and exclusivity) and the local and national opposition to their football association membership were overlooked by the modern-day (official) club historians.

The beginnings of the Edinburgh rivalry

The wider 'Edinburgh community' was not quite as welcoming as the official club account suggests. In addition to the 3rd ERV influence within the Edinburgh FA, Hearts' original hand of friendship was supplanted by two official protests lodged to the football authorities. The first one sought to prevent Hibs from competing in the prestigious Edinburgh Cup (Mackay 1986). The second protest occurred after Hibs defeated Hearts in the Edinburgh Cup, with Hearts protesting that Hibs had a player who was 'not local' (Mackay 1986: 22). This set the tone for the next century, with both clubs becoming major rivals.

The extent to which these respective origins continue to influence and shape modern fan identities is debatable. In attempting to understand this we now turn attention to the fans themselves, allowing them to express their club identities in contemporary times.

FANS' PERSPECTIVES

The following fans' accounts form part of a larger on-going study that began in 2004. A number of fans from both clubs were interviewed. Some interviews were individual, some group and others took the form of unplanned, unstructured, opportunistic 'interview-as-talk' (Spradley 1979) interviews like those often conducted in ethnographic research environments. All interactions occurred between 2004 and the present day. Unless stated, opinions expressed here were shared by some other fans of each respective club, allowing some corroborating evidence to exist. While it is always problematic generalising too much with small samples, these views are the perspectives of existing fans of both clubs and therefore undeniably represent some fans' perceptions of both clubs. A range of ages and both male and female respondents were interviewed.

Ethno-religious and national identities

While both sets of fans generally tried to stress that the Edinburgh rivalry was not a mini-Old Firm, analysing their views exposes subtle elements of religious, ethnic and national identities emerging. One Hearts fan illustrates these subtleties by first stating: 'Hearts and Hibs hate each other but there's not the same bitterness [as the Old Firm] and the rivalry is very much a football rivalry.'

But he later inadvertently reveals it *is* more than mere football rivalry, stating his reasons for viewing Hearts as Edinburgh's premier club as being linked to Hibs' Irish links: 'Maybe it's the Irish connection with Hibs and the roots they came fae and everything else . . . Hearts were formed in Edinburgh, by Edinburgh people.'

Both sets of fans generally agreed that there are some sections of both supporters' groups that contribute to the *impression* of both clubs being a mini-Old Firm. Most fans admitted that Hearts are or have been perceived as a 'Protestant club' and Hibs as a 'Catholic/Irish-Catholic club'. The majority of Hearts fans interviewed expressed the view that in some ways Hearts and Hibs are a smaller and less bigoted version of their Glasgow counterparts, as illustrated in the following example: 'A lot of Hearts supporters can become sectarian . . . there is a lot of Union Jacks that fly about and what have you . . . but that's just the way they have been.'

In agreeing that Hearts and Hibs can sometimes be perceived to be an 'Edinburgh Old Firm', another Hearts fan notes:

> They probably are but I wish they weren't. Because Rangers and Celtic and the reasons they hate each other, that is not what football is about. Football is about competing for football, not about religion . . . but there is a certain aspect in our support and the same with Hibs fans who take it to that level.

Reflecting common themes among the Hibs fans, one Hibs fan adds:

> Some people see Hibs and Hearts as a mini Rangers and Celtic, with Hibs being the Catholic team and Hearts being the Protestants. I can't speak for Hearts but I mean when I went to my school all the lads that supported them [Hibs] were all Protestants. Hibs have a unique identity in that they came ye' know they've got this Irish heritage that they were founded by you know, basically by Irish immigrants but that the difference between us and Celtic is we're proud of our history and we've got it there but we don't let it sort of impact on the present if ye' like. I don't think you could identify that Hibs have got a Catholic support as opposed to a Protestant support . . . Hibs are not seen as a Catholic club by Hibs fans . . . the religious aspect disnae come into it in any way shape or form. I can state that without fear of contradiction.

Some Hearts fans suggested that Hibs are still, to some extent, seen to be representative of an Irish-Catholic identity. Another Hearts fan notes that some Hibs supporters wear Republic of Ireland tops to matches, but he viewed this as not having 'religious' or 'sectarian' undertones:

> You still get Hibs supporters that go to the game with the Republic of Ireland tops on . . . not to be inflammatory or anything like that, but just because they wear them as sort of leisure tops. And I think because there is probably a small percentage of Hibs supporters that possibly because of their family and the family roots as much as the club roots and everything else, will have a sort of sneaking sympathy for the Republic of Ireland.

Another Hearts fan, however, emphasises the religious connotations some Hearts fans attach to Hibs fans wearing Republic of Ireland tops or even the wearing of green, stating: 'To the wider Hearts supporters it's [green] seen as Catholic. Some Hibs fans see it like that too. You'll see some of them going to football matches with Ireland tops on and stuff like that.'

It was overwhelmingly agreed by both sets of fans that sections of Hibs and Hearts fans continue waving Irish Tricolours and Union Flags at each other and sometimes due to religious and national identity reasons. Most Hearts respondents agreed that Hibs supporters fly the Irish Tricolour more widely during matches with Hearts and Rangers, who they believe Hibs fans view as British-Protestant clubs. The wider Hearts support were viewed by their own fans to share a mild preference for Rangers over Celtic, which some Hearts fans explained was linked to the perceived similarities between Hearts and Rangers in their political and religious identity markers. The clearest expression of this came from a fan who also illustrated the accompanying perception that Celtic and Hibs share aspects of their respective identities:

> Some fans, maybe a lot of Hearts fans, think there's a connection between Hearts and Rangers. They think that because, well they used to think that anyway because it used to be Hibs and Celtic and then it's Hearts and Rangers. Hearts and Rangers are the two Protestant clubs and Hibs, Celtic are the two Catholic clubs. When Hearts visit Ibrox there are virtually no police there. And you can walk through the Rangers fans. And when you go to Celtic Park, we are cordoned off and we are marched to our bus . . . they hate Hearts fans because they see us as a little Rangers. And with Hibs it's the other way about. . . . I see Rangers as not as bad as Celtic . . . I hate Celtic much more than I do Rangers . . . it's maybe just because of the Hearts Rangers thing, because we sing one of their songs. Rangers fans and Hearts fans have a special thing with their scarves . . . They share some of their songs, they're both Protestant as well . . . originally.

Many fans of both clubs demonstrated that supporter behaviour depends largely on the perceived identity of the opposition. For example, a majority of Hearts fans explained that against Celtic more unionist symbols and songs will be utilised against the perceived Irish-Catholic Celtic supporters. 'I think in many cases the Hearts fans will sing songs back that they would never consider singing under any other circumstances.' One fan highlights the flying of the Union Flag by Hearts supporters, noting a section of them will 'bring those flags out against Celtic and no' against anybody else . . . I suppose it's for them to hold onto their British identity.'

Modified behaviour occurs against Rangers too but with a different identity constructed to suit the preferred impression being fostered for the particular audience – the Hearts supporters construct a more Scottish-centred identity against the perceived Ulster-British identity attributed to Rangers:

> The Hearts fans sing 'Flower of Scotland' when the Rangers fans sing 'Rule, Britannia!' We sing 'Flower of Scotland' to show we are a Scottish club and that. See, that's all it is, they sing 'God Save the Queen' and 'Rule, Britannia!' and all this.

Explicitly illustrating this impression management maintained by Hearts supporters, this fan adds: 'the only time ye' hear "Flower of Scotland" getting sung by Hearts fans is when it's in retaliation to a Rangers song'.

It was agreed by all fans that a section of Hearts supporters fly the Union Flag primarily at matches involving Hibs and Celtic as a way of reinforcing their Scottish-British identity against a perceived (Irish-Catholic) 'Other'. All respondents agreed that Hearts are perceived by others as well as by many of their own supporters as being 'more British' in their identity than most other clubs. One Hearts fan remarked: 'I mean they are British and the [Hearts] supporters like to get that over to people.'

Although sharing aspects of a British Protestant identity, the type of unionism linked to Hearts and Rangers differed (see Bradley and McKillop in this volume for further discussion about Rangers' Protestant identity). Some Hearts fans explicitly suggested that Hearts' Britishness is Scottish-British as opposed to Rangers' which they see as more Ulster-British. Some fans explained that although some Union Flags are present at European away matches, most Hearts supporters prefer to display the Scottish Saltire when playing abroad. It was suggested their Scottish identity becomes reinforced abroad as a result of being 'foreign' and the desire of the Hearts supporters to portray Scottish football supporters in a positive light. Other Hearts fans emphasised the Scottish dimension to the club's British identity, as neatly summarised by one fan:

> I would say there is more a sense of Scottishness than a sense of Britishness. I would say the Britishness thing goes in cycles. I think it tends to revolve around other circumstances and what is happening elsewhere, whether it's a war or whether it's the Gulf conflict or whatever . . . I would say if you were to ask 90 per cent of Hearts supporters, the badge has a St Andrew's cross in it and that's not coincidence.

The divergent British Unionism between Hearts and Rangers was perhaps most sharply illustrated by one fan's comments regarding whether or not the Hearts supporters display the Red Hand of Ulster flag:

> There is an Ulster Hearts supporters club who did have a Red Hand of Ulster flag. They stopped bringing it because Hearts asked them to. But they did have a flag, 'Ulster Hearts', which people took exception to as well. It was a Hearts flag with Ulster Hearts. I remember it at East End Park a couple of years ago and the flag had to get taken down. Well it was at East End Park and some Hearts fans mibee were seeing something that wisnae there, coming to the conclusion that anything with any association with Ulster may have other ulterior motives. I dinnae see the Red Hand of Ulster very often. Mibee one or two maximum at a big game but the Union Jack is more prevalent than any Red Hand of Ulster.

City rivalry

While competing (perhaps opposing) national identities remain part of the fabric of the Edinburgh clubs' sense of self (and in relation to others), a local geographical habitus emerged in the views expressed by most fans of both clubs, with the importance of Edinburgh and Leith[4] appearing significant. One Hearts fan explained the rivalry with Hibs was based largely on coming from 'different sides of Edinburgh, with the outskirts and west of Edinburgh tending to be populated by Hearts fans while Hibs fans largely reside in the east of the city'. Another Hearts fan added: 'Hearts are as big a part of the city as the castle. When I was growing up it always seemed to me that Hearts were Edinburgh's team. Even the colours of the buses were maroon.'

Just as Hearts fans viewed Edinburgh as central to their sense of club identity, a number of Hibs fans viewed their modern identity and rivalry with Hearts in geographical, rather than religious or ethnic, terms. Representing a common position, one Hibs fan noted:

> Leith is seen as having a separate identity from Edinburgh . . . and people from Leith regard themselves as sort . . . of separate, as totally separate from Edinburgh. 'Leithers' is what everybody's called. So Hibs play in Leith now and I think it is important that if ye' ever move the club from this area of Edinburgh, I think the club would die pretty rapidly.

Another Hibs fan sums up the duality of Leith and Edinburgh for Hibs fans, noting:

> It's another part of the Hibs dual identity . . . is that they are seen as this big Leith club and they are in many ways. Yet they come from the Cowgate and their traditional support was always from the Southside of Edinburgh which was where the Irish immigrant population lived.

Although cursory analysis of some fans' comments suggests a geographically focused identity, on closer inspection the geographical habitus occasionally incorporates ethno-religious dimensions which intersect the stated geographical identities expressed by both clubs. For example, one Hearts fan stresses:

> For me it [Hearts] was the club that identified with Edinburgh whereas Hibs were in Leith . . . oh they're from Leith . . . so as far as I'm concerned Hearts is Edinburgh's club. Hibs came later. I dunno, maybe it's the Irish connection with Hibs and the roots they came fae and everything else. I mean Hearts were formed in Edinburgh, Edinburgh people and it's a bit of that I think.

The obvious implication therefore is that Hearts and its supporters are seen by this fan as the established group while Hibs and its supporters are seen as outsiders as a result of coming from Leith, having an Irish connection and not being formed in Edinburgh for Edinburgh people. Most fans of both clubs viewed each other as the major rival, though a significant minority within both groups viewed either Celtic, Rangers or both Glasgow clubs as the major rival. Curiously, for some (among both clubs), even when their Edinburgh rival was noted to be the major rival, they sometimes preferred their major rival to win against the Glasgow clubs.

While some Hearts fans admitted that most Hearts fans view Rangers and Celtic as important rivals – with Celtic being slightly bigger rivals – most Hearts fans were certain that Hibs are *the* major rival and the team most Hearts supporters like to beat. Most Hibs fans agreed that Hearts are the primary rival. One Hibs fan explained: 'I suppose the biggest rivals have got to be Hearts simply because they come from the same city. So I think your biggest rivals are going to be your local rivals.'

Some of the Hibs fans perceive the Edinburgh rivalry as being intensified in recent years due to the aborted amalgamation of Hearts and Hibs, which some Hibs fans see as a failed takeover.[5] One fan commented:

> For a lot of Hibs fans, myself included, if ye' finish above Hearts then that's success for a season. Ye' want Hibs to win all the time and Hearts to get beat all the time and there's this added animosity since they tried to put us out of business in 1990. But ehhh, it's down to eh, they are *the Other* without any shadow of a doubt.

There was evidence of an imagined Edinburgh–Glasgow rivalry impacting on fan allegiances. Some Hearts fans conceded: 'more and more Hearts fans dislike both Celtic and Rangers as much as Hibs. And a lot of Hearts fans will say they hate Rangers just as much as they hate Celtic.' However, one fan's alternative position was occasionally shared. When asked who Hearts' biggest rivals were, he emphatically stated: 'Celtic. In my eyes it's Celtic. I'd rather be a Hibs fan than a Celtic fan. Ninety-nine per cent of [Hearts] fans agree that Celtic are the major other.'

Demonstrating a common view, a number of Hearts fans claimed that most fellow fans would rather see rival club Hibs beat Celtic or Rangers in a hypothetical cup final. One fan noted:

> Now, if it came to Rangers or Celtic playing Hibs in a cup final, I'm not sure how that would work out. I think most of them [Hearts supporters] would have a sneaky feeling in the back of their minds that they would actually like to see Hibs win it.

Other Hearts fans endorsed the view that they would rather see local rivals Hibs beat Celtic. But when asked about Rangers (playing Hibs), a small number admitted they would prefer Rangers to win. Some Hibs fans also viewed their Edinburgh rivals favourably. Even when noting Hearts as the primary local rival, they expressed a large degree of camaraderie with them, subsequently viewing both Rangers and Celtic as the primary 'Other': 'I actually see Hibs and Hearts as two sides of the same coin and actually if I had to tell you who did I, if you were talking about disliking more, I would say Rangers or Celtic.' A fellow Hibs fan agreed: 'Yeah, ye' hate the Old Firm more than ye' hate Hearts.' However, clarifying her position, she added:

> I would rather see the Old Firm get beat because it's always funny . . . I actually don't mind the . . . the Hearts fans are like Hibs fans in a lot of ways. They could go through to Ibrox and Parkhead like half the people in Scotland do but they don't, so you've got to give them some kind of respect for that.

Paradoxically then, though some Hearts and Hibs fans concede their Edinburgh rivals are their main 'Other', these fans simultaneously express a large degree of camaraderie with the Other to such an extent that they prefer to see them win against either Celtic or Rangers. Attributing reasons for this is difficult and may be more related to a perceived joint Edinburgh unity in imagined opposition to the Glasgow clubs as much as it might be due to ethno-religious factors. The general antipathy towards Celtic and Rangers was evident throughout all of the interviews with both sets of fans, with a small minority of Hearts fans reserving it exclusively for Celtic and a small minority of Hibs fans reserving it exclusively for Rangers. Noting the particularly intense rivalry with Rangers, a Hibs fan adds:

> I don't say Hibs are any angels in this. There is a section of Rangers fans who know that the club [Hibs] is from an Irish background and they know that there are people who support Hibs who are Catholic and perhaps they may even attend Church, but the perception is that they are Catholic. And given the nature that Rangers is predominantly a club that people who are Protestant will tend to support, they will come with the intention of winding Hibs fans up . . . And when Rangers start singing songs that they know will antagonise the Hibs fans, when they start singing things like 'Rule, Britannia!' and singing the Sash they do it because they want to wind Hibs fans up.

There was an overwhelming belief in the Glasgow clubs' collective culpability for 'sectarianism', with many Hearts and Hibs fans expressing the opinion that many (sometimes 'the majority') of Rangers and Celtic fans were 'sectarian'. A Hibs fan captures this fully:

> We're now in the 21st century and people are still . . . I'm talking about both Rangers and Celtic here, ye' know the obscenity of still fighting battles that happened three or four hundred years ago just does ma' head in to be honest with ye'. Jack McConnell summed it up calling it Scotland's Shame . . . The people that attach themselves to the two Glasgow clubs continue to promote it every Saturday and ye' go to Ibrox where ye' have the obscenity of going to see the Scottish people wearing England football shirts and singing the songs, even promoted by the club. Ye' used to have Andy Cameron coming on five minutes before the game and he leads a sing song flying the Union Jacks and they play a medley of songs over the loudspeakers and it's the Dambusters and the Great Escape. And they used to have a fucking German goalie. And it's the same when ye' go to Parkhead . . . the bigot brothers, I'm afraid they've certainly destroyed Scottish football to a certain extent and they are a blight on Scottish society as far as I'm concerned.

In addition to the 'bigot brothers' label, some Hibs fans perceive Celtic supporters to be patronising towards Hibs. One Hibs fan comments that Celtic fans 'treat us like their little Irish brothers'. Another adds:

I think that Celtic see it almost patronising slightly at times if ye' like. Ye' know they see ye' as their wee cousins if ye' like, ye' know their wee cousins from Edinburgh because we play in green and white or some crap like that.

Although it seems fair to assert that for Hearts and Hibs the ethno-religious dynamic is distinct from and less obvious than that exhibited in Glasgow between the Old Firm, it does continue to lurk in the construction of imagined identities (and differences) for some of the Edinburgh clubs' supporters. But it appears that most fans of both clubs view their self and intra-city rival in Edinburgh terms first and ethno-religious terms second, if at all. What is clear, however, is that both clubs occasionally reveal elements of their ethno-religious past and this is as likely to occur against the Glasgow clubs as it is against their own Edinburgh rivals.

MAPPING THE FIELD IN THE TWENTY-FIRST CENTURY

In recent years, there have been some instances involving fans of the Edinburgh clubs that could be interpreted as 'sectarian' in nature. In April 2005, a minute's silence for Pope John Paul II was disrupted by Hearts supporters to such an extent that it was cut short by more than half (Stow 2005). Subsequently some Hearts supporters' spokespeople refused to condemn the actions of the Hearts supporters (Stow 2005). In more recent times, sections of Hearts supporters have worn scarves and t-shirts to matches decorated with Ulster Loyalism images, displayed Red Hand of Ulster flags and the Union Flag,[6] and in some cases aligned themselves with the British National Party (Jardine 2002). There has also been an apparent increase in fan tensions recently when Celtic play Hearts.[7] Although it is unwise to ascribe definite motives for these acts, it is reasonable to consider the possibility that some are linked to sectarianism.

With regard to the Edinburgh derby, in April 2011, a month after the so-called 'shame game' between Celtic and Rangers which precipitated the eventual Offensive Behaviour Bill, Hibs played Hearts at Easter Road in a controversial derby. Pre-match, Hibs' player Richie Towell (on-loan from Celtic) had angered some by claiming the alleged abuse he received from Hearts fans was worse than he experienced from Rangers fans and that it was linked to being an Irish Catholic (see Scotsman 2011). In a match that resulted in twenty fans being ejected for 'unruly behaviour' and three stadium arrests, scores of Hearts fans encroached onto the pitch at one point and around a dozen missiles were thrown from Hibs fans towards Hearts players taking throw-ins and corners in one part of the ground.[8] Hibs fans goaded Hearts' star player, singing en-masse 'Rudi Skacel's a fucking refugee', while the Hearts fans responded with their Gorgie Boys adaptation of the banned Billy Boys with the proscribed line, 'We're up to our knees in Fenian blood'. One Hibs fan had his Irish Socialist-Republican Starry Plough flag confiscated by police inside the stadium. Even before the match a small group of around thirty Hearts fans congregated outside a pub on Easter Road and sang the Famine Song, asking the Irish descendants in Scotland, 'Why don't you go home?' What this reveals is rather contradictory. On the one hand, the Edinburgh rivalry is about Edinburgh, Gorgie and Leith and is a local rivalry based on geographical factors. On the other hand, for some within both clubs, sectarian elements remain.

It is true that the Edinburgh rivalry is not a mini-Old Firm. It is also probably true that the vast majority of both clubs' fans place little or any importance on ethno-religious factors when imagining their respective identities. But there are dormant ethno-religious tensions that occasionally awaken, reminding us of both clubs' past and their lingering contemporary significance in particular situations. While some Hearts fans have a stronger antipathy towards Celtic than Rangers (some even preferring Hibs to Celtic) and some Hibs fans have a stronger antipathy towards Rangers than Celtic, most fans of both Edinburgh clubs disdainfully view both Celtic and Rangers equally, labelling them the bigot brothers, Scotland's Shame or the non-sectarian but equally pejorative 'slum-dwelling weegies'.[9]

Hibs fans tend to oscillate between either viewing the club's Irish-Catholic identity as having little place in modern Edinburgh/Scotland or having some (as yet) unarticulated part to play in the modern club. For example, the former position is characterised by some who actively seek to avoid any association for fear of being 'sectarian':

Although there is the Irish heritage . . . you don't have to go in for all that plastic Paddy stuff to be a Hibs fan. In fact most people are actually anti-that. They see themselves as an Edinburgh club. And with an Edinburgh identity and Scottish despite the roots . . . Hibs did actually turn away from that quite early on in their existence. They've been a lot quicker to let go of that kind of background than certain other clubs in Scotland. And I must admit that's one of my pet hates. I can't stand sectarianism or racism in any form at all. And if I felt the club was going down that route in any way I would be disillusioned with it. In the modern-day Edinburgh club the Irish Tricolour has no place. The whole Irish . . . I don't think it does Hibs any favours.

However, other Hibs fans who also agreed that the Irish-Catholic identity has little place in the modern club were less concerned that it might be perceived to be sectarian, but rather view it as an undeniable anachronism:

Given the history of the club coming from the Catholic community of Edinburgh and also from the Irish community . . . it's seen as being in the past, part of the Irish community and part Catholic, but today I think, given the nature of Edinburgh and society, I think that is a historical part of the club. And I think you will find that when people support Hibs, anything that has to do with religion is not seen as such a big part of it.

There remain, however, some Hibs fans who wish to embrace the club's Irish-Catholic identity. This ranges from those who wish to give a lukewarm, cautious welcome, to those who would emphasise the political contexts more openly. Well-known Hibs fan Charlie Reid captures the former position:

I'm glad the club is acknowledging its roots – in the past there's been some reluctance to do so. The club is now at peace with its culture in a way that maybe some other clubs are not and I would like to see more done to acknowledge our history, without that 'greeting into a beer glass' thing that so persists at Celtic . . . As a Scottish football club with Irish roots, that identity should be celebrated and integrated into what we all are as Hibs supporters. (cited in MacVannan 2011: 23)

Capturing the latter position clearly, Jim Slaven notes:

We need to create a space where Hibs can acknowledge its origins and those who want to can express their ethnicity, within the football stadium and within Edinburgh, without feeling somehow that they are doing something wrong or that it's illegitimate . . . The people who complain about the tricolour being flown at football games are the same people who would tell you there isn't any anti-Irish racism or that there isn't any sectarianism. (cited in MacVannan 2011: 78–9)

There is an uneasiness around embracing Hibs' Irish-Catholic linkages, with some fans describing feeling like 'an embarrassing uncle', while no such fear or embarrassment exists among the Hearts fans' embracing of their club's history. Hearts fans appear more comfortable and open about recognising their historical development and original traditions than Hibs fans, with McCrae's Battalion occupying a position of legitimacy that Irish-Catholic signifiers struggle to achieve in Scotland.

CONCLUSIONS

These fan relationships with the past and their respective collective representations in the present encapsulate some of the broader attitudes towards 'sectarianism' beyond the confines of Edinburgh. It is clear that many of the views expressed by these fans reflect and reinforce some of the dominant themes around 'sectarianism' in Scotland, with Irish-Catholic and Ulster-Loyalist symbols being anchored in sectarian terms, making their legitimacy in twenty-first-century Scotland problematic for many.

'Sectarianism' is viewed by most fans of the Edinburgh clubs as someone else's problem or, to be precise, a Glasgow/West problem sustained by the 'bigot brothers' of Rangers and Celtic (clubs and fans, see Rosie's chapter for similar findings). While a very small minority of Hibs and Hearts fans continue to embrace sectarianised elements of their clubs' identities, this presents problems for much of their combined wider support and reveals yet more common (and officially endorsed) attitudes towards ethno-religious identities and power dynamics beyond Edinburgh football culture, with a core hegemonic 'we' identity encouraged and legitimised in favour of the pejoratively viewed 'sectarian' Irish/Ulster identities. This selective construction of the imagined communities of Hibs and Hearts camouflages the reality of tradition, heritage, identity and legacy being contested terrain with selection/omission, location/dislocation and legitimising/demonising discourses occurring. Billig (1996: 2) reminds us that:

> To hold an attitude is to take a stance in a matter of controversy. The meaning of the stance derives both from what is being supported and from what is being rejected . . . An argument for an issue of controversy is also an argument *against* counter-views . . . [A]ffirmation and negation are intertwined, as the logoi of discourse are also anti-logoi, to be understood in relation to the context of controversy. (original emphasis)

There is a legitimised non-sectarian identity promoted at the expense of alternative ethnic, religious and political identities that, for some, are equally meaningful, relevant and legitimate.

NOTES

1. Alexander (2003: 311) claims that 'Heart of Midlothian's grasp of its own history leaves much to be desired.'
2. Some of this Hibs section was originally published as part of an article by the author published in *Sport in Society* in 2007 and entitled 'Hibernian Football Club: The Forgotten Irish?' Copyright permission has been granted.
3. Mackay (1986) states that it was the Young Men's Catholic Association (YMCA).
4. Leith was an independent municipal burgh prior to its incorporation within the city of Edinburgh.
5. In 1990 the then Chairman of Hearts, the late Wallace Mercer, made a £6.2m bid to take over Hibs. Resistance to the move, sparked by fears of an amalgamation and the ending of the individual identities of the two clubs, resulted in the high-profile 'Hands off Hibs' campaign. Mercer's attempt to form a united Edinburgh team was eventually defeated.
6. In the last four years I have attended a number of Hearts matches – against Hibs and Celtic – and have witnessed all of these symbols being displayed among a small minority of Hearts fans.
7. This is undoubtedly linked to the Green Brigade banner criticising the Earl Haig poppy being placed on the Celtic shirt. Hearts fans more than most reacted to this and the subsequent Hearts v. Celtic fixtures were among the most heated in recent times. Numerous references to British forces and 'Heroes' and 'remembrance' and numerous Red Hand and Union Flags have been visible among the Hearts fans, and Celtic fans have chanted anti-poppy slogans and 'I, IRA, Irish Republican Army' in a manner very uncommon in recent years.
8. I attended the match and witnessed this clearly as I was in the same section where it occurred.
9. A general non-'sectarian' Edinburgh–Glasgow rivalry was expressed by both groups of fans and is an additional layer of identification and rivalry that cannot be expanded upon here due to space.

REFERENCES

Alexander, J. (2003), *McCrae's Battalion: The Story of the Sixteenth Royal Scots*, Edinburgh: Mainstream.

Billig, M. (1996), *Arguing and Thinking. A Rhetorical Approach to Social Psychology*, Cambridge: Cambridge University Press.

Finn, G. P. T. (1994), 'Faith, hope and bigotry. Case studies of anti-Catholic prejudice in Scottish soccer and society', in G. Jarvie and G. Walker (eds), *Scottish Sport in the Making of the Nation. Ninety Minute Patriots?*, Leicester: Leicester University Press, pp. 91–112.

Hognestad, H. K. (1997), 'The Jambo experience: An anthropological study of Hearts fans', in G. Armstrong and R. Giulianotti (eds), *Entering the Field. New Perspectives on World Football*, Oxford: Berg, pp. 193–210.

Jardine, P. (2002), 'Fans banned as Hearts probe trouble', 4 January 2002, www.soccernet.co.uk.

Kelly, J. (2007), 'Hibernian Football Club: The forgotten Irish?', *Sport in Society*, 10: 3, 514–36.

Kowalski (2004), '"Cry for us, Argentina". Sport and national identity in late twentieth-century Scotland', in A. Smith and D. Porter (eds), *Sport and National Identity in the Post-War World*, London: Routledge, pp. 69–87.

Lugton, A. (1999), *The Making of Hibernian. Volume 1*, Edinburgh: John Donald.

Mackay, J. (1986), *The Hibees. The Story of Hibernian Football Club*, Edinburgh: Mainstream.

Mackie, A. (1959), *The Hearts. The Story of Heart of Midlothian F.C.*, London: Stanley Paul.

MacVannan, A. (2011), *We are Hibernian: The Fans' Story*, Edinburgh: Luath Press.

The Scotsman (2011), 'Bigotry "not unique to the Old Firm"', 5 April 2011, p. 3.

Spradley, J. P. (1979), *The Ethnographic Interview*, London: Holt, Rinehart and Winston.

Stow, N. (2005), 'Hearts fans leaders refuse to slam jeers', *Evening News*, 11 April.

4   'They Sing That Song': Football and Sectarianism in Glasgow during the 1920s and 1930s[1]

Andrew Davies

INTRODUCTION

The sectarian contours of football in Glasgow were firmly established before the First World War. As Bill Murray noted in his pioneering history of the 'Old Firm', the Celtic Football Club was founded 'for and by' Catholics in the city's East End in 1888.[2] The club was aligned with Irish nationalism and home rule politics from its inception and effectively served as the 'standard-bearer' of the city's Irish-Catholic community.[3] Rangers assumed a similar mantle among Protestants during the 1890s, and Old Firm matches quickly acquired the backdrop of religious bigotry which has characterised encounters between the teams ever since.[4] Murray claimed that football provided a social palliative in Glasgow during the early decades of the twentieth century. While he was fiercely critical of the way in which Rangers and Celtic together exploited the city's ethnic and religious divisions for commercial gain, he nonetheless saw the Old Firm rivalry as offering 'a release for sectarian hatreds in the relatively harmless atmosphere of a football match'.[5]

Other historians have echoed Murray's claim. Tom Gallagher depicted the Rangers–Celtic rivalry as a useful outlet for Glasgow's ethnic and religious antagonisms: 'the soccer rivalry which emerged at the start of [the twentieth] century may have been a useful tension-releasing valve – two rival working-class communities were able to assert their identity through sporting champions who had the fortunes of their own people on their shoulders.'[6] Seán Damer echoed Gallagher's claim, commenting that the 'ritual expression of hostility' between supporters of Celtic and Rangers helped to ensure that the city did not witness the larger-scale sectarian rioting seen in Liverpool in the early twentieth century.[7]

This chapter makes the opposite case. My argument is that the Old Firm rivalry inflamed sectarian hostilities in Glasgow throughout the interwar decades. Matches between Rangers and Celtic mobilised tens of thousands of football supporters into bitterly opposed camps, with expressions of national and religious allegiance inseparable from exchanges of sectarian abuse and violence. Like the annual 'Orange Walks', held to commemorate the victory of the Protestant William of Orange at the Battle of the Boyne in 1690, Old Firm matches brought ethnic divisions to the forefront of civic life and turned religious affiliations into the source of intense antagonism. On these occasions, over-arching Protestant and Catholic allegiances found expression in the sporting of blue (Rangers) and green (Celtic) colours and even momentarily eclipsed the fierce territorial loyalties that underpinned Glasgow's gang culture.[8] Far from providing a safety-valve, football added an incendiary spark to Glasgow's ethnic and religious divisions.

Like the Orange Walks – and church parades – football matches involved the movement of thousands of people across Glasgow in crowds that were clearly identifiable as Protestant or Catholic. Football, however, was played on a weekly basis for ten months of the year. By the 1920s, with supporters increasingly utilising motorised charabancs, it was common for followers of the Old Firm to travel to their team's home matches in groups forty- or fifty-strong. Any day when either Rangers or Celtic played in Glasgow saw potential flashpoints across the city. Many Rangers supporters drove through districts with substantial Irish-Catholic populations en route to Ibrox Park, Rangers' stadium in Govan. Likewise, Celtic followers frequently passed through the East-End Protestant stronghold of Bridgeton Cross on their way to Celtic Park. Neither set of supporters moved anonymously through the city. Rangers and Celtic supporters alike flaunted their teams' colours, sang 'party' songs and shouted abuse and threats at passers-by suspected of belonging to the rival faith. On days of matches between Rangers and Celtic, the thoroughfares leading to Ibrox or Celtic Park were crammed with supporters of both teams, and Glasgow's sectarian antagonisms were mobilised in full.

This chapter is divided into four sections. The first briefly sketches the development of sectarianism in Glasgow before 1914 and its nature and intensification during the 1920s and 1930s. The second examines violence perpetrated by and against Old Firm supporters travelling by charabanc during the 1920s, both within Glasgow and on journeys to and from matches elsewhere in the West of Scotland. The third section offers a wider exploration of violence between supporters of the Old Firm, in riots outside the stadiums, in ambushes of supporters travelling to matches on foot or by train, and in more spontaneous confrontations on non-match days. The fourth section presents a case-study of the trial of John Traquair, a Rangers supporter sentenced to four years' penal servitude following an attack on Celtic supporters in March 1934. Traquair's trial exposed both the nature of confrontations between followers of the Old Firm and the fusion of ethnic and religious antagonisms that informed them. As the Traquair case forcibly reminds us, concerns with violence and disorder among supporters of Rangers and Celtic are not new.

SECTARIANISM IN GLASGOW

Sectarianism was deeply rooted in many aspects of communal life in Glasgow by 1914. The city's Protestant community, which formed around three-quarters of the population, harboured long-standing anti-Irish and anti-Catholic prejudices. Moreover, the settlement of Ulster Protestants in Glasgow from the early nineteenth century led to the forging of many cultural and political ties with Ulster loyalism. The Orange Order established strongholds in many of the city's working-class districts, from Govan in the south-west of the city to Bridgeton in the East End.[9] Protestant migration from Belfast to Glasgow was renewed from 1912, when the Belfast shipbuilders Harland & Wolff opened a yard in Govan. A new wave of Ulster Protestants settled in the surrounding districts; their arrival coincided with the sharpening of ethnic divisions in Glasgow in the wake of the burgeoning home rule crisis.[10]

Glasgow's Catholic population, although largely Scottish-born by the turn of the twentieth century, was overwhelmingly of Irish descent and identified strongly with Irish nationalism. Irish Catholics were treated with disdain by many Scottish Protestants on grounds of both religion and ethnicity and suffered widespread discrimination in the labour market. Throughout the late nineteenth and early twentieth centuries, membership of Masonic and Orange lodges was used by Protestants to regulate entry into skilled trades and exclude Catholics from the better-paid and more secure manual occupations in many branches of industry. The effects of labour market discrimination were cemented by the development of an 'introverted' Irish-Catholic culture, in which a separate faith was augmented by a host of social and cultural institutions ranging from Catholic schools to the Ancient Order of Hibernians and the Celtic Football Club.[11]

Sectarianism intensified during the 1920s and 1930s. The War of Independence witnessed IRA activity in the city, leading to a violent Protestant backlash against the local Irish-Catholic population during the early 1920s.[12] The establishment of state support for separate Catholic schools under the 1918 Education (Scotland) Act led to prolonged protests from Protestants complaining of 'Rome on the Rates'.[13] Antagonism was stirred up further during the 1920s by the vehemently anti-Catholic campaigns of the Church of Scotland, which railed against the effects of Irish-Catholic settlement on the racial purity and ecclesiastical integrity of the Scots. Protestant anxieties were heightened by the growth of the Catholic church in Scotland during the interwar decades. Increasing Catholic church attendances contrasted sharply with the slow, relative decline of the Church of Scotland.[14]

In the early 1930s, anti-Catholicism became a significant force in Glasgow's municipal politics. Mass unemployment eroded the economic privileges of skilled Protestant manual workers and the economic downturn of the early 1930s was exploited by the militant Scottish Protestant League (SPL) under the leadership of Alexander Ratcliffe. In Ratcliffe's propaganda, the local Irish-Catholic population made a perfect scapegoat for the city's economic and social ills. The SPL enjoyed a short-lived surge of support in Glasgow's municipal elections, taking two council seats in 1931 and another the following year. In 1933, with adult male unemployment in Glasgow reaching 38 per cent, the SPL secured four more seats after polling 67,000 votes, nearly a quarter of the total cast.[15] The SPL's initial successes were in working-class wards with strong 'Orange' traditions. In the East End, in particular, the SPL appealed to Protestant manual workers who had previously voted for the

Unionist-led 'Moderates'.[16] The main beneficiary, ironically, was the Labour Party, which wrestled control of the city council from the Moderates for the first time.[17]

The demise of the SPL was as rapid as its rise. By 1934, Ratcliffe's autocratic leadership style had alienated his fellow SPL councillors, who began to defect amid much rancour. In November that year, following a botched electoral pact with the Moderates, the SPL's share of the votes in the municipal elections fell to just 7 per cent.[18] Labour's control of the city council for the remainder of the decade suggests that, within the realm of municipal politics, class loyalties ultimately triumphed over ethnic and religious divisions. Nonetheless, Ratcliffe's brief flourish highlighted the political capital to be made from militant Protestantism in periods of economic decline.

There was only limited residential segregation between Catholics and Protestants in Glasgow during the 1920s and 1930s. As Damer noted, many of the city's working-class residential neighbourhoods were predominantly Catholic or Protestant and widely recognised as such, but Glasgow never had near-exclusive religious ghettos on the scale of those in Liverpool.[19] Glasgow's Irish-Catholic community tended to be clustered in the impoverished districts on the fringes of the city centre such as the Calton, the Garngad and the Gorbals. Although renowned as 'Irish' districts, however, none was exclusively so. The Gorbals, for example, housed both a substantial Protestant population and a vibrant Jewish community during the interwar decades and an SPL candidate received 25 per cent of votes cast in the Gorbals ward in the municipal elections of 1934.[20] Bridgeton, renowned as the epicentre of militant Protestantism in the East End, likewise housed a sizeable Catholic minority.[21]

In these ethnically mixed neighbourhoods, religious parades tended to draw large crowds of both supporters and opponents. Processions organised by the various churches, along with those of the Orange Order and the Ancient Order of Hibernians, frequently spilled over into violence. The annual 'Orange Walks', held on a Saturday around 12 July, drew as many as 50,000 people during the interwar decades. Confrontations broke out across Glasgow on the Saturday evening as the processionists made their way home. Catholic residents hung Irish Tricolours from tenement windows in gestures of defiance and hostile crowds gathered in principal thoroughfares such as the Gallowgate in the Calton. Violence was easily sparked by the waving of orange or green colours or by the shouting of sectarian abuse.[22]

In the East End, feuds between rival street gangs frequently assumed sectarian overtones. Sectarianism among the East-End gangs stretched back into the late nineteenth century, in part as a result of the strong Orange presence in Bridgeton.[23] The Bridgeton Billy Boys, whose name proclaimed their allegiance to William of Orange, were widely recognised as the most powerful of Glasgow's gangs from the mid-1920s to the late 1930s.[24] During the early 1930s, they provided stewards for SPL election meetings in the East End to ward off disruption by local Catholic street gangs.[25] Their song, 'Hello, Hello, We are the Billy Boys', with its challenge to 'Fenians' to 'surrender or you'll die', was hugely inflammatory. Bellowed in the streets, at Rangers matches and on Orange Walks, it was guaranteed to cause uproar.[26]

Following the 12 July parades, the Billy Boys marched at the head of Orange processions through the Calton back to Bridgeton. The gang claimed that its presence was a defensive response to Catholic assaults on Orange marchers.[27] However, the appearance of this renowned group of Protestant street-fighters in turn demanded a response from the Catholic gangs of the Calton. The resulting clashes were eagerly anticipated on both sides.[28] Gang feuds in the city's East End provoked bitter sectarian hostility among those aged in their teens, twenties and even thirties. Skirmishes between gangs were by no means confined to the traditional tension points in the religious calendar. Quite the reverse: gangs sometimes fought on a weekly, or even nightly, basis in seemingly endless cycles of retribution.[29]

Gang conflicts on Glasgow's South Side were less overtly sectarian. The largest and most notorious of the Gorbals gangs, the South Side Stickers, were often assumed to be Catholics on account of the Gorbals' reputation as an 'Irish' district. However, the Stickers contained Catholic, Protestant and Jewish members, in contrast to the avowedly sectarian gangs of the East End.[30] The lack of a strong Orange tradition in the Gorbals might help to account for the comparatively low level of sectarianism among the South-Side gangs. Gorbals gangs pursued vendettas against each other, against their Catholic counterparts from the Calton, and against Protestant gangs from Bridgeton with equal vigour.[31]

Even territorial gang loyalties were momentarily eclipsed, however, on the days of Old Firm matches. Larry Rankin was a member of the Gorbals-based Beehive Boys during the 1930s. Like their rivals, the South Side Stickers, the Beehive Boys had Protestants and Jews among their ranks as well as Catholics.[32] Rankin was fiercely proud of his standing as a Beehive Boy. Nonetheless, he was also a proud Protestant and when Rangers played Celtic he would make his way to Bridgeton to join up with the Billy Boys. In Rankin's words:

> when it came to the Rangers and Celtic game, I always went over to Bridgeton and became one of the Billy Boys for the day ... you were always getting involved ... it was usually bottles that they were throwing, and you didn't know who was hit with them anyway so you didn't care so much ... .[33]

Rankin must have known that some of his fellow Beehive Boys were among the crowds of Celtic supporters that he was bombarding. Yet this form of violence was relatively impersonal and meant that his identity as a Beehive Boy could be reconciled with his allegiance to Rangers.

BRAKE CLUBS AND DISORDER

During the early 1920s, reports of rowdiness and violence among Old Firm supporters centred on the rival Rangers and Celtic 'brake clubs'. The clubs were first formed in the 1890s and named after the horse-drawn carriages, or brakes, hired by groups of supporters to travel to games at Ibrox and Celtic Park. As early as the 1900s, it was alleged that brakes were being used to ferry rival sets of 'hooligans' around the city.[34] Concern with the conduct of the brake clubs intensified during the early 1920s, by which time the supporters were hiring motorised charabancs capable of carrying fifty passengers. Brakes were festooned with flags and banners proclaiming allegiance to the rival national causes of Britain and Ireland.[35] Against the backdrop of the War of Independence and the creation of the Irish Free State in 1922, these were an incendiary presence on the streets of Glasgow.

Rangers brakes drove through the city's 'Catholic' districts on their way to matches, just as Celtic brakes crossed through the Protestant heartlands of Bridgeton and Govan. The conduct of the 'brakists' was calculated to antagonise those of the rival faith. The waving of flags, singing of songs, shouting of sectarian abuse and issuing of threats to passing pedestrians frequently met with violent ripostes and many brakists armed themselves before setting off to matches.[36] In October 1923, forty members of the Sally Boys, a Celtic brake club from Parkhead comprised of lads aged in their late teens, were arrested after their charabanc was witnessed driving through Govan following an Old Firm match at Ibrox with the occupants waving flags and banners and shouting threats. A store of stones and half-bricks was found on board the vehicle along with a hammer, a loaded stick and fourteen flagpoles.[37]

Brake clubs, however, were as much sinned against as sinning. In April 1925 there was a series of attacks on charabancs carrying Celtic supporters home from the Scottish Cup final between Celtic and Dundee at Hampden Park. Eighteen members of a Celtic brake club were arrested following an incident in Bridgeton. Police told how the occupants of the charabanc had been waving banners, playing bugles and shaking rattles. They were also holding aloft an imitation Cup trophy. They met a hostile response in Dalmarnock Road, as the Evening Citizen reported: 'a crowd of young men were lined up waiting for them, and bottles, stones, etc, were thrown at the occupants of the charabanc who jumped down to save themselves'. The ambushers promptly fled. Police apprehended the brakists, all of whom were subsequently fined for breaching the peace. Another Celtic brake club was attacked in the Plantation district, where their charabanc was bombarded with missiles by Rangers supporters returning from Ibrox.[38]

Brake clubs were frequently involved in outbreaks of violence when they travelled to matches outside Glasgow. Supporters of both Celtic and Rangers complained bitterly that their brakes were the targets of widespread hostility.[39] However, complaints of misbehaviour by the brakists themselves on their travels were legion. In effect, the brake clubs' return trips through the towns and villages of Lanarkshire, like their journeys through Glasgow, provided endless opportunities to antagonise those of the opposing faith. Some brake clubs knowingly took routes through towns and villages where they were likely to encounter a hostile response and they appear to have relished the violence that followed. In November 1922, Rangers brakists were involved in a spate of incidents in Broomhouse following a match at Hamilton. Police witnessed one brake stop as it entered the village to allow the passengers to gather stones for use as missiles. They waved flags, sang 'party' songs, yelled 'Kick the Pope!' and 'other such phrases' and threw bottles at the Catholic residents of the miners' cottages in Boghall Rows. Thirty-one brakists were arrested and subsequently fined five pounds each.[40]

Heightened efforts were made to combat the 'brake club menace' in the wake of incidents such as these. A special meeting of the Glasgow magistrates had been convened in September 1922, when it was noted that the police were only empowered to apprehend brakes when breaches of the peace took place.[41] On the instruction of the Chief Constable, attempts were made to prohibit supporters taking flags and flagpoles, banners, rattles, bugles and whistles into stadiums.[42] This was of limited effect, and in any case, most of the disorder sparked by the brake clubs took place outside the stadiums as supporters made their way to and from matches. In October 1925, Glasgow police chose the day of an Old Firm match at Ibrox to launch another campaign to combat 'brake club rowdyism'. Police motorcyclists tracked the brakes as they left the vicinity of the stadium, having issued warnings that rowdy conduct would not be tolerated. Three Celtic brakes were apprehended along with one carrying Rangers supporters. Police made 128 arrests and roundly condemned the brake clubs when the prisoners appeared at Glasgow's Southern Police Court, pointing both to the tendency for brakists to carry weapons and missiles, and to the disorder provoked by their 'bawling and shouting', obscene language, party tunes and banners. Fines of two guineas were meted out, with the option of twenty days' imprisonment, after the police called for exemplary sentences. The conviction of such a large batch of offenders made front-page news in the local press.[43]

However, the concerted efforts of the police and magistrates posed no immediate deterrent. Two weeks later, police tracked a charabanc carrying Celtic supporters from the Garngad on its way to Ibrox. Green-and-white flags were draped around the vehicle before it set off. The charabanc wound its way through the city centre and crossed the River Clyde, its occupants waving banners and singing 'My Bonny, Blue-Eyed Irish Boy' along with an improvised verse in which Celtic players formed an alternative royal family: Paddy Gallagher became king of Ireland, and Jimmy McGrory prince of Wales. Police apprehended the vehicle in the Gorbals and confiscated green-and-white banners, scarves, flags and painted bowler hats along with a concertina. Twenty-nine young men were arrested and charged with disorderly conduct.[44] Similar scenes were reported following brake club disturbances in Glasgow and beyond in the years that followed.[45] However, during the second half of the 1920s, concern with the conduct of brake clubs among the Glasgow police and press was eclipsed by the growing anxieties surrounding the city's street gangs. Brake clubs more rarely captured headlines after 1925, but hostility between supporters of the Old Firm continued unabated.

GEOGRAPHIES OF DISORDER

During the late 1920s and 1930s, violence continued to flare between supporters of Rangers and Celtic in riots outside the stadiums and in ambushes of supporters travelling to matches on foot, in brakes or by train. At Old Firm encounters, rival supporters were segregated inside Ibrox and Celtic Park, but routinely clashed both before and after matches in the surrounding streets. Outbreaks of stone-throwing appear to have been a ritualised occurrence on these occasions.[46] More spontaneous confrontations erupted on non-match days, both within the city's working-class

residential districts and in the city centre. Sectarian hostility between Old Firm supporters was thus woven into the fabric of everyday life in the city.

Members of sectarian street gangs often played a prominent role in violence
outside the stadiums. In October 1927, the Old Firm met at Hampden Park for the
final of the Glasgow Cup. A general melee in which sticks, stones and other missiles
were thrown caused a 'stampede' outside the stadium at the end of the match. The
Bridgeton Billy Boys were reportedly at the heart of the affray. The disturbance was
broken up by a detachment of thirty mounted and foot police, only for hostilities to
resume when the Billy Boys spotted a Celtic supporter sporting a green handkerchief
and scarf. The man was punched, knocked down and kicked.[47] The following season
a riot broke out on Broomloan Road, one of the principal thoroughfares leading to
Ibrox. Thousands of people were crossing a patch of vacant land following an Old
Firm match when rival supporters began stoning each other and passing tram cars.
Mounted police were again required to restore order.[48] Almost identical scenes, on
the same patch of open ground, were reported eight years later. Police described a
'running fight' with missiles being thrown among a vast crowd of supporters.[49]

Supporters of both Rangers and Celtic were routinely at risk of assault as they
made their way across the city to matches, whether by public transport or on foot.
In March 1935, trains carrying Rangers' supporters back from Motherwell were
stoned as they reached Glasgow's East End. According to railway officials, this was
a 'common practice'.[50] More common still were assaults on Celtic supporters as
they made their way through Bridgeton before and after matches at Celtic Park. In
September 1934, twenty-year-old James Boyle was stabbed in the leg and severely
wounded as he walked to Celtic Park with two companions.[51] Celtic supporters were
especially vulnerable as they passed the Billy Boys' gathering place at Bridgeton
Cross. Pedestrians were assaulted and buses were stoned. In April 1937, four Celtic
supporters suffered head and facial wounds after their bus was 'showered' from both
sides with bottles and stones. Police had been positioned at the Cross to safeguard
supporters' buses, but to no avail. A twenty-eight-year old Billy Boy with five previous convictions was jailed for thirty days for his part in the stone-throwing.[52] The
following year, a full-scale gang fight between two hundred men broke out as Celtic
supporters entered Bridgeton. Police found thirty-year-old Hugh Fanally from the
Gorbals lying on the pavement with severe head injuries.[53]

Even the Bridgeton Billy Boys came under attack if they ventured into rival districts such as the Gorbals, as they found to their cost in April 1930 following the
Scottish Cup Final replay between Rangers and Partick Thistle at Hampden Park.
The match attracted 103,000 spectators. Only one-fifth of the crowd was able to fit
onto trains, buses and trams back to the city centre after the match, leaving tens of
thousands, most of whom were Rangers supporters, to walk. Their route took them
through the Gorbals. One group of Billy Boys paraded through Crown Street, one
of the main Gorbals thoroughfares, with orange-and-blue banners and flags, Union
Jacks and a cardboard replica of the Scottish Cup. Their conduct could hardly have
been more provocative. As they reached Govan Street, they entered the territory
of the South Side Stickers, many of whose members were Catholics. A fifty-strong
group of Stickers launched an immediate attack and in the ensuing melee, bottles,

sticks, bricks and other weapons were used by both sides. The street was filled with 'a seething mass of men fighting', halting traffic and forcing passers-by to rush into nearby shops. Robert Cotton, a Rangers supporter easily identified by his blue rosette, was felled by a blow on the back of the head and kicked repeatedly as he lay on the ground. Four Stickers were jailed for nine months for their part in the assault.[54]

More spontaneous violence broke out within Glasgow on non-match days. Apparently trifling remarks about Rangers or Celtic sparked confrontations among men who had been drinking heavily, and assaults, woundings and occasional fatalities resulted. Fights broke out at the various locations where men congregated at pub closing-time: the streets, fish and chip shops, bus shelters and urinals.[55] In August 1934, Alexander Craig-West, a thirty-year-old Protestant from King's Park on Glasgow's South Side, died following a fracas outside a city-centre fish and chip shop. West and his companion exchanged words with two Catholic gangsters. In the ensuing fight, twenty-one-year-old John Kerr stabbed West in the neck with a broken bottle, severing an artery. West died four days later. Kerr was convicted of culpable homicide and sentenced to three years' penal servitude. As the trial unfolded, it became clear that the spark for the confrontation had been remarks about Celtic, which led one of West's assailants to exclaim, 'I am a Roman Catholic and you are a Protestant—.' Threats were muttered about what would happen 'after the match tomorrow'. As the judge, Lord Blackburn, remarked in his summing-up: 'For some mysterious reason that [he] could not understand, football and religious prejudice seemed to be very much mixed up in the minds of the particular class of people with whom they were dealing.'[56]

THE CASE OF JOHN TRAQUAIR

The mutual antipathy between followers of Rangers and Celtic was starkly highlighted at the trial of a Rangers supporter, John Traquair, convicted of mobbing and rioting and assault in April 1934. The judicial proceedings illuminated both the nature of confrontations between Old Firm supporters and their relationship to the wider culture of sectarianism in Glasgow.

On Saturday, 3 March 1934, a crowd of five to six hundred Rangers supporters gathered in Bridgeton Cross station to wait for the 2.10 p.m. train to Ibrox. Many were wearing blue rosettes and scarves. Some were carrying weapons. At around 1.50 p.m. a train carrying Celtic supporters to a game against St Mirren in Paisley pulled into the station. As the train came to a halt the rival supporters hurled insults at each other. Celtic supporters claimed that they were met with shouts of 'You Papish bastards' and 'Irish bastards', while the train's guard heard cries of 'To hell with the Celtic', 'Papists' and 'A lot of papish buggers'. A station porter heard shouts of 'Good old Celtic' from supporters on the train interspersed with more aggressive cries 'running down' Rangers.[57]

A group of Rangers supporters led by Traquair then burst into one of the carriages. Traquair struck at John McVey, a twenty-one-year-old carter from Saracen Street,

Glasgow, who raised his arm to ward off the blow. Traquair then punched McVey's companion, Ranzo Buonaccorsi, in the face. The train's guard ran into the carriage, grabbed Traquair and wrestled him off the train. The guard then promptly signalled for the train to depart, ahead of schedule, as he was afraid of the Celtic supporters spilling out of the carriages to confront their adversaries. Traquair 'disappeared' into the crowd on the platform. Following the disturbance, station porters saw a group of men run up the stairs from the platform and out of the station. As the train pulled out, McVey's fellow passengers noticed that he was bleeding from a cut on his left forearm. He got off the train at the next station, and was taken to the Royal Infirmary, where his wound was stitched.[58]

John Traquair, a thirty-eight-year-old, unemployed rivet-heater from Bridgeton, was identified by one of McVey's fellow passengers. Traquair's description was circulated by the police and he was taken into custody at 10.30 p.m. that night. Police officers found him leaning against a wall in Main Street, Bridgeton, surrounded by a crowd of onlookers. He was drunk, and bleeding from several injuries. Traquair told the officers that he had fallen, but they were convinced that he had been fighting. Traquair was initially charged with being drunk and incapable. On Monday, 5 March, he was charged in connection with the incident at Bridgeton Cross station on the Saturday afternoon.[59] Traquair subsequently stood trial at Glasgow High Court on 30 April. He was charged with mobbing and rioting, assaulting John McVey with a knife or razor and his fists, and assaulting Ranzo Buonaccorsi with his fist. His membership of the Billy Boys was cited in the indictment.[60] Traquair pleaded not guilty, although he admitted to assaulting John McVey with his fist.[61]

The story that unfurled at the trial was that of an organised ambush on a train carrying Celtic supporters carried out by a gang of Billy Boys who exploited the cover provided by the larger group of Rangers supporters gathered at the station. There was no agreement among the witnesses as to the weapons wielded by the gang: knives, razors, hammers, 'tools', hatchets, bayonets, wooden batons, sticks and stones were all mentioned. Accounts of the threats and insults exchanged by the rival supporters left no doubt that the violence was sectarian. 'Papish' and 'Irish' were used interchangeably as terms of abuse by the Rangers supporters, starkly capturing the fusion of national and religious conflicts embedded in the Old Firm rivalry.[62] Buonaccorsi and a series of fellow passengers testified to Traquair's central role in the fight in the carriage. Traquair's blow against McVey was described as a downward, sweeping motion, suggesting the use of a razor or knife, rather than a punch with a fist. A surgeon from Glasgow Royal Infirmary testified that McVey had suffered an incised wound on his forearm.[63]

Police witnesses emphasised Traquair's involvement with the Billy Boys. Lieutenant Paterson told the court that Traquair regularly frequented Bridgeton Cross, the gang's recognised 'headquarters'. Asked by the Advocate Depute to describe the nature of the Billy Boys, Paterson responded:

They are a so-called Orange organisation. There is a crowd sometimes of them of about 100 strong. They are known as Rangers' supporters and follow the Rangers everywhere and one of their songs is 'We are the Billy Boys'. They hang about Bridgeton Cross and cause great trouble. When there are matches at Parkhead and Celtic [supporters] going there . . . wearing a Celtic scarf, there is a disturbance. We have instructed special policemen to be there on Saturday afternoons to keep down disorder. Q.- Caused by the Billy Boys?- A.- They do. They sing that song.[64]

Pressed further by the Advocate Depute, Paterson was adamant that the Billy Boys formed 'a definite body'. Their members were easily distinguished at football matches since they were 'usually dressed with orange colours and blue Rangers' colours'. In cross-examination, Traquair's counsel asked Paterson: 'Don't you know that the chief reason for [the existence of the Billy Boys] is to protect the band at the Orange Walk?' Paterson responded that he '[did] not think the Orange Lodge would admit that' and in any case, the Orangemen were well protected by the police. Asked where the gang got the name 'Billy Boys', Paterson replied, 'Followers of King Billy I would say.'[65]

Following a strong steer from the Judge, Lord Moncrieff, the jury unanimously found Traquair guilty on all three counts.[66] Moving for sentence, the Advocate Depute highlighted Traquair's eleven previous convictions for crimes of violence. The most recent, in September 1933, followed a gang fight in Bridgeton. Traquair had been jailed for three months for assault, having fractured a man's skull with a hatchet.[67] Traquair's counsel portrayed him as a First World War veteran who had fallen on hard times and was now living in a household bereft of a woman's nurturing presence: he had been unemployed for twelve months; he lived with his seventy-five-year-old father 'without the assistance of any female in the house'; he had served for twenty-one months in the Cameron Highlanders during the Great War.[68] Lord Moncrieff was unmoved. He passed sentence of four years' penal servitude.[69]

Traquair appealed both against his conviction, on the grounds of insufficient evidence, and against the 'excessive' sentence.[70] Lord Moncrieff submitted a report to the appeal judges in which he explained that the severity of the sentence reflected the evidence that Traquair had aimed a blow with a knife at McVey's face and might thus have struck his neck. Moncrieff added that he had been influenced by Traquair's previous convictions and, in particular, the 'startling' sentence of just three months' imprisonment imposed in September 1933. He pointed out: 'I have subsequently been told that the case was tried summarily on that occasion because there was reason to distrust the courage of a jury, and because conviction was regarded as of more moment than sentence.'[71] In Moncrieff's view, the administration of justice in Glasgow was tempered by the fear that juries were intimidated in 'gang' cases. Traquair's appeal was heard at the Scottish Court of Criminal Appeal on 17 July. Lord Anderson pronounced that Traquair's conviction was 'well warranted', while the sentence of four years' penal servitude 'was not a day too long'.[72]

In addition to Traquair's own appeal, two petitions were launched on his behalf in the fortnight following his trial. The first, addressed to the Home Secretary, was libellous in the accusations it levelled at Lord Moncrieff. Alexander Ratcliffe, leader of the SPL and councillor for the East-End ward of Dennistoun, quickly launched a more judiciously worded alternative addressed to the Secretary of State for Scotland,

Sir Godfrey Collins. Ratcliffe's petition pleaded for a reduced sentence, highlighting the disparity between the term of four years' penal servitude imposed on Traquair and those of twelve months' imprisonment passed on five Catholic gang members at the same sitting of the High Court. The Catholic youths had been convicted of mobbing and rioting following a fight in a Gorbals dance-hall in which a man died after being stabbed in the neck. Ratcliffe's petition claimed that 'so-called religious differences' had been the cause of both disturbances and added that the disparity in the sentences, especially in relation to the injuries sustained, had caused grave disquiet among Glasgow's Protestant community.[73]

Ratcliffe clearly viewed the Traquair case as an opportunity to rally popular support at a moment when he was losing control of the SPL group in the city council.[74] As Graham Walker has pointed out, Protestant youths convicted in the wake of sectarian street fights may well have seen themselves as enduring punishment for 'standing up for Protestantism and loyalty to the Crown and constitution'.[75] The perception of judicial bias in the Traquair case therefore probably fed on a prior sense of grievance. In any case, Ratcliffe no doubt felt a more tangible obligation to the Bridgeton Billy Boys, not least for their services as stewards at SPL meetings.

Under the auspices of the SPL, Ratcliffe organised meetings in support of Traquair across Glasgow over a period of three weeks. The petition was submitted in June with 40,000 signatures gathered throughout Scotland and Northern Ireland and a promise of support from James Maxton, Independent Labour MP for Bridgeton.[76] The scale of support for Traquair indicated that he was no pariah among militant Protestants, whatever his record of violence. However, the petition received short shrift from the Secretary of State, who saw no grounds to commute Traquair's sentence.[77] Despite the failure of the criminal appeal and petition alike, for a brief period in the summer of 1934 John Traquair was a Protestant martyr, championed by militants on the city council as well as on the terraces at Ibrox.

CONCLUSIONS

The Old Firm rivalry was not the root cause of the sectarian antagonisms that scarred communal life in Glasgow during the 1920s and 1930s. The origins of sectarianism lay deeper in the fabric of Scottish society and, in Glasgow, stretched back into the nineteenth century at least. However, football inflamed hostilities between the city's Irish-Catholic community and its Protestant majority. Old Firm matches, like the processions organised by the Orange Order, the Ancient Order of Hibernians and the various churches, served to fuse ethnic and religious divisions, splitting many parts of the city into two opposing factions.

Encounters between the Old Firm drew football supporters from across Glasgow into conflicts in which sport, nationality and religion provided, in Murray's words, 'an explosive mixture'.[78] Gang members were prominent in the disturbances, but others who were generally law-abiding frequently entered into them too. As Sheriff Robertson commented when sentencing five youths from 'good' homes in 1934: 'The spirit of faction . . . frequently carries away people who are otherwise respectable.'[79] Far from providing a safety-valve for the release of sectarian tensions, football mobilised ethnic and religious antagonisms. The movement of large crowds of supporters across Glasgow led to furious exchanges of abuse and to frequent outbreaks of violence. Larger-scale disorder, sometimes spontaneous but often planned, erupted when groups of rival supporters confronted each other at railway stations and in the streets surrounding the stadiums. The violence that marred Orange Walks and church parades alike generated untold bitterness in Glasgow, as did sectarian feuding among street gangs in the city's East End, but it was the Old Firm rivalry more than any other factor that incessantly divided large swathes of the city into two mutually hostile ethnic and religious camps. The legacy of these antagonisms is still encapsulated in 'that song', first sung by the Bridgeton Billy Boys during the 1920s.

NOTES

1. A longer version of this chapter appeared in *Irish Historical Studies*, XXXV, 138 (2006), pp. 200–19.
2. Bill Murray, *The Old Firm: Sectarianism, Sport and Society in Scotland* (Edinburgh: John Donald, 1984), pp. 60–1.
3. Ibid., pp. 60–75.
4. Graham Walker, '"There's not a team like the Glasgow Rangers": football and religious identity in modern Scotland', in Tom Gallagher and Graham Walker (eds), *Sermons and Battle Hymns: Protestant Popular Culture in Modern Scotland* (Edinburgh: Edinburgh University Press, 1990), p. 138; G. P. T. Finn, 'Racism, religion and social prejudice: Irish Catholic clubs, soccer and Scottish society – I: The historical roots of prejudice', *International Journal of the History of Sport*, 8: 1 (1991), pp. 83–7; Murray, *Old Firm*, pp. 165–6.
5. Murray, *Old Firm*, p. 139.
6. Tom Gallagher, *Glasgow: The Uneasy Peace. Religious Tension in Modern Scotland* (Manchester: Manchester University Press, 1987), p. 3.
7. Seán Damer, *Glasgow: Going for a Song* (London: Lawrence and Wishart, 1990), p. 96.
8. Andrew Davies, 'Sectarian violence and police violence in Glasgow during the 1930s', in Richard Bessel and Clive Emsley (eds), *Patterns of Provocation: Police and Public Disorder* (Oxford: Berghahn, 2000), pp. 43–5.
9. Graham Walker, 'The Orange Order in Scotland between the wars', *International Review of Social History*, 37: 2 (1992), pp. 204–5.
10. Walker, 'Glasgow Rangers', pp. 140–1.
11. Gallagher, *Glasgow*, pp. 49–53, 99–100; Damer, Glasgow, 57–8, 95, 129; Walker, 'Orange Order', pp. 198–9.
12. Andrew O'Hagan, *The Missing* (London: Picador, 1995), pp. 22–8.
13. Gallagher, *Glasgow*, p. 104.
14. Callum Brown, *Religion and Society in Scotland Since 1707* (Edinburgh: Edinburgh University Press, 1997), pp. 147–8, 192–3; Michael Rosie, *The Sectarian Myth in Scotland: Of Bitter Memory and Bigotry* (London: Palgrave Macmillan, 2004), pp. 75–6.
15. Gallagher, *Glasgow*, pp. 152–3; Ministry of Labour, *Local Unemployment Index*, monthly returns (1933).
16. Rosie, *Sectarian Myth*, p. 133; William S. Marshall, *The Billy Boys: A Concise History of Orangeism in Scotland* (Edinburgh: Mercat Press, 1996), p. 144.

17. Steve Bruce, Tony Glendinning, Iain Paterson and Michael Rosie, *Sectarianism in Scotland* (Edinburgh: Edinburgh University Press, 2004), pp. 48–50.
18. Gallagher, *Glasgow*, pp. 156–7; Rosie, *Sectarian Myth*, pp. 128, 136.
19. Damer, *Glasgow*, p. 95; Bruce et al., *Sectarianism*, pp. 94–5.
20. *Vanguard*, 29 January 1936; T. M. Devine, *The Scottish Nation, 1700–2000* (London: Penguin, 2000), p. 519.
21. Bruce et al., *Sectarianism*, p. 95.
22. Murray, *Old Firm*, pp. 154–6; *Sunday Mail*, 9 July 1933.
23. *Glasgow Weekly Herald*, 5 July 1884.
24. Davies, 'Sectarian violence', pp. 45–7.
25. *Evening Citizen*, 31 October 1931, 26 January 1932; Bruce et al., *Sectarianism*, p. 49.
26. See Walker, 'Glasgow Rangers', p. 143; *Sunday Mail*, 10 July 1927; *Weekly Record*, 20 December 1930.
27. *Glasgow Herald*, 1 May 1934.
28. Davies, 'Sectarian violence', pp. 44–5.
29. Sir Percy Sillitoe, *Cloak Without Dagger* (London: Cassell, 1955), pp. 129–30; Davies, 'Sectarian violence', pp. 49–56.
30. *Evening Citizen*, 4, 6 August 1930; *Weekly Record*, 21 March 1931; *Evening Citizen*, 10 January 1955.
31. Andrew Davies, 'Street gangs, crime and policing in Glasgow during the 1930s: the case of the Beehive Boys', *Social History*, 23: 3 (1998), pp. 254–5, 258.
32. Davies, 'Street gangs', p. 258.
33. Interview with Larry Rankin (pseudonym) by Stephen Humphries, undated (British Library, National Sound Archive, C590/02/177-180).
34. Murray, *Old Firm*, pp. 26, 169–71.
35. *Evening Times*, 7 September 1922; *Glasgow Herald*, 31 October 1923; Murray, *Old Firm*, p. 123.
36 Murray, *Old Firm*, p. 175.
37. Murray, *Old Firm*, p. 173.
38. *Evening Citizen*, 13, 14 April, 16 June 1925.
39. *Evening Times*, 1 May 1922; *Evening Citizen*, 6 September 1922.
40. *Evening Times*, 8 December 1922.
41. *Evening Times*, 11 September 1922.
42. *Evening Times*, 29 September 1922.
43. *Evening Citizen*, 7 October 1925.
44. *Evening Citizen*, 19, 21, 22 October 1925.
45. *Evening Citizen*, 26 September 1927.
46. *Evening Citizen*, 2 January 1937.
47. *Evening Citizen*, 10 October 1927.
48. *Evening Citizen*, 3 September 1928.
49. *Glasgow Herald*, 30 September 1936.
50. *Sunday Mail*, 10 March 1935.
51. *Sunday Mail*, 23 September 1934.
52. *Sunday Post*, 4 April; *Evening Citizen*, 7 April 1937.
53. *Sunday Mail*, 6 March 1938.
54. *Evening Citizen*, 17 April, 11 July; *Glasgow Herald*, 12 July 1930.
55. *Evening Times*, 9 May 1930.
56. *Glasgow Herald*, 25, 26, 29 October 1934; *Sunday Mail*, 28 October 1934.
57. 'Application for leave to appeal against conviction and sentence by John Traquair', Notes of evidence, 30 April 1934, National Archives of Scotland (NAS), JC34/1/179, pp. 17, 29, 31, 36, 43, 45–7, 50. (Hereafter cited as 'Notes of evidence'.)

58. Ibid., pp. 18, 25, 44, 46, 49–50.
59. Ibid., pp. 39–40, 52–5.
60. 'H. M. Advocate v. John Traquair: mobbing and rioting and assault and prev. cons', 30 April 1934, NAS, JC34/1/179.
61. 'Lord Moncrieff's charge to jury', 30 April 1934, NAS, JC34/1/179, pp. 4–5. (Hereafter cited as 'Charge to jury'.)
62. 'Notes of evidence', pp. 14, 16–17, 23, 29, 31, 36–7, 43, 46–7, 58.
63. Ibid., pp. 14–16, 24, 30, 38, 58.
64. Ibid., pp. 12, 55–7.
65. Ibid., pp. 56–8.
66. 'Charge to jury', pp 1–8.
67. Ibid., pp. 8–9.
68. Ibid., p. 9.
69. Ibid., pp. 9–10.
70. 'Note of application under S.1 (b) for leave to appeal against a conviction and sentence, Criminal Appeal (Scotland) Act, 1926', 28 June 1934, NAS, JC34/1/179.
71. 'Confidential report by Lord Moncrieff', 19 May 1934, NAS, JC34/1/179.
72. *Glasgow Herald*, 18 July 1934.
73. *Vanguard*, 16 May 1934; *Glasgow Herald*, 28 April 1934.
74. On the fragmentation of the SPL, see Rosie, *Sectarian Myth*, p. 128.
75. Walker, 'Orange Order', pp. 204–5.
76. *Vanguard*, 23 May, 13, 27 June 1934.
77. *Glasgow Herald*, 20 August 1934.
78. Murray, *Old Firm*, p. 59.
79. *Evening Times*, 4 June 1934; Murray, *Old Firm*, p. 177.

5 History and Memory in Scottish Football

Joseph M. Bradley

INTRODUCTION: BEYOND THE SURFACE — USING THE PAST TO EXPLAIN THE PRESENT

This chapter looks beyond prevalent, often suffocating, narratives regarding so-called 'sectarianism' in Scottish society, particularly in football but especially with regards to Rangers and Celtic, the so-called 'Old Firm'. Such catch-all words and phrases often result in descriptions and explanations of areas of Scottish life that have in reality frequently remained obscure, misrepresented, unrecorded and poorly understood, as well as disguised and concealed. The term sectarianism has powerful connotations in terms of behaviour, beliefs and identities. The expression is often used as a tool to explain or portray two sectarian tribes on the opposite sides of a wall of ignorance: groups subsequently discounted on the basis of simply reflecting each other as 'two sides of the same coin', defined essentially by their outdated identities. However, this crude and one-dimensional view means that many people discount and disregard the multi-faceted nature of ethnic and religious identity in Scotland.

The chapter seeks to use football to look at the multicultural and plural nature of Scottish society, but also to consider varied insights into the identities involved in the mainstream cultures of the two clubs and beyond. It reflects on historical memories and perspectives as well as their symbolic manifestations and how these inform the identities of many Rangers and Celtic supporters, as well as others throughout Scottish football and elsewhere, including fans, officials, politicians, police and media. It also looks at the relevance of these memories, perspectives and identities and reflects on how deeply significant they are to Scotland's social, cultural and political past and present.

BRITISH COLONIALISM AND THE INFLUENCE OF IRELAND IN SCOTTISH FOOTBALL

Over the past few hundred years the history of British colonised Ireland has produced one of the western world's most significant dispersals of people. Since before the cataclysmic Great Hunger (an Gorta Mor) of the mid-nineteenth century, but particularly as a result of that event and after, millions of Irish have been forced to flee and have chosen to leave their native shores to survive and in search of a better life. Although this diaspora has spread around the globe, North America, Australia and Great Britain have been the most significant recipients of several million of these immigrants. As one of the nearest accessible countries with a tradition of providing employment due to its strong and often vigorous economy, Scotland has been a noteworthy site of settlement for Ireland's scattering.

Scots have also had a crucial role in the history of modern Ireland in that it was from Scotland that tens of thousands of Protestants came to be planted in Ireland's conquered Ulster province under terms that allowed them, for the benefit of the British crown, government and military, to acquire land and power and to dominate and control native Irish Catholics in religious, cultural, economic, military and political terms (Gibney 2008):

> Ireland was conquered, dominated, and governed by the British from the end of the twelfth century until the third decade of the twentieth (and even the creation of Northern Ireland guaranteed that a segment of Ireland would remain in the United Kingdom that had emerged from the eighteenth century onward).

In this context Kowalski (2004) notes 'Scots soldiers came to play a prominent and at times savage role in the army of Empire', historian A. T. Q. Stewart (1977) recognises that 'the core of the Ulster problem is the problem of the Scots', while Walker (1995) concurs: '"the problem of the Scots" is indeed central to any analysis of Ulster or Irish history'.

After Ulster was conquered, usurped, settled and controlled, many Scottish-British colonists, referred to as 'Scots-Irish' or 'Ulster-Scots', left frontier Ulster for the new society that was North America, especially during the eighteenth century where they became central to accounts of the European colonial enterprise that developed into the USA. While many descendants of the Scots plantation community in the north of Ireland remain, other Scots-Irish also 'returned' to Scotland in times of economic advances and disruptions in the late eighteenth and early nineteenth centuries as well as periods thereafter.

The history of Scots conquest and colonising in Ulster prior to thousands from that community returning to Scotland several generations later is important to understanding numerous contemporary political and cultural identities in Scotland. As part of a dispersed colonial community, returning Ulster-Scots have long been distinctive, indeed separate, from the diaspora that comprises Irish Catholics with whom they inhabited the island of Ireland. Over two centuries Ulster-Scots inter-married and assimilated with other Scots, thus continuing to share and maintain Protestant religious, cultural and political attributes and characteristics while self-identifying as British as well as Scots and Ulster-Scots. Despite such religious, cultural and political commonalities, there is also adequate evidence demonstrating that the specific history, experience and influence of this once-frontier Scottish-British plantation community remains important in Scottish society. For example, the existence of the Orange Institution is the most obvious, significant and distinguishable legacy of Ulster-Scots Protestant migration (Bradley 1996). Given birth from within the colonist population in the north of Ireland as a loyal British institution, in Scotland Orange membership and affiliation has been shared mainly by descendants of Plantation Ulster-Scots and lowland Scots Protestants. Indigenous Scots and English already had their own anti-Catholic histories, cultures and associations (see Flint and Powell in this volume). Indeed, one commentator relays that in the late eighteenth century there were only thirty-nine Catholics in Glasgow but forty-three anti-Catholic societies (Gallagher 1987: 9; Devine 1988: 154 notes sixty anti-Catholic societies in 1791). However, although the Orange Institution was cultivated in a fertile anti-Catholic environment in Scotland, not all in society welcomed its marching and confrontational disposition (Bradley 1996). Orangeism has been built on anti-Catholic and pro-colonist ideology, which gives strong backing to all things Protestant, British and Royal within the north of Ireland and Britain (Bradley 1996). As well as an inherent local Scottish inspiration and influence, Ulster-Scots' colonial, cultural and political identities have also provided stimulus to the narrative of at least one famous Scottish football club, Glasgow Rangers.

RANGERS FOOTBALL CLUB

Rangers formed in 1872 at a time of a growing affection of the working classes for football. By the turn of the century the club had begun to amass honours that confirm its contemporary claim as one of the world's most successful football institutions. Its growing success, massive number of supporters, the religious and socio-political make-up of its officials, correlating with it becoming a symbol of a number of dominant, privileged and institutional features of Scottish-British life, particularly in terms of allegiances and affinities with royalty, empire, unionism, freemasonry and Protestantism, proved highly attractive to Ulster-Scots in Scotland's central belt. Subsequently, many Ulster-Scots joined with lowland Scots to give their sporting loyalties to the Glasgow club, although numerous others have also given backing to other Scottish football clubs (see Bradley 1995).

The successes of Rangers and the convergence of similar allegiances and affinities has resulted in Rangers supporters in Scotland and Ulster-Scots Rangers fans in parts of the north of Ireland sharing much by way of culture, politics, nationalism and faith. Although all members of the Orange Institution are not Rangers fans and indeed are affiliated with a variety of other football clubs in Scotland and the north of Ireland, by far the most significant sporting link that members have is with Rangers. This is expressed overtly in, among other ways, displays of Rangers memorabilia at Orange parades, in Orange symbolism at Rangers football matches and in sharing oral, singing and musical traditions.

In the past Orange, loyalist and/or anti-Catholic songs have characterised supporters of a number of clubs in Scotland, including most notably Airdrie, Falkirk, Dundee, Motherwell and Hearts (see Kelly's chapter). In 2005 thousands of Hearts fans booed and the referee reacted by cutting short a minute's silence intended to respect the death of Pope John Paul II prior to a Scottish Cup semi-final against Celtic. Outwith Rangers fan culture this was one of the most high-profile anti-Catholic expressions in Scottish football and which, on this occasion, attracted headlines in parts of the world's media. However, although still evident, in recent years such public expressions in football have seemingly reduced and most fans who previously sang such songs in public have either ceased, minimised or privatised their use.[1] Some of this change in Scottish life has resulted from Protestantism becoming less important, secularism proliferating markedly, and since the 1970s and 1980s a singular Scottish identity increasing in importance, often replacing a British or Scottish-British affiliation (which remains significant). Nonetheless, Rangers remain numerically the biggest-supported club in Scotland with widespread support throughout society, although the number of 'other' fans that look sympathetically towards the club seems to have declined markedly, culminating spectacularly in the widespread animosity attracted during the club's liquidation process in 2012.

While there are other factors, the monumental change in Scottishness at the expense of Britishness is important in understanding the decline in backing and affection for Rangers on the part of supporters of other football clubs who no longer share many of their British and Protestant affiliations, inclinations and preoccupations (see Rosie in this volume). Indeed, in the context of secularisation, a weakening of a once-strong Scottish Protestant identity, vociferous anti-Catholicism within Rangers culture and widespread increases in affinity for singular Scottishness, it might be argued that many have become uncomfortable about some of these previous popular identities.[2] The increase in Scottishness apparent in a number of relevant surveys is also evidenced in Scottish football, particularly seen in a range of changed symbols and songs of football supporters: for example, a manifest decline in the use of the Union flag and other similar insignia among many clubs' supporters (and some Scotland supporters) and in the emergence of a gradual widespread booing of the British national anthem at Scottish international football matches from the 1970s. In more recent years at club level this has also been evident on occasion when, among others, Aberdeen fans – considered as among the most passionate Scotland adherents – have sung to Rangers supporters the Scottish nationalist anthem 'Flower of Scotland', in opposition to Rangers fans' British or loyalist songs (Styles 2000, see Kelly's chapter for Hearts fans doing likewise).

Rangers' fans' song repertoire is frequently dominated by pro-British and Unionist themes and is pro-British military and paramilitary, especially in terms of the historical Irish-British colonial conflict. Although a number of these songs refer to historical events, individuals, groups and battles vital to the emergence of the British state, empire and British-Scottish cultural and political formations, narratives and identities, and which are in turn imperative to understanding the Northern Ireland troubles, it is clear also that others in Scottish society are critical of these songs and what they consider to be an importation of 'Irish problems' to Scotland. In 2011, during a debate on the Offensive Behaviour in Football and Threatening Communications (Scotland) Bill, Scottish Conservative and Unionist MSP David McLetchie stated that 'sectarianism' in Scotland was 'born out of the history of Ireland'.[3] It was also in such a context that a caller to a relevant BBC Radio Scotland programme said:

If we all came out with the fact and said we were Scottish instead of half Celtic fans thinking they're Irish and half Rangers supporters thinking they're British. That this is the answer to sectarianism . . . It all boils down to the fact that people need to stand up and be counted as Scottish.[4]

Such pronouncements reflect historical ignorance as well as lack of acknowledgement regarding Scotland's multicultural character. Despite a widespread tendency to describe and couple Rangers and rivals Celtic as two sides of the same coin, partly signalled in the use of the term 'Old Firm', neither club nor their respective supporters have much in common in terms of national, ethnic or religious social and cultural identities. For example, historically Rangers have been viewed and identified as, and represented numerous features and facets of, Protestant, Scottish and British identities that mirror aspects of the common, routine, privileged and dominant historical, social, cultural and political narratives of wider society, and indeed, to an extent, of national and public memories and official histories of the state itself. This partly accounts for the club's significant social and cultural ascendancy in relation to football in Scotland. For many Scots, Rangers have been the sporting epitome and embodiment of popular Scottish British and Protestant identities and few groups or communities have been as articulate, numerically significant, vociferous or as passionate about these as Rangers supporters (see McKillop, this volume).[5]

Although there has been social decline in the importance of the noted identities, the important theme in this chapter is not so much the cultural, religious and political spaces shared by Rangers and their supporters with much of the rest of Scottish football and society, but also to specific notions of memory and identity which are inherent to any sense of these. Rangers' identities can only be appreciated in the context of religious and political history, particularly in relation to British colonial domination of Ireland, while relationships between and within Ireland and Great Britain are critical to understanding various aspects of wider Scottish football fandom and society.

Banners, flags and chants referencing fourteenth-century Scottish historical events and figures such as the Battle of Bannockburn and William Wallace at Scottish international matches, the booing of the British national anthem from the early 1970s until a change to playing 'Flower of Scotland' in the 1990s, and a range of other such examples from across the global game, demonstrate that the importance of socio-cultural and political history to clubs or national teams is not unique to Rangers or Scottish football. However, memories based on readings of history are contestable socially constructed terrain, particularly in terms of what is remembered, what is forgotten or consciously discarded, and also as to how and when something might be remembered or celebrated. In late 2012 British Prime Minister David Cameron stoked controversy when he spoke of plans to commemorate the 1914 War, believing that this would say 'something about who we are as people' (Bell 2012). In this light, Carlow (2007) stresses how individual and social memory can be 'selective and malleable' and when enmeshed with historical and political events can make commemoration 'difficult'. Gillies (1994: 5) writes that:

Commemorative activity is by definition social and political, for it involves the coordination of individual and group memories, whose results may appear consensual when they are in fact the product of processes of intense contest, struggle, and, in some instances, annihilation.

Hobsbawm's work (with Ranger 1983) on the study of the construction of invented traditions for the benefit of the nation state (to justify its importance and existence) is one of the most influential pieces of such literature in the twentieth century. Memory, that is, what is remembered rather than what is not known or what is 'forgotten', is of course fundamental to the construction of individual, group and community identity. It is clear that memory also makes a significant contribution to the production and formation of narratives around any football (as well as a number of other sports) club or country where the game has social, cultural, religious, ethnic or political meaning. International football can be an apt demonstration of the importance of historical narratives and contexts in producing matches that have significance beyond the football field: the previously annual Scotland against England, Iran versus the USA in the World Cup in 1998, and the intercontinental rivalry between Argentina and England beginning with on-field occurrences during the 1966 World Cup but escalating beyond the football field with the short war between Britain and Argentina over the Falkland/Malvinas Islands in 1982, which then took added meaning with both Argentina and England playing against each other in three World Cup matches post the 1982 conflict, are all examples.

As with international teams, the depth of meaningfulness of club sides increases the more significant religious, social, cultural or political identities, narratives and experiences are considered intrinsic to history and the people that constitute relevant supporting communities. In Scotland, as well as the magnitude relating to huge numbers that associate with the club and its world record trophy-winning achievements, Rangers have long been distinctive for the strength and intensity of their connections with, indeed their capacity to contribute to and be a part of, the construction and sustenance of popular British-Scottish Protestant identities.

Like other such noteworthy, sizeable and indeed distinctive football clubs, the dominant narratives of Rangers fan culture are partly constructed via knowledge and understanding of the distant and recent past, utilising memories of historical events and figures, added to the implications and outcomes of readings of history, and the meaningfulness of these for contemporary ideologies and identities. The club has enjoyed massive success, popularity and encouragement on the football field and in wider society and is supported by a fanbase largely characterised by its Protestant, British and Scottish cultural, political and military identities, Ulster Unionism and Loyalism. The knowledge that informs this culture and these identities arises from formal education processes, the mass media, oral representations of history and the 'in-culture' of Rangers football environment constructed around matches, social events, functions, paraphernalia, symbols, song traditions, family and community narratives. Rangers' supporters are no different from any other community in that they possess a collective dominant memory, born from specific narratives which feed and enlighten the principal identities of the club and its support. What distinguishes

Rangers fans is the specificity of what is remembered, with what significance these memories are given and in how they are manifested and celebrated.

Dependent on the context, occasion and environment and through narratives relayed via practices and performances involved in, for example, group names, banners, attitudes, perspectives, social media, dialogue and discussions, symbols, music and song, Rangers and their support utilise historical readings, understandings and knowledge actively to remember, honour and celebrate the importance of the British-Scottish conquest and plantation of Ireland-Ulster, the British crown as a protector and symbol of the status of Protestantism in Great Britain and the north of Ireland, links with Orangeism, the British Empire, and a hegemonic faith, nationality, ethnicity, culture and social standing over what is perceived to pertain to Catholicism, Ireland and Irish ethnicity in Scotland, especially as represented and embodied in Celtic FC and its supporting community. Common celebratory chants, among them 'We are the people', and songs at public and private occasions like 'Rule, Britannia!', 'The Sash my Father Wore', 'Derry's Walls', 'The Famine Song', 'No Pope of Rome' and 'Build My Gallows', as well as the British national anthem, 'God Save the Queen', constitute cultural and ritualistic performances of Rangers' identities.

Although a number of these songs, chants and identities can be expressed outwith a Rangers social, cultural or match environment, and by other football fans and associations in Scotland, and as with the general population almost all Scotland's football clubs can look towards a similar heritage and apposite historical and contemporary narratives can be connected and correlated with the production of culture and identity, these expressions acquire exceptional prominence in the context of Rangers and Scotland's most popular team sport. In relation to football, relevant acts, symbols, performances and rich and vibrant memories are constructed around what is considered important in historical and contemporary cultural, political and religious terms, thus constituting Rangers' identities.

With such vast numbers contributing to the Rangers-minded environment, uniqueness is constructed partly because of what is memorialised, for example in song and chant, as well as to how this memorialisation has come to define the club and supporters. This uniqueness is particularly defined with regard to narratives concerning the British-Irish colonial encounter and the importance that Rangers supporters place on this as a primary marker in the construction of the club's pre-eminent identities. It might also be contemplated that as some of these identities have declined in importance in wider Scottish society, the likelihood arises that Rangers have moved away from their central role traditionally played in Scottish life to one where the club retains enormous meaning, but the numbers of those sympathetic and supportive has declined. Noting such decline is important because it also points towards historical perspectives and identities changing in Scotland, while 'Rangers memories' and ensuing identities have continued to be characterised and governed by more 'traditional' events and narratives (see McKillop's chapter).

'Other memories' and identities are emphasised by other football clubs and fans, and in wider society. These are partly shaped by marginalising or even rejecting the aforementioned traditional memories and identities, by not choosing to acknowledge, know or be reminded about, much less preserve and celebrate, specific matters that relate to Scotland as an intrinsic part of the state of Great Britain, its history as a junior partner alongside England fashioning Britain as a major colonising world power from the eighteenth century, and especially Scotland's role in colonising Ireland, particularly during the plantation of the northern province of Ulster. As many fans of other football clubs in Scotland have apparently moved away from such memories and identities, for Rangers and their supporters these remain fundamental.

HISTORICAL NARRATIVES AND MEMORY

Symbols and emblems can be popular and unsophisticated practices for expressing and celebrating important and meaningful historical narratives, events and people from the past. A football club's name, colours and the make-up of its players and supporters are among the most obvious examples of a social and cultural formation reflecting the importance of origins and identities: the connections and links between Barcelona and Catalan history, politics and identities are among the most obvious examples in terms of world-renowned football clubs.

Reflection on Rangers' identities allows us to appreciate associations, links and connections with significant features and narratives of Protestantism, royalty, Scottishness, Britishness and the Empire: at the same time being mindful of how changed and contested these have become in recent decades. This raises an enquiry as to how different identities, indeed identities that are sometimes oppositional to more indigenous and prevalent constructions, can emerge and become counter-cultural in terms of what at first sight dominates. Rangers' greatest rivals Celtic's hybrid nature and identity, born from within the Irish Catholic diaspora as an Irish football club to additionally develop as a Scottish institution, constitutes the essence of its distinctiveness and uniqueness and the resultant football contest offers a window to discern often misrepresented or ignored aspects of Scottish history and society.

For Rangers, the club's supporters and a majority of people in Scotland, formal narratives of history are central to the construction of their Scottish and British national and cultural identities (Johnson 1992). However, diasporic peoples are more often than not cut off from native representations of important strands of their histories by a series of absences from spaces of cultural reproduction, in education, memorials and popular culture more widely. At least some aspects of this culture can be passed on in the intimate space of child-rearing, but at school age in particular the children, grandchildren and great-grandchildren of immigrants are thrust into a public sphere where their background culture is under-represented or may be missing altogether.

For colonised populations this may even entail a more active suppression of dissident identities in order to avoid contestation and speed up the process of incorporation into the national mainstream – and with this the adoption of the national and cultural practices, beliefs and identities of the host nation. Hickman (1993, 1996) shows that Irish history has been conspicuously excluded from the curriculum in Britain since the nineteenth century, not only of state schools, but also from the Catholic school arrangement, where the majority of children of Irish descent are educated. She argues that this has been a key element in the denationalisation of the Irish in Britain and their construction as 'good' Catholic British (English or Scottish) citizens.

However, there is also evidence to suggest that knowledge of their cultural background in relation to Ireland cannot entirely be erased. It continues to be handed on and rediscovered by British-born Irish offspring both consciously and unconsciously. This knowledge can result in Irishness being manifest among those of Irish descent in Britain. Most strikingly, the case of Celtic Football Club's supporters has been used to demonstrate how people born in Scotland can have a passionate identification with, affinity for and disposition towards Ireland, their country of origin (Bradley 2004, 2006, 2009). In this context the Irishness around Celtic may also be seen as an outward expression of the way cultural, national and identity impositions can be resisted and alternatives maintained, sustained and celebrated.

PUBLIC ACCOUNTS OF IRISH HISTORY IN BRITAIN

This section of the chapter reflects on aspects of this resistance and how Irishness, particularly elements of an historical and political Irishness, remains central to Celtic supporter culture and identities. This entails ways in which Irish histories are passed to second, third and subsequent generations, enabling them to acquire a varied perspective on dominant national narratives being told in the 'diaspora space' in which they live. Because the national stories of Britain and Ireland continue to clash, this de-centred knowledge has an ongoing political significance for many people of Irish descent in Britain. One of the key purposes of the introduction of the Prevention of Terrorism Act in 1974, for example, was to dissuade British residents from expressing views sympathetic towards Irish nationalism in Ireland and questioning the British state's political and military strategies there. Since 'the propaganda war' ensured that strict British censorship was being practised in the public sphere, access to alternative constructions was largely confined to sources found within private or semi-private family, community, cultural and, in the case of Scotland, additionally where most football-minded Irish and their offspring congregated (Bradley 2004, 2006, 2009). The production and reproduction of narratives of Irish history among the Irish diaspora in Scotland, specifically those that comprise the majority of Celtic football supporters, is a qualitatively different version of the Irish-British colonial conflict from that which dominates in Britain, particularly in much of the media.

In a recent Economic and Social Research Council (ESRC)-supported study focusing on second- and third-generation Irish in Britain, respondents were asked about their knowledge of, and interest in, Irish history.[6] For most people the study of national histories is primarily connected with compulsory elements of formal education, possibly supplemented in adulthood with voluntary activities including courses, reading and other popular media forms. Of course, the mass media is a further significant source of learning. However, the most striking aspect of the ESRC participants' encounters with Irish history outside the home was its absence from the school curriculum. Even in Catholic schools, history lessons were about British history and most could not remember Ireland being mentioned. This absence has been analysed closely by Hickman (1993, 1996) in her study of the experiences of London and Liverpool children of Irish descent.

It transpired that some interviewees used a variety of formal and informal methods to gain an understanding of Irish history as adults: for example, a number reported searching for Irish history books in the public library or finding websites. Most respondents made a point of watching documentaries and dramas about Ireland when they were shown on television, as well as accessing films such as *Michael Collins*, *Some Mother's Son*, *The Wind that Shakes the Barley*, *Hunger*, etc. For many families, the family home is a place where Irish issues can be most safely discussed (Walter 2001). However, the ESRC study showed that the knowledge that people had acquired about Irish history within the family was fragmentary in most cases. But even where there was little factual knowledge of wider historical events imparted on the part of parents and grandparents, children often grew up with a strong sense of an alternative story in their family's past. But many people also experienced silence at home and only picked up more indirectly on the sense of an oppositional history. For the purposes of this chapter, the ESRC study partly reflects the important point that the national story being painted, however faintly, for children in households that were to some extent 'Irish' was often different, at least varied, from that being promoted by, and absorbed from, the dominant English/Scottish and British mainstream.

HISTORY AND THE IRISH DIASPORA IN SCOTLAND

Throughout the post-Great Hunger years of the mid-nineteenth century, during the first quarter of the twentieth and more erratically for the rest of that century, substantial numbers of immigrant Catholic Irish entered Scotland, most eventually settling in the west central belt in and around Lanarkshire and greater Glasgow. Collins estimates that around 8 per cent of all Irish-born emigrants went to Scotland during the period 1841 to 1921, and most Irish immigration to Scotland took place during this time, with the peak of Irish born in Scotland in the 1880s (Collins 1991). After 1921 Scotland declined as a significant focus of settlement. However, a post-Second World War economic boom in Britain once again increased migration from Ireland and resulted in thousands of Ulster, and in particular Donegal, people arriving in the Glasgow area. The Irish in Scotland are a multi-generational ethnic community.

The ESRC research informs us of the potential for alternative representations, images and narratives of 'Irish' history among the Irish diasporic section of the British population. We can assume that in more numerically significant areas and towns of Irish settlement, as there is for example in and around Glasgow and Lanarkshire, there will be a greater likelihood of this awareness, as well as possibly an increased depth, knowledge and understanding of Irish perspectives on Irish-British history in particular. This can also be seen as having an influence in increasing Irish 'alternative' identities that are maintained, developed or manifest, in contrast to those which dominate in other Scottish locales, and that reflect more prevailing indigenous Scottish/British identities. Although throughout Britain people of Irish descent have not been able, or have found it demanding, to access the histories of their country of origin through formal channels of education, and although individuals and families occasionally overcome this, it is the case that in Scotland a unique space does exist to access aspects of these histories. For many Celtic supporters the historical narratives, awareness and counter-culture that exist around the club are significant. This is critical to the acquisition of insights, knowledge and understanding regarding alternative versions of the Irish-British historical cleavage and struggle from those that dominate in Britain.

Of course, various Irish nationalist identities, feelings, attitudes and activities had characterised the Irish in Scotland prior to the foundation of the club in 1887/8 and today individual and family Irish nationalist identities, feelings, attitudes and activities retain resonance among parts of the Irish-descended community. Celtic's founding, evolution, success and supporter culture are reflections and aspects of the story of the Irish in Scotland. As a football club founded by men of an Irish nationalist disposition, followed by many people of a similar outlook, and where since its foundation corresponding attitudes significantly shaped the club's character and culture, Irish nationalist ethno-cultural and political identities remain markedly relevant to understanding Celtic.

Irish social and political awareness, as well as Irish nationalist and/or republican identities, have been prominent features of the Irish diaspora in Scotland and in other countries with a history of Irish immigration. In Scotland, although the days of mass meetings, demonstrations and activities in relation to Irish nationalism have passed (Bradley 2000), resistance against loss of Irishness and the assertion of diverse historical perspectives and understandings from the mainstream remains. The clearest public evidence of this is manifest through popular renditions of Irish songs that reflect and resonate with themes around Irish historical events and patriotic personalities and ideologies that are ultimately significant with regard to challenging not only British colonialism, but also historical and contemporary interpretations of British economic, social, cultural, political, religious and, specifically, military involvement on the island of Ireland.

HISTORY, IDENTITY AND FOOTBALL

Most football clubs reflect facets – economic, social, religious, cultural, symbolic, ideological and political – of the prevalent and ascendant features of the wider society and more specific community that they spring from and inhabit. Although all football clubs and their fans are 'distinctive', to a greater or lesser degree most share the ideas and identities that govern and reflect, for example, widespread and established religious, ethnic and state identities as well as in relation to the prevalent ideologies of the national mass media and relevant political landscape. In such terrain, having a collective identity that deviates markedly from principal and mainstream socio-cultural tendencies can create and constitute an unconventional and non-conformist character for a football club and its support.

Although attracting support and including staff, players and supporters from various ethnic, national and religious backgrounds, a majority of Celtic's support are part of the multi-generational Irish diaspora in Scotland. However, this community's Irishness is largely cut off in society from positive and informative representations 'by a series of absences from spaces of cultural reproduction, in education, memorials and popular culture more widely' (Walter et al. 2002). As Hickman (1993, 1996) has demonstrated with regard to the Irish descended in England, for the community of Irish descent in Scotland knowledge of their cultural background in Ireland is partly erased through the state education system. Added to this, we should also acknowledge exposure to the media and its role as a primary source of information and 'education', shaped largely by British/Scottish-centric specifics and contexts, especially in terms of politics, economic affairs, perceptions of other countries, ideology and military matters.

However, just as the family unit can be viewed as a counter-cultural influence in relation to the acquisition of a different perspective on among other things (for example, morality) the centuries-long colonial and anti-colonial struggle between Britain and Ireland, the Celtic football environment represents a similar diasporic space. This has long provided a point for disrupting the established and prevalent social and cultural hegemony, to congregate as a community, and to construct alternative narratives, understanding and knowledge that challenge British versions of Britain's military, political, economic and cultural participation in Ireland. As with many in the wider community of Irish descent, much of the character of the Celtic support reflects interpretations and viewpoints more akin to the broad assortment of Irish nationalist thinking that exists across Ireland and its diaspora, rather than the more dominant colonialist and British unionist ones more frequently reproduced in wider society, particularly through families, communities, education, media, ideologies and identities.

The Irish nationalist dimension involved in the establishment of Celtic is emphasised by Wilson (1988: 13), who notes that although the decision:

> to form Celtic Football Club is rightly identified with the needs of Catholic charity in the East End of Glasgow . . . the early nature of the club, and the direction it pursued, owe at least as much to the influence exercised by the political organisation which spoke for the vast majority of the Irish in Scotland in the 1880s, the Irish National League, and specifically one of its branches in Glasgow, known as the Home Government Branch.

The club's obvious political symbolism remained evident until at least the 1960s when it launched its own newspaper, the *Celtic View*. Prominent adverts were included for 'Irish Rebel Records', including 'The Merry Ploughboy' (which topped the charts in Ireland) and 'James Connolly'.[7] Commemorative concerts for

Irish patriots 'Sean South' and 'Kevin Barry' were also advertised, as was a Glasgow concert to celebrate the fiftieth anniversary of the 1916 Easter Uprising, which included the appearance of readers' favourite Celtic stars.[8] Beyond Irish political concerns, in 1968 Celtic refused to travel to play in the then Soviet Bloc because of the invasion of Czechoslovakia by Warsaw Pact countries. Since at least the 1970s much of the Celtic support has been partly characterised by 'alternative' notions and non-mainstream identities with regard to other ethnic, national and political conflicts. Among the causes noticeably sympathised with, promoted or supported within the Celtic support have been those of Black South Africans (particularly anti-Apartheid and pro-ANC), Basque separatists, Nicaraguan Sandinistas, Catalan nationalists and the Palestinian cause against the perceived colonialism and hegemony of the Israelis. Consciousness concerning and/or support for these causes can be manifest among fans through wearing apposite t-shirts, waving flags and wearing various scarves and badges, as well as within the narratives of numerous Celtic fanzines, websites and other supporter discourses, including through music and song. In November 2010 several hundred fans brought to the fore much Celtic supporter disquiet against their club joining with others in wearing a British commemorative red poppy by displaying an oppositional banner at a match which stated with regard to the British military, 'Your deeds would shame all the devils in Hell. Ireland, Iraq, Afghanistan. No bloodstained poppy on our hoops' (see the chapters by Kelly and Flint and Powell).

IRISH TRADITIONS: MUSIC, BALLADS AND SONGS

Generally, many popular Irish tunes, songs and ballads reflect an array of aspects of Ireland's anti-colonial struggle against invasion, conquest and domination. These rebel and revolutionary songs refer to a resistance struggle characterised by a yearning for Irish liberation and independence. They are accessed, listened to and sung by many people within the Celtic support and reflect an alternative reading and interpretation of individuals, groups and events in Irish-British history from those excluded, or referred to, via a standard British education and the military-political complex and media. Traditionally many thousands of people of Irish descent in Scotland have come together and expressed these alternative identities in the context of the culture that surrounds Celtic Football Club.

There are many different kinds of 'rebel' songs, their variety infused with contexts and narratives relating to poverty, love, family, death, despair, celebration and aspirations. Many can be categorised in terms of the periods they refer to, the patriots and events reported and the knowledge they contain and convey. As alternative accounts of the historical cleavage and conflict, they can be defiant, joyous, educational and celebratory: they can also refer to the sacrificing, defending and/or taking of human life.

Since the birth of the club and as an important part of the Irish diasporic community in Scotland and beyond, as well as chants about on-field events, players and winning trophies, Celtic supporters have collectively sung Irish rebel and resistance songs: at varying family and community gatherings as well as publicly whenever Celtic play or privately on the many more occasions where and whenever support-ers gather. The ESRC-supported *Irish 2 Project* recognises not only 'alternative' Irish identities from those of mainstream British/Scottish/English ones, but also identifies how family and community can be seen as additional and alternative forms of education and knowledge regarding Irish history and politics. Likewise, the Celtic-supporting environment provides a site for learning: of cross-generational communications, a sharing of collective memories, histories, and alternative under-standings and identities in relation to several ethno-cultural and political conflicts and struggles, none more so than Ireland, the country where most of them have their ethnic origins.

CONCLUSIONS

For many Rangers fans, the club and its cultural attributes are meaningful with reference to Protestant, British, Scottish, Ulster-Scots and/or royalist identities and history: it is these that provide the club with the tools and implements that con-stitute the dominant narratives and which in turn help describe Rangers' culture. Rangers' supporters can be seen as being among the most overtly pronounced in terms of manifestations of popular British, Scottish-British, Protestant and imperial identities in public spaces like that which constitutes football in Scotland.

For many Irish Catholics descended in Scotland, particularly evidenced in the Celtic supporting culture, awareness of their ethnic and national past highlights a strong memory of what they recognise as the unfinished process of the decolonisation of Ireland. This is not unique among the Irish diaspora in Scotland, Britain or else-where. Lennon et al. (1988) reviewed the life stories of Irish-born women in Britain:

> A sense of our own history is very strong amongst Irish people in a way which people in Britain often find mystifying. Most women we talked to felt this. The need to locate ourselves historically also appears to be reinforced by living over here and confronting that lack of information which so many British people have about Ireland and also, about their own history.

That this is contrary to what dominates culturally and politically, and also what has resulted from decades of armed conflict within and beyond the north of Ireland, is undoubted. This was stressed by a university conference organiser in 2012 who discussed the legacy of the troubles from a British perspective. Graham Dawson explained some of the rationale behind the occasion when he said that 'over the years posing any questions regarding the political arguments around the troubles risked getting you a name as an IRA sympathiser in this country'.[9]

Many Celtic supporters have traditionally accessed different sources of histori-cal memory and discourses that challenge those that have produced a hegemonic belief in Britain that the 'problem' was not a well-established colonial one, and further, was the inability of two religious tribes to live peacefully together, which necessitated the peacekeeping input from the even-handed, justice-seeking British Government and military. Such perceived censorship and propaganda is often vigorously challenged by many within the worldwide Irish diaspora and from within the multi-generational Irish communities in west central Scotland (and who often incline towards the various forms and genres of Irish rebel music, song and culture, especially manifest in the Celtic-supporting environment). The culture around Celtic is a site of struggle for ethnic and political identities that provides the Irish descended in Scotland with a space to express and celebrate their Irishness, to resist hostility against Irishness in Scotland, and to remember people and events that have partly shaped who they are and where they are. The existence and presence of Celtic allows those of Irish descent in Scotland a sense of cultural, social and political empowerment otherwise difficult to acquire in other spheres of life.

This chapter does not condemn or condone but rather seeks to explore and illuminate. It reflects on the importance of historical perspectives, interpretations, narratives and identities in Scottish football, particularly for many supporters of Rangers and Celtic, matters often overlooked, treated superficially or used as a tool to construct accounts which simply marginalise or negatively characterise. History and how it is viewed and represented is contested terrain. Nevertheless, it is necessary to see beyond conventional popular and dominant descriptions of Scottish football, particularly of the cultures that comprise Rangers and Celtic, to facilitate enhanced consideration of critical aspects of society. This chapter highlights the importance of recognising Scotland's formidable anti-Catholic past, the Scotland-England partnership that comprised the British Empire and particularly the history-altering epoch of the colonisation of Ireland's Ulster province, of Ireland's Great Hunger, Irish and Ulster-Scots migration to Scotland, and in how resultant national, ethnic, religious and cultural relationships have produced a range of memories and identities which contribute to the mosaic that comprises life in Scotland.

NOTES

1. For Motherwell fans celebrating in an Orange Hall, see http://www.youtube.com/watch?v=sCDDjTMQ5ul (last accessed 6 November 2012).
2. Alan Bairner (2001) reports Graham Walker (1995: 146) as noting that Rangers were in the past part of 'a celebration of Scottishness which was underpinned by a strong unionism or loyalism' but that 'in recent years, however, particularly as conflict in Northern Ireland intensified, many Scottish Protestants have felt increasingly uneasy about a sports club with an essentially exclusive ideology'.
3. Scottish Parliament, Official Report, 23 June 2011.
4. Broadcast on BBC Radio Scotland, 2 August 2002.
5. Rangers historians R. Ferrier and R. McElroy (1996) claim that Rangers is the 'flag carrier of what the majority of Scots would consider to be national virtues – Protestant, Monarchist tradition and Unionist.'
6. An ESRC-funded research project, 'The Second-Generation Irish: A Hidden Population in Multi-Ethnic Britain' (reference number: R00023836); see http://www.londonmet.ac.uk/research-units/iset/projects/esrc-hidden-population.cfm (last accessed 24 January 2013).
7. See issues of the *Celtic View* for 9 March 1966, 20 July 1966 and 19 April 1967.

8. *Celtic View*, 6 April 1966.
9. Quoted in *The Irish Post*, 4 August 2012, p. 14. It might be argued that recent legislation regarding the Offensive Behaviour in Football and Threatening Communications (Scotland) Bill has partly been passed, intentionally or otherwise, to keep the issue of British colonialism or the legacies thereof with regard to Ireland/Northern Ireland 'off' any social, political or cultural agenda in Scotland and to limit and restrain debate or expressions, particularly Irish nationalist, with regard to this long-term conflict. In addition, the Bill might also serve a function of absolving, through a process of silencing, Scotland of its historic responsibility in creating the problem in the first place.

REFERENCES

Bairner, A. (2001), *Sport, Nationalism, and Globalisation*, New York, NY: State University of New York Press.

Bell, I. (2012), 'Why I refuse to buy into politics of the poppy brand', *The Herald*, 27 October 2012, p. 15.

Bradley, J. M. (1995), *Ethnic and Religious Identity in Modern Scotland: Culture, Politics and Football*, Aldershot: Avebury.

Bradley, J. (1996), 'Identity, Politics and Culture: Orangeism in Scotland', *Scottish Affairs*, 16: Summer, 104–28.

Bradley, J. M. (2000), 'Wearing the green: a history of nationalist demonstrations among the diaspora in Scotland', in T. G. Fraser (ed.), *The Irish Parading Tradition: Following the Drum*, London: Macmillan, pp. 111–28.

Bradley, J. M. (ed.) (2004), *Celtic Minded: Essays on Religion, Politics, Society, Identity and Football*, Glendaruel: Argyll Publishing.

Bradley, J. M. (ed.) (2006), *Celtic Minded 2: Essays on Religion, Politics, Society, Identity and Football*, Glendaruel: Argyll Publishing.

Bradley, J. M. (ed.) (2009), *Celtic Minded 3: Essays on Religion, Politics, Society, Identity and Football*, Glendaruel: Argyll Publishing.

Carlow, J. (2007), 'Memoria, memory, and commemoration', *Mortality*, 12: 2, 103–8.

Collins, B. (1991), 'The Origins of Irish Immigration to Scotland in the Nineteenth and Twentieth Centuries', in T. M. Devine (ed.), *Irish Immigrants and Scottish Society in the Nineteenth and Twentieth Centuries; Proceedings of the Scottish Historical Studies Seminar*, Edinburgh: John Donald, pp. 44–66.

Devine, T. M. (1988), 'Urbanisation', in T. M. Devine and R. Mitchison (eds), *People and Society in Scotland, vol. 1, 1760–1830*, Edinburgh: John Donald, pp. 27–52.

Ferrier, R. and McElroy, R. (1996), *Rangers: The Complete Record*, Glasgow: Breedon Books.

Gallagher, T. (1987), *Glasgow: The Uneasy Peace*, Manchester: Manchester University Press.

Gibney, J. (2008), 'Early Modern Ireland: A British Atlantic Colony?', *History Compass*, 6: 1, 172–82.

Gillies, J. R. (1994), 'Memory and Identity: The History of a Relationship', in *Commemorations: The Politics of National Identity*, Princeton, NJ: Princeton University Press, p. 5.

Hickman, M. J. (1993), 'Integration or segregation? The education of the Irish in Britain in Roman Catholic voluntary-aided schools', *British Journal of Sociology of Education*, 14: 3, 285–301.

Hickman, M. J. (1996), 'Incorporating and denationalizing the Irish in England: the role of the Catholic church', in P. O'Sullivan (ed.), *The Irish Worldwide Volume 5: Religion and identity*, Leicester: University of Leicester Press, pp. 196–216.

Hobsbawm, E. and Ranger, T. (1983), *The invention of tradition*, Cambridge: Cambridge University Press.

Johnson, N. (1992), 'Nation-building, language and education: the geography of teacher recruitment in Ireland, 1925–55', *Political Geography Quarterly*, 11: 170–89.

Kowalski, R. (2004), '"Cry for us, Argentina": Sport and national identity in late twentieth-century Scotland', in A. Smith and D. Porter (eds), *Sport and National Identity in the Post-War World*, London: Routledge, pp. 69–87.

Lennon, M., McAdam, M. and O'Brien, J. (1988), *Across the Water: Irish Women's Lives in Britain*, London: Virago.

Stewart, A. T. Q. (1977), *The Narrow Ground: Aspects of Ulster, 1609–1969*, London: Faber and Faber.

Styles, S. C. (2000), 'The Non-Sectarian Culture of North East Scotland', in T. M. Devine (ed.), *Scotland's Shame: Bigotry and sectarianism in modern Scotland*, Edinburgh: Mainstream, pp. 115–23.

Walker, G. (1995), *Intimate Strangers: Political and Cultural Interaction between Scotland and Ulster in Modern Times*, Edinburgh: John Donald.

Walker. G. and Gallagher, T. (eds) (1990), *Sermons and Battle Hymns: Protestant Popular Culture in Modern Scotland*, Edinburgh: Edinburgh University Press, pp. 137–59.

Walter, B. (2001), *Outsiders Inside. Whiteness, Place and Irish Women*, London: Routledge.

Walter, B., Morgan, S., Hickman, M. and Bradley, J. M. (2002), 'Family stories, public silence: Irish identity construction amongst the second-generation Irish in England', *Scottish Geographical Journal*, 118: 3, 201–18.

Wilson, B. (1988), *Celtic: A Century with Honour*, Glasgow: Collins Willow.

6 Scottish Enlightenment and the Sectarianism Civilising Offensive

John Flint and Ryan Powell

INTRODUCTION

> If posterity were to judge the present times by their general character, they would be somewhat amazed at our late rejection of the Catholic petition. The age is more generally refined than any preceding era in modern history. (Leigh Hunt, 1808, quoted in Tomko 2011: 1)

This chapter locates sectarianism and its governance in Scottish football and society within theories of civilising offensives and moral panics. It argues, like Andrew Davies' chapter, that historical precedents may be uncovered if we frame the recent emergence of sectarianism as a specific social (and economic) problem to be tackled as a project of government (see the introduction and Flint 2008) within continuing long-term attempts to regulate conduct (Rohloff 2011). The chapter identifies how the definition of sectarian conflict and identity as outmoded in a modern and enlightened Scotland is not new and suggests that economic imperatives are central to government rationalities, combined with an increasing utilisation of legal remedies. We then describe the ambiguous relationships between popular cultural expressions of sectarianism and nationalism and the role of state authorities, and how these need to be understood as being embedded in urban space. We illustrate this by examining the bonfire celebrations in Lewes and conflicts over memorials and commemoration. The chapter concludes that we should reframe our understanding of sectarianism and its regulation from temporary and sporadic events linked to football and urban disorder towards struggles over our history and the right to occupy physical, virtual and imaginary spaces in Scotland.

CIVILISING OFFENSIVES

Mitzman (1987: 663) defines a civilising offensive as the relationship between traditional popular mentalities and the 'normative psychology of secular and religious authorities' in the upper orders of society. In this relationship between the *culture populaire* and *culture des élites* (Muchembled 1978), modernising and 'archaic' mental structures both combine and conflict and are characterised by complex, paradoxical and ambivalent processes (Powell 2007; Rohloff 2011). Work on civilising offensives has often been located in the sociology of Norbert Elias (2000) and his theory of civilising processes. Elias traces the normative concept of civilisation whereby particular groups define categories of 'civilised' and 'uncivilised' behaviours and populations and how these become linked to connotations of progress: civilisation came to express the 'self-consciousness of the West' (Elias 2000; see also Powell and Flint 2009; and for an introductory discussion of this and its relationship to sport, see Molnar and Kelly 2013, Chapter 7). A second element of Elias' project was to link long-term changes in behaviour to state formation and wider social developments. We have previously sought to apply Elias' theories of civilising processes to the governance of sectarianism in Scottish football (Flint and Powell 2009, 2011). Theories of civilising offensives have been linked to the conceptualisation of moral panics, viewed as intensive episodes that arise from longer-term projects of regulating conduct (Cohen 1972; Foucault 1977; Hier 2008; Hunt 1999).

Elias (2000) argued that shameful behaviour and violence were gradually and increasingly shifted behind the scenes of everyday and public life and that what he termed the 'social constraint towards self-constraint' resulted in individuals' orientations and conduct increasingly being characterised by foresight, mutual identification and increasing restraint. As social constraints are gradually internalised there is a corresponding change in thresholds of shame and repugnance: behaviours that were once unremarkable (including violence, the bodily functions and various eating habits for instance (see Elias 2000)) bring about shame in the perpetrator and repugnance in the observer (see Powell and Flint 2009). In this understanding, one explanation for why sectarian behaviour in the arenas of Scottish football becomes the subject of a specific civilising offensive is precisely because it shifts social tension and violence from 'behind the scenes', often into the media spotlight in more recent times, and represents the antithesis of mutual identification (see Waiton in this volume; Fletcher 1997) and self-restraint.

Stuart Waiton (2007 and this volume) explores moral panics as a form of elite disdain towards the cultures and behaviours of working-class football supporters (see also Jones 2010) and addresses the paradox of this occurring when other forms of sectarian conduct or ethno-religious disadvantage appear to be declining in Scottish society (see the chapters by Davis and Rosie). However, as Rohloff (2011) illustrates, moral panics need not be related to actually occurring decivilising processes within society or a weakening of state authority, but only a *perception* of such developments in which exaggeration and distortion are inherent features. Civilising offensives may include '*decivilising*' techniques – such as challenges to civil liberties (Elias 2000; Powell and Flint 2009; Rohloff 2011; Waiton in this volume), epitomised by the debates in this book about The Offensive Behaviour at Football Matches and Threatening Communications (Scotland) Act 2012 – as well as decivilised or barbarous *outcomes* (see van Krieken 1999; Powell 2007) exemplified most obviously in the colonial projects of Western nations.

Elite (including intellectual) disdain of the masses is nothing new (Carey 1992) and is particularly intensified when the crowd (especially the football crowd) generates a physical presence and intrusion of public space by the 'masses' who are usually understood as a metaphor for the unknowable and invisible and given imagined attributes (Carey 1992: 21). The actual sectarian behaviour of elements of the football crowd may then be used to confirm the attitudes and morals of a larger imagined 'psychological crowd' (Le Bon 1896; Allport 1979), such as the lower orders of society; or contrasted with the different standards of behaviour of another psychological crowd – the nation or 'civilised majority' of the population (see Flint and Powell 2011).

The broader context of sectarianism in Scotland is one in which competing groups attempt to define and give legitimacy and/or primacy to these psychological crowds and imagined communities (Anderson 1983): the construction of an Irish-Catholic diaspora or unionism/Britishness/loyalism (visibly and physically mani-fested in elements of the support and rituals of Celtic and Rangers football clubs); and a Scottish national identity promoted by the Scottish Government and made visible, to some extent, in the support of the national football team and the contra-Old Firm identities of some supporters of other Scottish football clubs. Overlapping these identities are other fault lines of class, gender and religious and secular forms of authority (see the chapters by Crawford, and Goodall and Malloch).

ABSOLUTISM

For Mitzman (1987: 664) a major historical tendency of the last five hundred years has been steadily increasing control by centralising political and ideological authorities over traditional cultures and mentalities, premised on a 'disenchanted and goal-orientated modern consciousness'. The civilising offensive has thus been charac-terised by both an intensification of national consciousness and efforts to reform the vulgarity of the lower classes. The defining technique of this centralising project of absolutism has been the condemnation of local and regional diversity and the repres-sion of popular culture (for example, the prohibitions on dancing by both Calvinist and Catholic regimes). The French Revolution resulted in a struggle to replace 'priest-ridden' local rituals, cultures and beliefs with a national language, school system and scientific reason (Mitzman 1987). Similar attempts to sublimate sectarian identities to national unity occurred in Britain in the same period (Tomko 2011: 30).

The Offensive Behaviour at Football Matches and Threatening Communications (Scotland) Act 2012 follows previous legislation in Scotland making religious hatred an aggravating offence, both primarily framed as a response to sectarianism (see Flint 2008) and the emphasis on utilising Football Banning Orders (see the chapter by Hamilton-Smith and McArdle). In some respects, this marks a signifi-cant shift from the previous governance of sectarianism, where, according to Tomko (2011: 12), legislation was viewed as insufficient and 'performative requirements for joining the nation' became linked to determining the cultural parameters of national identity through:

Models that regulate the place of a religious minority within the modern public sphere . . . projects that transfer the burden of quelling sectarian energies from the legal to the cultural world. Whether by erasure or obsolescence, they . . . overcome difference by eliminating difference.

While we may be witnessing a re-emergence of legal burdens for 'quelling sectarian energies', the focus on cultural parameters and the attempt to use both erasure and obsolescence to overcome difference by eliminating difference have been key techniques in the civilising offensive against sectarianism in Scotland and particularly Scottish football (see introduction and Kelly's chapter).

AGES OF ENLIGHTENMENT

According to Chandler (1998), the Scottish Enlightenment looked back to a pre-modern, pre-commercial past as an alien culture with different manners and norms. As Tomko (2011: 2–11) argues, at various stages in history Catholicism, anti-Catholicism and religion itself have been constructed in elite discourses as 'vestigial remnants from an obsolete or primitive stage of history', and these 'archaic remnants' are to be removed from the social order within a project of continually re-enacting modernity and national identity through a rejection of the past. Tomko (2011: 183) describes Catholic emancipation as being viewed as 'a triumph of liberty and enlightenment over the antiquated powers of religious tribalism'. For Edmund Burke (1855), no popery bigotry was a 'shameful ghost' which 'haunted an enlightened age'; while Wolfe Tone (1791) argued that anti-Catholicism belonged to the 'dark ages of superstition' and not 'the days of illumination at the close of the Eighteenth Century' (quoted in Tomko 2011: 23). As Elias (2000) describes, these motifs of civilised superiority were applied against foreign populations as well as the domestic lower classes. 'Rule, Britannia!' (written by James Thomson, a Lowland Scot) includes a line pitying 'Nations not so blest as Thee' (Groom 2006: 317). The notion of national superiority again resonates with Scottish sectarianism, dependent as it is on a selective and imagined history which appeals to group and national identifications, and thereby disidentifications, reinforced through the songs and imagery of past battles and victories (see Flint and Powell 2009: 222–3).

This unburdening of a divisive past was linked to motifs of the state, ideas of liberty and the primacy of commercial imperatives (Tomko 2011: 17). In addition to 'God Save the King' wishing Marshall Wade 'rebellious Scots to Crush', early verses of Oswald's national anthem also called for the Pope to be 'confounded' and: 'Protect our Church and State/And make true Britons hate/Priests with bald-headed Pates'. Crucially, this explicit entwining of state, patriotism and anti-Catholicism was also explicitly linked to commerce through a closing verse exalting that 'Heavens grant the wars to cease/That trading may increase' (quoted in Groom 2006: 319–21). Thus, sectarianism was to be overcome through a Protestant supremacy and uniformity achieved through unionism removing religious and ethnic conflict as a barrier to commerce and industry. The Union Flag itself became the acme of capitalism: an unrivalled advertising opportunity (Groom 2006). Similarly, Beaven (2006) describes how local processions in the early twentieth century increasingly became shorn of civic symbolism and were reconstituted as commercial and advertising enterprises.

These themes of modernity and commercialism continue to dominate the contemporary governmentalities of responses to sectarianism in Scotland which equally conceptualise our own period as one of illumination and enlightenment. The 'new Scotland' and 'modern Glasgow' (Braiden 2009) reject sectarianism as 'an anachronism', 'Neanderthal' or 'a cultural backwater mired in its own past' (Garavelli 2009; O'Sullivan 1999). Sectarianism is viewed as 'holding back Modern Scotland' and sectarianism must be confined to 'the dust-bin of history' so that Scotland may play a 'full part ... in the global economy' (Scottish Executive 2006a: 1).

Glasgow City Council's attempts to reduce the number of Loyal Order Parades in the city by 90 per cent are explicitly framed within the disruption caused to businesses and consumers, and the Orange Order itself has countered by seeking to rebrand the traditional July parade as a tourist attraction and therefore as a boost to the local economy (Hammil 2008). Such explicit economic considerations resonate with Weber's notion of the internal pacification of society as a prerequisite for the functioning of a capitalist economy dependent on forethought and calculability. Of course, the link between sectarianism and economy has always been central to Celtic and Rangers and explicitly epitomised in the very term 'Old Firm' with its connotations of extracting profit from ethno-religious tensions (Murray 1984; see McVey in this volume). As Joe Crawford argues in his chapter, economic drivers must never be neglected in an examination of the rationalities underpinning the governance of sectarianism. Becker (1991) defines those engaged in moral crusades as 'moral entrepreneurs' and there is undoubtedly a direct link between moral entrepreneurship and the economically entrepreneurial Scotland envisaged by its elites. Arnold Toynbee (1884) long ago recognised that the modern city dissolved old attachments and replaced them with a fierce competition for wealth among strangers. There is no city without a market (Braudel 1967; Weber 1921). But, as Lamennais (quoted in Burleigh 2005: 138) claimed, a bazaar is not at all the same thing as a city.

We may identify three key governmentalities that have framed contemporary responses to sectarianism in Scottish football: a problematisation of sectarian expression within a wider long- term project of the moral regulation of the working class; an imposing of the commercial and economic imperatives of a 'modern' Scotland; and a concern with regulating football supporters as primarily a problem of urban disorder (on the latter, see Flint 2008; and also its powerful illustration in the Hillsborough disaster). We may also identify historical precedents and parallels for each of these governmentalities. We now examine the complex and ambiguous relationship between official and popular expressions of sectarian identities which deny a simplistic dichotomy of the state and prominent institutions either colluding in sectarian nation-building or, conversely, merely regarding sectarianism as a problem to be 'eradicated' (Scottish Executive 2006b: 2–3).

BONFIRES, REVELS AND RIOTS

The British state has always had an ambiguous and problematic relationship to the popular expression of sectarian identities and, more specifically, anti-Catholicism. The history of anti-Catholicism is one often manifested through 'bonfires, revels and riots' (Paz 1992: 265) and there was also significant rioting in Scotland in protest against the Act of Union (Groom 2006: 184). The historical embedding of anti-Catholicism in popular celebrations occurred throughout Britain. At parliamentary elections patriotic songs were sung, free beer was served and the Pope was burnt in effigy, as with Guy Fawkes' Day and Queen Elizabeth's birthday (Groom 2006: 183).

But the state has viewed with suspicion, and at times repressed, the organisations, institutions and secret societies of religious groups and working-class populations (see Burleigh 2005; Thompson 1968). Contemporary characterisations of sectarian disorder, especially linked to football, are dominated by accounts of 'thuggish', 'drunken' and 'ignorant' behaviour that is divorced from any 'legitimate' religious or political affiliation (see Flint and Powell 2009, 2011). Again, this is not new. The Gordon Riots of June 1780 were the largest outbreak of urban violence in British history, fuelled by Lord George Gordon's Protestant Association and protests against the Catholic Relief Act, in which over three hundred people were killed (Haywood and Seed 2012). There was also violence in Edinburgh that delayed the introduction of similar legislation in Scotland (Tomko 2011). Burke (1855) described the rioters as 'a bigoted multitude' enflamed by 'obscure clubs', and Daniel Defoe wrote that 'horror possesses the Minds of the common people about it [Popery], that I believe there are 100,000 stout Fellows who would spend the last Drop of their Blood against Popery, that do not know whether it be a Man or a Horse' (quoted in Groom 2006: 184).

But, despite their Protestant and patriotic basis, such outbreaks of sectarian rioting were primarily regarded by urban authorities as plebeian revolts (Tomko 2011) and a threat to the authority of the governing elite and their attempts to project an imagined image of a chivalrous and harmonious society (Beaven 2006). These outbreaks were not confined to Scotland and Britain, however, but were exported alongside migration and colonialism (see Bradley in this volume). Colonial administrators in Melbourne in 1847 enacted legislation (The Party Processions Bill) to reduce disorder occurring at St Patrick's Day parades, and disturbances between Irish nationalists and loyalists were still occurring at parades in the city in 1920 (Groom 2006). The Orange Riot in New York in 1871 occurred after city authorities rescinded an order (imposed after violent clashes resulting in fatalities the previous year) banning Irish Protestants from parading in commemoration of the Battle of the Boyne. Heavily protected by soldiers and police officers, the parade proceeded and fighting broke out, resulting in the deaths of sixty people after troops fired on the crowd (Fairfield 2010: 112–13). The events were perceived by the *New York Times* as the 'proletariat and dangerous classes showing their revolutionary head'. The current prominence given to the policing of English (and Scottish) Defence League demonstrations and counter-demonstrations (see Copsey 2010; Jackson 2012; Treadwell and Garland 2011) illustrates how social movements appropriating emblems and discourses of loyalty and patriotism can be viewed by elites as challenging both urban order and the authority of the state and its ability to address social problems, a defining feature of decivilising processes in Eliasian theory.

This ambiguity between popular culture and the normative positions of authorities is exemplified in the history of St George's Day in England. From the fifteenth century it had become an annual mandatory festival which one could be fined for not attending – it was a carnival that embodied and supported, rather than challenged, the existing order (Groom 2006: 78). But in 1645, the Puritans' 'Directory for the Public Worship of God' banned observation of the event (Groom 2006: 145). Yet, by the twentieth century it had again become a popular holiday (Groom 2006: 231). Similarly, the history of Caribbean carnival in Britain is one of a contested social event inscribed in the landscape (Jackson 1988), having been appropriated from colonial powers in the Caribbean, developed into a symbol of resistance to Empire, and then re-emerging as a (multi)cultural event celebrated by local authorities and tied to economic considerations. Historical outbreaks of violence serve as a reminder of its ambiguity.

Festivals were often regarded by both religious and secular authorities as explosions of popular culture that acted primarily as safety valves and could therefore be tolerated (Burke 1978). It is often suggested that Old Firm football matches perform a similar social function in the west of Scotland. But urban crowds always had the potential to subvert or realign official commemorations. Public processions developed in Britain throughout the nineteenth century as social groups and institutions staked their claim for a place in the social body of an urban locality (Gunn 2000). The national Peace Day celebrations of 19 July 1919 were designed to forge national unity, yet they resulted in serious disturbances in several English cities and towns (Beaven 2006) and were perceived to be a direct challenge to the legitimacy and authority of urban elites. Up to ten thousand people were involved in disturbances in Coventry and Luton (where the town hall was burnt to the ground) and rioters were referred to in official reports as 'riff raff'.

Lewes bonfires

There is a tendency in studies of sectarianism in Scotland to focus on the specifics of the Scottish (or often west of Scotland) context and its linkages to Ireland, or to refer to historic sectarianism in England and Wales, through its connection to Irish migration in cities such as Cardiff and Liverpool. This negates the very long history of religious antagonism and anti-Popery in England (Hogge 2005) that pre-dates the British state and was often not directly linked to Anglo-Irish relations but which has been manifested in popular rituals and culture through to present times. One illustration of this is the history of conflict surrounding bonfire celebrations in the East Sussex town of Lewes, including the 1847 Lewes Bonfire Riot (Etherington 1993; Leith 2011). The previous year *The Sussex Advertiser* had called, in language resonating with current depictions of sectarian crowds in Scotland, for a ban of the 'riotous and brutalising orgies celebrated by a class of men taken from amongst the lowest ranks of society'. Following petitions to the Bench of Magistrates to ban the celebrations, a large police force, including reinforcements from London, was drafted in and the reading of the Riot Act led to disturbances and the arrest of eight individuals, with further disturbances occurring for several weeks. By 1850 *The Sussex Express*' description was of 'a scene [that] reminded one far more of the orgies of infuriated savages than of the amusements of an even semi-civilised people'. In the 1930s, the Mayor of Lewes requested that societies dispense with 'No popery' banners and the burning of the Papal effigy. In the 1950s, the Cliffe Society was banned by the town's Bonfire Council from the United Grand Procession for its refusal to desist from carrying a 'No popery' banner, which the society displays to this day, along with banners commemorating the sixteenth-century Protestant martyrs of Lewes. Contemporary controversy continues to be associated with the Lewes Bonfire Societies and competing definitions of traditionalism and bigotry (BBC News 2004; Lewes Forum 2010).

The example of Lewes illustrates the civilising offensive as a relationship between authority and popular culture, but also how this relationship is ambiguous and contested within, as well as between, groups. Popular rituals that appear to support the existing premises of the state: Protestantism and patriotism become reframed as working-class events that pose challenges to the urban and moral order. The response by groups subject to new forms of regulation which seek to minimise the visibility of sectarian sentiments becomes divided and tensions develop between officially sanctioned forms of commemoration (linked to maximising tourism and the local economy) and the rights of other groups to express 'popular' or traditional sentiments which may be regarded as offensive to others and risk breaches to the urban peace. Similar debates emerge as other forms of traditional popular culture become problematised as sectarian, for example the controversies over the 'Hokey Cokey' song (Cramb 2008); or new groups become folk devils in traditional rituals, such as the burning of effigies of Gypsy Traveller caravans during bonfire celebrations (Townsend 2003).

'A Celtic Row in a Saxon metropolis': Commemoration and the urban landscape

Contemporary debates about sectarianism and its governance in Scotland, including several of the contributions to this book, often focus on concepts of free speech and (in)tolerance and abstract national-level constructions of identity and national belonging. However, these debates, we would argue, also have to be viewed through the lens of conflicts over the right to the city (Harvey 1973; 2008; Fainstein 2011; Lefebvre 1968): that is, the right to appropriate, participate in and occupy urban space (and the spaces of the virtual city through the internet which have a complex relationship with physical geography, including sectarian tension, see O'Dochartaigh 2007). This enables us to recognise how the informalised spaces associated with Scottish football represent particular constructions of territory and belonging made visible in a dramatic aural and spatial experience which is less regulated by official authority (Caudwell 2011; Davies, this volume; Flint and Powell 2011). In doing so, we can examine how forms of sectarian behaviour and reactive civilising offensives act as mechanisms of socio-spatial exclusion against specific groups along the lines of class, gender and sexuality as well as ethno-religious and political identities (Crawford, and Goodall and Malloch in this volume; Caudwell 2011). To date, most studies of sectarianism in Scotland have not engaged with concepts of hate crime in the context of urban space (Iganski 2008); or conceptualised supporters' groups as social movements, using both urban space and the internet as forms of mobilisation seeking to secure cultural ownership of their clubs and to legitimate their identities in wider society (Millward 2012). Viewing attempts at regulating/eradicating sectarianism through the theoretical lens of the civilising offensive opens up new avenues for inquiry in terms of resistance to such governmental projects and the conflicts inherent therein.

The urban landscape is not a neutral 'flat' territory in which sectarian and other social conflicts play out. Rather, various acts and techniques of commemoration, such as street names and monuments, transform urban arenas into political settings and attempt to impose an authorised version of history and of 'civilisation' onto the ordinary settings of everyday life (Azaryahu 1996; Doyle 2010; Jackson 1988) – what Billig (1995) terms 'banal nationalism'. Groom (2006) argues that the Union Flag became omnipresent in Britain and its Empire, subtly informing all aspects of everyday life. Indeed, the New Town in Scotland's capital was deliberately designed by James Craig in 1767 (during the Scottish Enlightenment) as a symbol of unionism (progress and patriotism) made physically manifest in the pattern of the Union Flag and the street names. Edinburgh's example was subsequently replicated by Lord Kitchener in Khartoum and by the market place and bazaars of Faisalabad, where patriotism and commerce were literally entwined and embedded in the urban form (see Groom 2006: 224).

However, these processes are contested, for example Doyle (2010) describes how Belfast's Victorian urban geography acquired popular sectarian meanings that were independent of official imperial ideology and were heavily influenced by riots in the 1850s, which the *Belfast Telegraph* termed 'a Celtic row in a Saxon metropolis' (quoted in Doyle 2010: 853).

The links between patriotism, militarism and allegiance that are increasingly prominent in discourses of sectarianism in Scottish football also have historical precedents in Belfast (Doyle 2010). In 1854 the *Newsletter* criticised the Catholic Church for failing to hold special services on an anointed day of prayer and commemoration in April 1854 for the Crimean War. Catholics were accused of not being significantly patriotic and countered with evidence that Catholic churches across the United Kingdom were saying prayers for the British army. It should also be noted that working-class Protestants and Catholics were equally enthusiastic in celebrating news of the Sebastopol victory in 1855. Loyalty to the Empire or army was not a Protestant monopoly and was, in part, driven by a Catholic bourgeoisie attempting to demonstrate their respectability in a Protestant city (Doyle 2010; see Hogge 2006 on similar controversies of Catholic loyalty in Elizabethan England).

These conflicts over symbols and patriotism have gained primacy in debates about sectarianism in Scottish football in recent years. The first campaign in Britain to 'support the colours by wearing the colours' and the first national flag day was proposed by a Glaswegian and was instigated on 3 October 1914 (Groom 2006). Controversies over flags have been a regular feature of Scottish football history, including the attempt by the Scottish Football Association to ban the flying of the Tricolour over Celtic Park in 1952 (Celtic were supported by Rangers in this dispute); and Scotland's Lyon Court decision in 1978 to fine an individual for using the Lion Rampant on souvenirs sold to Scottish football supporters and to admonish both the Scottish National Party and Rangers FC for using the St Andrew's cross with a red lion (Groom 2006).

Military commemorations have become sites for conflicts over identity and allegiance. An Armed Forces Day event in Glasgow in 2009 resulted in arrests as a result of confrontations, a protest and sectarian singing. There were also disputes between Celtic and Rangers supporters about the presentation made to Falklands War veteran Simon Weston at Ibrox during an Old Firm game in March 2010 (Walker 2010). Rangers FC has been prominent in its support for the Tickets for Troops charity which provides armed services personnel with tickets to a range of sporting and cultural events (see www.ticketsfortroops.org). In contrast, sections of the Celtic support have staged a range of protests in recent seasons against the club's decision to wear poppies on their strip (see Flint and Powell 2011 and Kelly in press). The prominence of this direct support of, or opposition to, British militarism among football supporters, clubs and authorities is, to our knowledge, a relatively new phenomenon. But it has occurred within a wider recent politicisation of war commemoration ceremonies (for some related discussions on these themes, see Kelly in press for a UK-specific one and Silk and Falcous 2005, Falcous and Silk 2005 and Scherer and Koch 2010 for international ones). The immediate spark for the formation of the English Defence League was a protest by the Ahlus Sunnah wal Jamaah group against the public and visible endorsement of returning troops in Luton in 2009. The Home Secretary has banned the Muslims Against Crusades group after they threatened to repeat their 2010 demonstration of burning poppies on Remembrance Sunday (Casciani 2011). These protests coincided with an emergence of popular rituals and expressions of support for the British military,[1] such as crowds lining the streets of Wootton Bassett for the return of soldiers killed in action.

The lines between officially sanctioned commemoration (and the forms of allegiance and patriotism that they legitimise) and unofficial sentiments of sectarianism to be condemned are often blurred. Heart of Midlothian FC provides a good example of this (see also the chapters by Kelly and Rosie). In the aftermath of the attack on Neil Lennon by a Hearts supporter at Tynecastle on 10 May 2011 and concerns about the increasing presence of sectarian emblems and singing at derby games between Hearts and Hibernian, a spokesperson for Hearts stated that the Red Hand of Ulster had 'no relevance' at Tynecastle. But the statement also said that Hearts had no objection to the Union Flag, adding 'no club deserves more the right to fly the Union Flag' (Hannan 2011; Rangers have also officially sanctioned the Union Flag as an expression of being 'a Scottish club that is proud to be British', see Flint and Powell 2009).

The Hearts statement was a reference to the club's history, which is presented in a section on the club's official website entitled 'The Proudest Moment of a Proud

Club' (Heart of Midlothian 2004) and is excellently documented by Alexander (2004). In November 1914 sixteen first team players enlisted in the British army, with seven subsequently being killed (their names, along with a Poppy, were embroidered into a commemorative strip worn by the Hearts players in a match against Aberdeen in 2007). In 1922 a memorial was erected in the Haymarket in Edinburgh where a commemoration service occurs on each Remembrance Sunday. The Hearts memorial, like the New Town of Edinburgh nearby, inscribes the urban landscape with particular civic and political vocabularies and memories.

This memorial is largely viewed as uncontested and unproblematic, although the uneasy relationship between popular and civic commemoration and commercial forces is again evidenced by the formation of a campaign group to influence Edinburgh City Council's relocation of the memorial as a part of the new Edinburgh tram system (Friends of the Heart of Midlothian Memorial 2008). However, in contrast, the memorial in Carfin, Lanarkshire to victims of the Irish potato famine became the subject of controversy in 2006 when a planned dedication of the monument by Irish Premier Bertie Ahern was cancelled due to fears of sectarian violence. Glasgow City Council has currently established a working group to develop a memorial to the victims of the potato famine (in both Ireland and the Scottish Highlands) as 'physical recognition' of the city's diversity (Braiden 2012).

These examples illustrate how urban space is not simply a neutral grid on which cultural difference, historical memory and social organisation are inscribed (Gupta and Ferguson 1992). Rather, it is a site of conflict and negotiation and is itself productive of identity and difference (see Flint 2012). They reveal the inherently political nature of commemoration: that the Hearts memorial and Edinburgh New Town are viewed as unproblematic reflects a relative convergence of dominant political expression and popular culture.

CONCLUSIONS

Controversies over commemoration and memorials enable us to reframe our understanding of the relationships between sectarianism, football and Scottish society. 'Sectarian' conduct is not only visible in the arenas of football. It is not merely a temporary aberration fuelled by alcohol, crowd mentalities or ninety-minute animosities. Nor is its governance simply a dichotomy of elite vertical power being imposed on elements of popular culture, as some proponents of moral panic theory suggest.

Rather, we need to understand how the contemporary governance of sectarianism is part of the long history of the regulating project of the modern state and how sectarianism is not merely a problem of urban disorder or unenlightened dispositions, but rather reflects groups' attempts to secure a position in the physical and imagined constructions of contemporary Scotland (and in some cases to deny this space to others). Their techniques include securing officially sanctioned forms of remembrance and commemoration (through monuments, commemoration days, symbols on football strips or permission for processions and flags) or challenging these. They also extend to legitimating their presence within the actual science and official understanding of the state, for example the campaigns of the Federation of Irish Societies and the Muslim Council of Britain, and to maximise the count of their respective groups in the 2011 Census (Federation of Irish Societies 2011; MCB News 2011).

The context of the new anti-sectarianism legislation in Scotland is one in which there is no law against desecrating the Union Flag or St Andrew's Flag, as there is with the national flag of the United States (indeed, there have been proposals to extend this legislation to the singing of the US National Anthem following controversies at major sporting events, Michaels 2012). There is also no legal status for the term 'hate crime' in the United Kingdom and the hate crime concept is inadequately defined (Iganski 2008). It is equally worth remembering that popular culture has always resisted and subverted officially sanctioned forms of national identity expression – very soon after the composition of 'God Bless our Lord the King' there were alternative versions desiring 'that Scotland we may see freed from vile Presbytry' (Groom 2006: 180). But we also should never forget that there have been periods in our history when disgracing the flag was a criminal offence (Groom 2006). The civilising offensive is, after all, a perpetual (not necessarily progressive) process and, to paraphrase Steven Johnsen (2001), through commemorative architecture, football, government and internet communication, Scotland continues to do battle with history and with itself.

NOTE

1. Kelly (in press) refers to this and other such events as contributing to the post-'war on terror' '"hero"-fication of British militarism'.

REFERENCES

Alexander, J. (2004), *McCrae's Battalion: The Story of the 16th Royal Scots*, Edinburgh: Mainstream.

Allport, G. A. (1979), *The Nature of Prejudice*, London: Addison-Wesley.

Anderson, B. (1983), *Imagined Communities: Reflections on the Origins and Spread of Nationalism*, London: Verso.

Azaryahu (1996), 'The Power of Commemorative Street Names', *Environment and Planning D: Society and Space*, 14: 3, 311–30.

BBC News (2004), 'Bonfire Sparks anti-Catholic claims', 2 January 2004, http://news.bbc. co.uk/1/hi/england/southern_counties/3362175.stm (last accessed 2 August 2012).

Beaven, B. (2006), 'Challenges to civic governance in post-war England: The Peace Day disturbances of 1919', *Urban History*, 33: 3, 369–92.

Becker, H. S. (1991), *Outsiders: Studies in the sociology of deviance*, New York, NY: Free Press.

Billig, M. (1995), *Banal Nationalism*, London: Sage.

Braiden, G. (2009), 'Orange Order "under attack" over parades, claims chief', *The Herald*, 20 August 2009.

Braiden, G. (2012), 'Famine memorial study approved', *The Herald*, 14 September 2012, http://www.heraldscotland.com/news/home-news/famine-memorial-study-approved.18876069 (last accessed 18 October 2012).

Braudel, F. (1967), *Civilisation and Capitalism, 15th–18th Century. Vol. 1*, New York, NY: Harper and Row.

Burke, E. (1855), *The Works of the Right Honourable Edmund Burke*, Vol. 2, London: H. G. Bohn.

Burke, P. (1978), *Popular Culture in Early Modern Europe*, New York, NY: New York University Press.

Burleigh, M. (2005), *Earthly Powers: Religion and Politics in Europe from the Enlightenment to the Great War*, London: Harper Perennial.

Carey, J. (1992), *The Intellectuals and the Masses: Pride and Prejudice among the literary Intelligentsia, 1880–1939*, London: Faber and Faber.

Casciani, D. (2011), 'Muslims Against Crusades banned by Theresa May', BBC News, 10 November 2011, http://www.bbc.co.uk/news/uk-15678275 (last accessed 17 October 2012).

Caudwell, J. (2011), '"Does your boyfriend know you're here?" The spatiality of homophobia in men's football culture in the UK', *Leisure Studies*, 30: 2, 123–38.

Chandler, J. (1998), *England in 1819: The Politics of Literary Culture and the Case of Romantic Historicism*, Chicago, IL: University of Chicago Press.

Cohen, S. (1972), *Folk Devils and Moral Panics: The Creation of the Mods and Rockers*, Oxford: Martin Robertson.

Copsey, N. (2010), *The English Defence League: Challenging our country and our values of social inclusion, fairness and equality*, Faith Matters.

Cramb, A. (2008), 'Doing the Hokey Cokey "could be hate crime"', *The Telegraph*, 21 December 2008, http://www.telegraph.co.uk/news/newstopics/howaboutthat/3883838/Doing-the-Hokey-Cokey-could-be-hate-crime.html (last accessed 17 October 2012).

Doyle, M. (2010), 'The Sepoys of the Pound and Sandy Row: Empire and Identity in mid-Victorian Belfast', *Journal of Urban History*, 36: 6, 849–67.

Elias, N. (2000), *The Civilizing Process*, Oxford: Blackwell.

Etherington, J. (1993), *Lewes Bonfire Night*, Lewes: SB Publications.

Fainstein, S. (2011), *The Just City*, New York, NY: Cornell University Press.

Fairfield, J. D. (2010), *The Public and Its Possibilities: Triumphs and Tragedies in the American City*, Philadelphia, PA: Temple University Press.

Falcous, M. and Silk, M. (2005), 'Manufacturing Consent: Mediated Sporting Spectacle and the Cultural Politics of the "War on Terror"', *International Journal of Media and Cultural Politics*, 1: 1, 59–65.

Federation of Irish Societies (2011), *How Irish Are You?*, London: Federation of Irish Societies.

Fletcher, J. (1997), *Violence and civilization: An Introduction to the Work of Norbert Elias*, Cambridge: Polity Press.

Flint, J. (2008), 'Governing Sectarianism in Scotland', *Scottish Affairs*, 63: Spring 2008, 107–24.

Flint, J. (2012), 'Catholic Schools and Sectarianism in Scotland: Educational Places and the Production and Negotiation of Urban Space', *Policy Futures in Education*, 10: 5, 507–17.

Flint, J. and Powell, R. (2009), 'Civilising Offensives: Education, Football and "Eradicating" Sectarianism in Scotland', in A. Millie (ed.), *Securing Respect: Behavioural expectations and anti-social behaviour in the UK*, Bristol: Policy Press, pp. 219–38.

Flint, J. and Powell, R. (2011), '"They Sing That Song": Sectarianism and Conduct in the Informalised Spaces of Scottish Football', in D. Bursey (ed.), *Race, Ethnicity and Football: Persistent Debates and Emerging Issues*, London: Routledge, pp. 191–204.

Foucault, M. (1977), *Discipline and Punish: The Birth of the Prison*, London: Penguin.

Friends of the Heart of Midlothian War Memorial (2008), http://heartofmidlothianwarmemorial.com/0001.html (last accessed 16 October 2012).

Garavelli, D. (2009), 'Orange circus is out of order', *Scotland on Sunday*, 22 November 2009.

Groom, N. (2006), *The Union Jack: The Story of the British Flag*, London: Atlantic Books.

Gunn, S. (2000), *The Public Culture of the Victorian Middle Class: Ritual Authority and the English Industrial City 1840–1914*, Manchester: Manchester University Press.

Gupta, A. and Ferguson, J. (1992), 'Beyond "Culture": space, identity and the politics of difference', *Cultural Anthropology*, 7: 1, 6–23.

Hammil, J. (2008), 'Orange Order bids to turn walk into week-long festival', *The Herald*, 5 July 2008.

Hannan, M. (2011), '"Irrelevant" Ulster Flags Discouraged at Tynecastle', *The Scotsman*, 4 June 2011.

Harvey, D. (1973), *Social Justice and the City*, Athens, GA: University of Georgia Press.

Harvey, D. (2008), 'The right to the city', *New Left Review*, 53: September–October, 23–40.

Haywood, I. and Seed, J. (2012), *The Gordon Riots: Politics, Culture and Insurrection in Late Eighteenth Century Britain*, Cambridge: Cambridge University Press.

Heart of Midlothian FC (2004), 'The Proudest Moment of a Proud Club', http://www.heartsfc.co.uk/page/WarMemorial/0,,10289,00.html (last accessed 2 August 2012).

Hier, S. (2008), 'Thinking beyond moral panic: Risk, responsibility, and the politics of moralization', *Theoretical Criminology*, 12: 2, 173–90.

Hogge, A. (2005), *God's Secret Agents: Queen Elizabeth's Forbidden Priests and the Hatching of the Gunpowder Plot*, London: HarperCollins.

Hunt, A. (1999), *Governing morals: A social history of moral regulation*, Cambridge: Cambridge University Press.

Iganski, P. (2008), *Hate Crime and the City*, Bristol: Policy Press.

Jackson, P. (1988), 'Street life: the politics of carnival', *Environment and Planning D: Society and Space*, 6: 2, 213–27.

Jackson, P. (2012), *The EDL: Britain's New Far Right Social Movement*, Northampton: RNM Publications.

Johnsen, S. (2008), 'Political Not Patriotic: Democracy, Civic Space, and the American Memorial/Monument Complex', *Theory and Event*, 5: 2: http://muse.jhu.edu/journals/theory_and_event/v005/5.2johnston.html.

Jones, A. (2010), *Chavs: The Demonization of the Working Class*, London: Verso.

Kelly, J. (in press), 'Popular Culture, Sport and the 'Hero'-fication of British Militarism', *Sociology*.

Le Bon, G. (1896), *The Crowd: A Study of the Popular Mind*, New York, NY: Macmillan.

Lefebvre, H. (1968), *Writings on Cities*, Oxford: Blackwell.

Leith, A. (2011), 'The 1847 Lewes Bonfire Riot', http://www.lewesbonfirecelebrations.com/bonfire-night-history/1847-bonfire-riots/ (last accessed 2 August 2012).

Lewes Forum (2010), 'Anti-Catholic Sentiment Was Not Bigotry', http://www.lewes.co.uk/Forum/Post/Re:_Anti-Catholic_Sentiment_Was_Not_Bigotry/68527 (last accessed 2 August 2012).

MCB News (2011), 'The MCB urges Muslim households to complete the 2011 Census form', *MCB News*, 14 March 2011.

Michaels, S. (2012), 'Fine Proposed for botching US national anthem', *The Guardian*, 5 January 2012, http://www.guardian.co.uk/music/2012/jan/05/us-national-anthem (last accessed 16 October 2012).

Millward, P. (2012), 'Reclaiming the Kop? Analysing Liverpool Supporters' 21st Century Mobilizations', *Sociology*, 46: 4.

Miztman, A. (1987), 'The Civilizing Offensive: Mentalities, High Culture and Individual Psyches', *Journal of Social History*, 20: 4, 663–87.

Molnar, G. and Kelly, J. (2013), *Sport, Exercise and Social Theory: An Introduction*, London: Routledge.

Muchembled, R. (1978), *Culture populaire et culture des élites dans la France Moderne XVe – XVIII siècle*, Paris : Flammarion.

Murray, W. (1984), *The Old Firm: Sectarianism, Sport and Society in Scotland*, Edinburgh: Mainstream.

O'Dochartaigh, N. (2007), 'Conflict, territory and new technologies: online interaction at a Belfast interface', *Political Geography*, 26: 4, 474–91.

O'Sullivan, J. (1999), 'I'm a Catholic in a football sense', *The Independent*, 4 June 1999.

Paz, D. G. (1992), *Anti-Catholicism in Mid-Victorian England*, Stanford, CA: Stanford University Press.

Powell, R. (2007), 'Civilising offensives and ambivalence: the case of British Gypsies', *People, Place and Policy Online*, 1: 3, 112–23: http://extra.shu.ac.uk/ppp-online/issue_3_281107/documents/civilising_offensives_british_gypsies.pdf.

Powell, R. and Flint, J. (2009), '(In)Formalisation and the Civilising Process: Applying the Work of Norbert Elias to Housing-Based Anti-social Behaviour Interventions in the UK', *Housing, Theory and Society*, 26: 3, 159–78.

Rohloff, A. (2011), 'Shifting the focus? Moral panics as civilizing and decivilizing processes', in S. P. Hier (ed.), *Moral Panic and the Politics of Anxiety*, London: Routledge, pp. 71–85.

Scottish Executive (2006a), *Action plan on tackling sectarianism in Scotland*, Edinburgh: Scottish Executive.

Scottish Executive (2006b), *Calling Full Time on Sectarianism*, Edinburgh: Scottish Executive.

Scherer, J. and Koch, J. (2010), 'Living with War: Sport, Citizenship and the Cultural Politics of Post-9/11 Canadian Identity', *Sociology of Sport Journal*, 27: 1, 1–29.

Silk, M. and Falcous, M. (2005), 'One Day in September/A Week in February: Mobilizing American (Sporting) Nationalism', *Sociology of Sport Journal*, 22: 4, 447–71.

Thompson, E. P. (1968), *The Making of the English Working Class*, London: Penguin.

Tomko, M. (2011), *British Romanticism and the Catholic Question: Religion, History and National Identity, 1778–1829*, Basingstoke: Palgrave Macmillan.

Townsend, M. (2003), 'A Burning Issue in the Village', *The Guardian*, 16 November 2003, http://www.guardian.co.uk/society/2003/nov/16/raceintheuk.uknews (last accessed 17 October 2012).

Treadwell, J. and Garland, J. (2011), 'Masculinity, Marginalization and Violence: A Case Study of the English Defence League', *British Journal of Criminology*, 51: 4, 621–34.

Toynbee, A. (1884), *Lectures on the Industrial Revolution in England*, Newton Abbot.

van Krieken, R. (1999), 'The barbarism of civilization: cultural genocide and the "stolen generations"', *British Journal of Sociology*, 50: 2, 297–315.

Waiton, S. (2007), *Amoral Panics: The Politics of Antisocial Behaviour*, London: Routledge.

Walker, D. (2010), 'Twisted', *Scottish Sun*, 10 October 2010, http://www.thesun.co.uk/sol/homepage/news/scottishnews/2872402/Celtic-fans-sick-Falklands-War-stunt.html (last accessed 17 October 2012).

Weber, M. (1921), *The City*, Glencoe, IL: Free Press.

Constructing and Governing 'Sectarianism' and Football

7 The New Sectarians

Stuart Waiton

> My duty to be tolerant towards the Other effectively means that I should not get too close to him, intrude on his space. In other words, I should respect his *intolerance* of my over-proximity. What increasingly emerges as the central human right of late-capitalist society is *the right not to be harassed*, which is a right to be kept at a safe distance from others. (Žižek 2009: 35)

INTRODUCTION

This chapter will argue that the rise of anti-sectarianism in Scotland in the last decade confusingly appears to be a progressive struggle against bigotry and divisions in society. Framed within the idea of tolerance, this modern concern is in reality predicated on both a new form of 'intolerance tolerance' and also on a late-modern conception of 'vulnerable autonomy'. The former is in many respects the opposite to the classical liberal notion of tolerance which lays the foundations of free speech, while the latter similarly undermines the liberal ideal of the robust moral and autonomous individual that was fundamental to ideas of liberty and to the practical advancement of democracy. Being 'tolerant' today means not speaking, acting or behaving in a way that would be upsetting to others – others who are deemed to be fundamentally vulnerable. Through this more fragile understanding (and construction) of the human subject, freedom of speech and expression has been undermined and at times criminalised, and a new form of caring authoritarianism has been, and is being, established in what is often described by politicians north of the border as our 'modern tolerant Scotland'.

The argument made below is that anti-sectarianism, within this context, is no longer fundamentally about challenging religious (or political) sect-like behaviour but is part of a wider framework of psychic protection, where everybody, but especially those defined as 'vulnerable groups', is protected from emotional hurt, that is from being offended. Twenty-first-century anti-sectarianism should consequently be understood as part of a *protection racket* and as a new basis for connecting fragmented groups and individuals to state institutions. In this respect anti-sectarianism can be seen as part of a re-legitimising process by the authorities in Scotland.

As this protection racket develops, as Slovoj Žižek (2009) observes, a new frag-mented or distant form of behaviour is being encouraged. We are increasingly, and in law, 'kept at a safe distance from one another', as our intolerance of other peo-ple's 'over-proximity' and our newly found 'right' not to be harassed (or offended) is institutionalised. The chapter concludes by looking in detail at a significant, and to some extent ironic, outcome of these developments – the creation of the 'new sec-tarians'. Through the increasing protection of the 'offended', new forms of division are being constructed or reinforced with the rise of what is best described as a kind of *nimbyism of the self* developing among increasingly asocial individuals, coupled with groups who have an inward- looking concern with defending 'their culture'. Both are developing a 'sect'-like approach to the over-proximity of others and are increasingly looking (and being encouraged to look) to the authorities for 'respect'. For those who are defined as acting 'inappropriately', the modern state is at the ready to listen out for anyone who cries out, 'Arrest him', because, 'I'M OFFENDED'.

THE RISE OF INTOLERANCE

Despite much talk about the need to create a 'modern tolerant Scotland' by politi-cians today, intolerance about certain things, like 'sectarianism', has risen dramati-cally. Searching Scotland's broadsheets for articles about both 'sectarianism' and the 'Old Firm', what is fascinating is that it wasn't until 1997 that there was any significant increase in interest in this interlinked topic of Celtic and Rangers with the issue of sectarianism.[1] Sectarianism in general existed as a discussion point to some extent, but particularly significant periods of interest emerge after this time, with, for example, over four hundred articles about sectarianism appearing in 1998 and 2002, and then over 550 such articles appearing in *The Herald* and *The Scotsman* in 2011 following the SNP campaign around offensiveness in football. The focus on 'sectarianism' and the 'Old Firm' was limited and appears to have been of little significance as a political debating point before 1997. There were only two articles on the subject in 1992 and 1993, for example, but after 1997 there were around forty articles each year on the Old Firm and sectarianism. There was then a doubling of the number of articles in 2001 and a peak of interest in 2002, with 117 articles on the subject. Old Firm sectarianism remained of some significance until 2006 and then declined. In 2011, following the SNP's campaign, a new high of almost two hundred articles were written about this 'problem' – one hundred times more articles than had been written in 1992.

The increased interest in sectarianism in football does not appear to bear any rela-tion to an actual rise in this 'problem', rather the perceived problem of sectarianism and especially sectarianism in football grew as a result of what could be described as a new form of governing *through* anti-sectarianism (Flint 2008). Another way to describe this would be to recognise that the behaviour of Old Firm fans did not change for the worse (indeed, a strong argument could be made that the reverse was the case), what changed was the behaviour of the Scottish authorities who became less tolerant of Old Firm fans' behaviour. From an issue that attracted relatively little political interest, it became a significant topic and one that was increasingly campaigned around.

The changing attitude towards sectarianism in football can be seen in the arguments made by key individuals within politics and the press over this period of time. One stark example can be seen in the writing and arguments of the celebrated sports writer Graham Spiers. During one of the Scottish Parliament's Justice Committee debates on the Offensive Behaviour at Football and Threatening Communication Bill in 2011, Spiers made a strong case to outlaw sectarian songs at Old Firm games. Graham Spiers rhetorically asked the committee (and myself, as I was also in attendance), 'Do you want to live in a country where thousands of people can shout "F" the Pope?' Spiers felt strongly that something more needed to be done to stop songs that were 'downright discrimination and prejudice' and consequently he was supporting the proposed Offensive Behaviour Bill – a bill that could imprison an individual for offensive behaviour for up to five years.[2]

Spiers' position on the need somehow to stop the singing of sectarian songs is now a mainstream position to take regarding the Old Firm. However, this concern about fans singing songs was less clear cut in the not-too-distant past. Writing in 1996, Spiers had a very different understanding about sectarianism and indeed about anti-sectarianism, and challenged the exaggerated idea of bigoted football fans. Insightfully observing the middle-class preoccupation to go on and on about sectarianism, he noted for example that:

> In Glasgow, in the pubs and wine bars and especially around the hearths of the chattering classes, you wonder if we can't let go of the tough subject-matter of bigotry. You wonder if some of us would feel stripped naked if we couldn't continually hark on about this 'hate-filled' city of ours. For a community that has made great strides in softening the divide, too many of us crave the expression of a bygone era.

Despite the comparatively more limited discussion about the 'sectarian Old Firm' in 1996, Spiers recognised that, even still, there was an exaggerated concern about this issue among his own colleagues in the press: 'We lay thick the heaving vocabulary of hate and venom and rancour', he observed, 'and before you know it word is back on the streets of the further disfigurement of society wherever Rangers and Celtic meet.'

Describing in lucid detail the myth of sectarianism as he saw it at the time, Graham Spiers explained to his readers that:

> There is a richly-titillating, but utterly empty, ritual about much of the Old Firm environment today. Remarkable and unremarkable men, who have good jobs and bad and who couldn't practice bigotry if they tried, nonetheless get swept into the firmament of these occasions. Before they know it they are hollering their heads off about the Queen or the Pope or both . . .

Many of these people work together, drink together, play their five-a-side football in bantering friendship together, but for the Old Firm, for 90 minutes of screaming, they take choir stalls at opposite ends of the ground. Some of us who feel the fiery indignation well up within us misunderstand this aspect of contemporary Glasgow life.

Spiers went on to mock the English for taking the Old Firm fans at their word and also challenged the idea that violence at games was a problem. Having asked Strathclyde Police for the arrest figures for an Old Firm game he found that only twenty-four people were arrested. These are 'stupendously paltry statistics', he pointed out, 'for peoples supposedly needing to tear the skin off each other'. The police officer giving Spiers these statistics even pointed out that 'A Rangers–Celtic game can sometimes be like a Sunday picnic.'

Yet by 2011, Spiers no longer appeared to be able to see that these men 'couldn't practice bigotry if they tried', or that they 'worked together and drank together' and had 'bantering friendship', and no mention was made by him about the 'stupendously paltry' level of violence. Now the very concerns about the 'chattering classes' harking on about our 'hate-filled' city – discussing Old Firm fans with 'hate and venom' – had become the concerns of Graham Spiers himself, and indeed the concerns of the media, the police and the political elite more generally.

Something had changed. But it was not punters on the terraces that had changed for the worse. Rather it was 'right-thinking people', indeed 'tolerant' right-thinking people, who became profoundly intolerant. The Old Firm 'Sunday picnic' of 1996 by 2011 had become a major political and police concern, something that needed more surveillance cameras, listening equipment and indeed new severe laws to lock up perpetrators of offensive song-singing for up to five years.

THE 'MYTH' OF SECTARIANISM

An additional and fascinating aspect of the rising concern about sectarianism is that the dynamic for sectarianism in Scotland – both religious and political divisions and tensions – has less of a basis in society than it has had for decades, indeed for centuries. At exactly the time when religion was and is in serious decline, and when political divisions have little or indeed no meaning or depth in society, the problem of sectarianism was rediscovered anew and anti-sectarianism became institutionalised.

To some extent the argument can be made that sectarianism, at least at an institutional and structural level, has never existed in Scotland. Steve Bruce, Tony Glendinning, Iain Paterson and Michael Rosie have done Scotland a great service by writing *Sectarianism in Scotland* (2004), in which they question the myth of sectarianism. Their evidence that Catholics in Scotland are not, and generally speaking have not, been discriminated against is compelling.

Sectarianism in Scotland was written in part to look into the claims of individuals like composer James MacMillan who in 1999 argued that Catholics in Scotland were still seriously discriminated against. But what is the evidence for this claim? What Bruce and his co-authors do is examine the issue of oppression and discrimination. Are Catholics discriminated against in the workplace, in politics and in unions? Are Catholics and Protestants living separate lives? Is religion an important feature of people's lives in Scotland? Are Catholics discriminated against in education and housing or cut off from mainstream Scottish society? Are Scottish institutions biased against Catholics? The answer they give to each of these questions is a resounding no.

There is no space to discuss the historical question of sectarianism in Scotland but looking at today and specifically at the issue of religion, Steve Bruce and his colleagues noted that in all recent surveys there is only a very small percentage of people who oppose inter-marriage between Catholics and Protestants – most of those who oppose it being elderly. Half of Catholics under the age of thirty-five marry a non-Catholic. Indeed, religion has been eroded considerably as a force in Scottish society and is less significant than it ever has been (see Rosie in this volume).[3] Given all this, it would be difficult to argue that religiously grounded sectarianism was likely to increase, rather the opposite conclusion must be drawn, that whatever this thing 'sectarianism' is it is not driven by religion.

However, perhaps more importantly when looking at the conflicting symbols, songs and indeed tensions surrounding the Old Firm over the last half a century, we must also note the potential significance of what can be called 'political sectarianism'. Books like *Sectarianism in Scotland* often ignore or give only a limited significance to the potential political tensions seen most visibly at Old Firm games. But it would be hard to over-estimate the significance of the 'troubles' in the north of Ireland for the British Government and British state in the conflict with Irish republicanism. It was arguably the most important and explosive political (indeed military) issue of the time, one which animated the animosity between Glasgow's two biggest football clubs.

It was within this charged context that Celtic flew an Irish Tricolour above their ground while some of their fans sang IRA songs at games and bought copies of magazines sold outside the ground with pictures of paramilitaries on the front cover. Meanwhile, these fans faced 'loyalist' opponents allied to Rangers singing the British national anthem and 'No Surrender to the IRA'. We might see then that the issue of 'sectarianism' was anything but a myth; there may not have been a war in Scotland, but there will have been a distinct animosity among at least certain sections of both Celtic and Rangers fans. Added to this is the fact that thousands of Rangers and Celtic season ticket holders are from parts of the north and south of Ireland and many will have had strong opinions and allegiances regarding the conflict in the north.

This is not to argue that this proves a strong existence of 'sectarianism' in Scotland: political allegiances, at least when it came to elections, did not express themselves decisively through the conflict in Ireland. Again space limits the opportunity to elaborate on this point, but, as with the case of religion and its decline, the crucial point to note here is that *whatever the tensions in the past, today, the war is over*. Some tensions remain but there is no longer a serious political and military struggle for the right to rule in Ireland. Consequently, what was by far the most important issue for potentially encouraging 'sectarian' rivalries in Scotland is of little significance except as a historical legacy. The point of greatest significance to note here is not the question of sectarianism as such, but more importantly the strange rise of anti-sectarianism: strange because anti-sectarianism emerged – or re-emerged with a vengeance – at precisely the time when religion was and is in serious decline, and when the conflict in Ireland regarding 'Irish freedom' came to an end. Despite some tensions and divisions in the north of Ireland remaining, the central importance of Ireland as a political and indeed as a military question across the whole of the UK has all but disappeared, as has the 'traditional' basis for possible heightened 'sectarian' tensions in Scotland.[4]

THE ANTI-SECTARIAN INDUSTRY

Anti-sectarianism became something of an 'industry' in Scotland in the new millennium. Indeed, today it has become part of the fabric of life in Scotland, not just in politics, law and football, but also in education. In schools, anti-sectarianism is now described as something that is at the heart of the new Curriculum for Excellence. 'Education', the Scottish Government notes, 'can play a pivotal role in challenging sectarian attitudes and religious intolerance.'[5] As such, anti-sectarian initiatives are crucial for developing 'informed responsible citizens'. It is not only children who need awareness-training about sectarianism. In prisons this attempt to develop 'positive attitudes' was given a boost in 2011 when the funding for anti-sectarian training of prisoners was doubled (Rose 2011). By November 2011 it was announced that anti-sectarian training would also be available for the staff of the Scottish Parliament (Hutcheon 2011).

To be against sectarianism is a new norm in Scottish society, an unquestioned good, something that can unproblematically become part of school curriculums and the training of prisoners, even parliamentary staff. Sectarianism is also something that all politicians in parliament oppose and indeed something that has come to be vocally denounced by Scottish governments for the last decade. As Ruth Davidson, the Scottish Conservative leader, explained at a debate in parliament, every single one of her MSPs is opposed to sectarianism.

The dynamic growth in concerns about sectarianism began in the late 1990s and continued into the new century. By 2002 the Labour leader and First Minister Jack McConnell started his own campaign against sectarianism in Scotland. Sectarianism now became 'Scotland's Shame'.[6] New laws were also passed to tackle sectarianism at this time. For example, section 74 of the Scottish Criminal Justice Act 2003 covers religiously aggravated offences, and part 2, chapter 1 of the Police, Public Order and Criminal Justice (Scotland) Act 2006 introduced Football Banning Orders for a variety of offences, including stirring of hatred.

In the new century initiative followed initiative, incorporating councils, schools, football teams, the SFA, the Scottish Government, youth groups and the police in the 'fight against bigotry'. A National Club Licensing Scheme was even introduced, making it a necessity for Scottish football league clubs to show evidence of their policies to fight racism and sectarianism in football. And, in 2006, the Scottish

Executive launched Calling Full Time on Sectarianism, a government initiative set up to challenge misbehaviour and abusive chanting.[7] By 2011 it was hard to imagine what else could be done to 'fight sectarianism in Scotland', and yet the SNP Government, with significant gusto, launched their very own campaign to tackle Scotland's shame with their proposal to introduce the Offensive Behaviour at Football and Threatening Communications Bill.

GOVERNING THROUGH TOLERANCE

Many commentators were taken aback by the sudden re-energising of anti-sectarianism by the SNP government and by the proclamations that 'something needed to be done' in the form of a new severe law to lock up offensive and sectarian football fans: after all, wasn't this what all the existing laws and initiatives were already about? However, the apparent transformation of Alex Salmond's SNP into *the* anti-sectarian party was simply an action replay of what had happened with the Labour Party under the leadership of Jack McConnell and his own discovery of 'Scotland's Shame'.

Professor John Flint has described the various anti-sectarian activities as the 'most intensive and sustained focus on governing sectarianism in the post-Second World War period' (Flint 2008: 121). He is right. However, this is not simply about sectarianism, but rather, sectarianism fits into the wider and more important development of 'tolerance' as a governing framework: anti-sectarian politics, journalists, initiatives, campaigns, education, awareness, training, policing, groups and laws all act as a flagship of tolerance in Scotland.

Being 'tolerant' is the badge you must now wear if you are going to be successful in politics, or in any key institution in Scotland. It has become an unquestioned good, and politicians fall over themselves to claim the tolerance mantle. But today tolerance means something very different from the original idea which constituted the foundation of the defence of free speech. Now tolerance means 'respecting difference'; it also embodies a therapeutic dimension, one that recognises that words hurt, and one that demands respect for people's fragile individual and cultural identities. Given this, you can already see the problem that exists for football fans who are often offensive to one another. Respecting difference is not usually the first thing on a supporter's mind as they unfurl their banners and take on the local rivals.

For over a decade, the promotion of tolerance has become an essential aspect of being part of the new Scottish establishment. The answer to the question 'Who are we?' raised by Michael Rosie in *The Sectarian Myth in Scotland* (Rosie 2004: 144) is that we are a 'modern tolerant Scotland'.

The buzzword 'tolerance' is accompanied by 'respect' and 'awareness', the correct form of behaviour being to 'accept others', to be multicultural and to be non-judgemental. This norm of tolerance explains why the Scottish police began to see themselves as a force for 'Celebrating and Valuing Difference' and why the Association of Chief Police Officers in Scotland produced their own Equality & Diversity Strategy (ACPOS 2009). A key aspect of this new idea of tolerance is the emergence of vulnerable autonomy within political theory (Ramsay 2012) and the development of the understanding that people are fundamentally vulnerable (Furedi 2004), that they need recognition and that the state must play a role in ensuring our psychic well-being.

Within this context we can start to see how a new form of anti-sectarianism emerged when it did: a form of tolerance that was less about politics or religion than it was a form of therapeutic protection. It is no accident, for example, that the new 'anti-sectarian' law in Scotland is called the *Offensive* Behaviour Act: this is because being sectarian is now simply equated with being offensive. In a sense anti-sectarianism gets its moral authority today not from the fight against sectarianism as such (which arguably is largely a myth), but rather as part of a tolerant fight against *offensiveness.*

As philosopher Joel Feinberg has noted, we have moved from the 'harm principle' to the 'offence principle'.[8] In the 1980s and early 1990s, for example, sectarianism (or what people saw as religious bigotry or politically based prejudices associated with loyalism and Irish republicanism) was tolerated. This does not mean that it was supported – rather there were plenty of people opposed to sectarianism – but it was tolerated – disagreed with, challenged, argued against and so on, but not out-lawed as long as no physical harm occurred. However, as 'tolerance' transformed its meaning towards an understanding of 'respecting difference' and increasingly about protecting groups and individuals from offensive or 'hateful' words, sectarianism was reconstructed as a form of hate crime – something that could no longer be tolerated. Consequently, individuals like Graham Spiers shifted their position – not because the position of the offenders had changed but because what was seen as 'banter' suddenly became seen as far more important, more dangerous, more damaging to individuals and to society. Now arresting people for the words they spoke became not only acceptable but celebrated.

THE NEW SECTARIANS

A tragic irony of the rise of the new form of intolerant tolerance is that new problems are being created. These problems are not related to any increase in old-fashioned bigotry or sectarianism, but are emerging because of a new kind of sectarian or sect-like behaviour being encouraged by the authorities themselves. This new 'sectarianism' relates to the rise of identity politics in Scotland and to the already growing importance of offensiveness and the protection of the offended; trends that are encouraging an insular, thin-skinned, tell-tale culture that could heighten divisions between fans.

The elevation of 'offence' within politics, culture and even law both reflects and creates a world where being offended becomes significant. In many respects, this appears to be a more caring approach – showing a concern about people's feelings and attempting to stop certain hurtful things being said. However, as with the criminalisation of football songs, a major consequence of this approach is that more things come to be seen as unacceptable and even against the law. The more society treats people as vulnerable and assumes we need to be protected from offence, the more it becomes authoritarian. As a result, society begins to resemble a school, with adults being treated like children who constantly need to be protected from one another and told how to behave. And, like children, we start to be genuinely outraged and 'hurt' by words that for previous generations would have been water off a duck's back.

Here, a modern-day character type is formed – fragile, self-preoccupied and totally disconnected from people around them. This character type has been educated to understand the world only with reference to his or her private emotions and consequently is profoundly inward-looking and intensely asocial. This is an individual who experiences any form of questioning or challenge as a personal insult and threat to their 'self-esteem'. The offence laws and initiatives actually help to protect and create this very type of person – antisocial narcissists who lack any sense of camaraderie or solidarity with other people, engaged only by 'How I Feel', they are the hub of the chronically offended complainers, often found down at the local police station reporting their friends, neighbours and even family for 'offences' against themselves.

Similarly, at the level of groups and cultures a trend has developed to feel genuinely offended and also to play the 'offence card', a situation that Josie Appleton argues has become a tactic used by an increasing array of groups, regardless of their size or strength, and something that replaces ideas and public debate with counterclaims of feeling hurt by others' words.[9] It also encourages a tendency both to search for evidence of offensive comments being made and of looking to the authorities both to recognise your hurt and to punish the 'offenders'.

At one level both the individual and group claim for offence is inter-connected. If individuals can be understood to increasingly live in their own bubble the same can be said for 'groups' or at least advocates of 'groups' who tend to be less engaged with society, social change and breaking down barriers through universal ideas and aspirations, than with the more introspective defensive protection of their more statically defined 'culture'.[10]

If society educates us that 'words hurt', it is likely that they will do just that. When certain words are given priority treatment by the authorities and within the culture of society, they are likely to create a particularly acute response – the forging of offended people. Indeed, being thin- skinned and being offended is the 'correct' response today, as the Evra–Suarez and Terry– Ferdinand sagas illustrate. We expect and encourage people to be 'offended' and to report colleagues and fellow professionals to the authorities for name-calling.

In Scotland, being offended and reporting your fellow fan to the police has become institutionalised and is likely to become an increasing source of tension between fans – a new 'sectarian' divide. Kevin Rooney (2011) notes that despite the significant decline in 'offensive' songs at Old Firm matches, fans have taken to 'more sinister methods of playing out their hostility towards rival teams' (see McKillop in this volume). As Rooney explains: 'Now we have the situation where fans are using new media including YouTube, Twitter and Facebook to monitor the behaviour of rivals and expose every expression of sectarianism or "offensive" remarks made.'

Rangers Football Club and fans have come under severe pressure in the last decade from a plethora of sources to stop singing certain songs. The criminalisation of religious and racially based terms has meant that Rangers fans have noticeably changed the songs they sing. The variant of the 'Billy Boys' song incorporating the line about being up to 'our' knees in 'Fenian blood' is noticeably absent from games today, as are other songs and chants that can be labelled as racist or sectarian.

A major source of anger among some Rangers fans about the criminalisation of their songs is that they believe Celtic Football Club and their fans have acted as 'grasses' for the last ten years, reporting Rangers fans to the authorities and trying to get songs outlawed. After a press release I sent out in September 2011 arguing that the Old Firm should unite to defeat the Offensive Behaviour Bill, the response from some Rangers fans was one of outrage and incredulity.[11] A debate erupted on *Follow Follow*, a Rangers fan site, about this call for unity: a number of comments reflected the one below:

> Sorry but reap what you sow, their mob brought this s**t on with complaints and the media complaining about the big bad huns (sectarian in its own right) but when the spotlight shines on their song sheet then you're being 'persecuted'??? Sorry but if it wasn't for the mortally offended Celtic support this knee jerk reaction by the government wouldn't be in the pipelines. I don't agree with the legislation but remember who brought this on, Celtic FC and their forever offended fans. We're already being persecuted for our song book, we have been under the spotlight for over 10 years. (BarLoch76)[12]

For some Rangers fans, the Celtic supporters cannot be trusted to fight for fans' freedoms as they are seen as the ones who have pushed for laws and regulations of songs at games; as BarLoch76 argues, they brought this 's**t on'. Looking at the history of the legislation introduced in Scotland to regulate fans, these Rangers supporters have a point. Various high-profile Celtic supporters and members of Celtic Football Club have argued for, and supported, legislation to outlaw some of Rangers' songs. Some fans have also helped to encourage new legislation by complaining about Rangers fans to the authorities.

Despite some Celtic supporters having encouraged the criminalisation of Rangers songs, it is nevertheless a mistake to understand this development as something that has been created by 'their' side. The anti-sectarian and the 'offence' industry both go to the heart of the new elites and their approach to regulating public life. The example of the 'Famine Song' being labelled racist and criminal is not particularly illustrative of the persuasive powers of Celtic supporters. It reflects, rather, the changing and increasingly flexible framework of 'offensiveness' and the growing use of law to regulate and enforce 'correct' behaviour in society in general and for football fans in particular. Nevertheless, the culture of complaint where fans take on the persona of the offended victim is an important and a worrying indication of a breakdown in basic solidarity between even rival fans.

Today, many Rangers fans take a relatively principled position on the freedom of fans to sing their songs. However, as Kevin Rooney observed, it is not only

Celtic fans who have acted as 'snitches', with, for example, 'hundreds of Rangers fans' reporting Neil Lennon to the police 'for making supposedly racist remarks to Rangers' controversial player El-Hadji Diouf'. Following this 'snitching' by Rangers fans, lip readers were brought in to study TV footage and Lennon was questioned by the police (Rooney 2011).

With the passing of the Offensive Behaviour Act, the framework for the new sectarianism is firmly established and all fans will now be encouraged to find offence in their opponent's songs and behaviour. Mark Dingwall of the Rangers Supporters Trust made this very point at the Justice Committee discussion on the bill in the Scottish Parliament when he observed that everything was now up for grabs in terms of being offended. Dingwall oscillates between wanting other fans to be treated as harshly as Rangers have been, especially Celtic fans, and recognising that there is an 'air of unreality' about the creation of a chronically offended climate. As he observed, 'Now we have a situation where there's almost an incitement to escalate your offendedness.'[13] Speaking at the *Battle of Ideas* in London, Mark Dingwall explained that:

> It's turned us, me, into a grass . . . What we're doing is handcuffing ourselves to Aberdeen fans and Celtic fans and saying if you find things we say offensive we are going to start complaining about you. People are literally sitting there with stop-watches and videoing games . . . you write to the match commander, you write to the police because that's the only way we see we can get out of this corner is to handcuff ourselves to other fans and pull them over the edge with us.[14]

This new sectarianism is sanctioned by the state and is one of the most worrying developments in Scottish football and perhaps even in Scottish society more widely. We now have a situation where the most anti-social and self-preoccupied, chronically offended individual has become the model citizen. The likely outcome is that complaints to the police about an increasing array of 'offensive' comments will rise. This reporting is likely to be about not only opposition fans but also fans of your own team. Indeed, some fans are already doing just that. Some Celtic fans, for example, are no longer arguing the toss about the rights and wrongs of singing Irish republican songs at games and instead make complaints to stewards and the police about other Celtic fans singing IRA songs (BBC Sport 2011). Indeed, clubs across the UK are starting to hand out leaflets advising their own fans to 'call this number' and report the seat number of the fan you find offensive.

At the same time, in Scotland there is also the likelihood that the minority of old-fashioned sectarians will now spend their time searching the internet to find offensive words written by people they hate. As one editorial comment noted, the new law can actually give the moral right to bigots to express their intolerance by being offended (*Scotland on Sunday*, 26 June 2011). Law is often a blunt instrument to deal with social problems; when it is backed by an unthinking 'zero tolerance' approach, the potential for unintended and reactionary outcomes is escalated further.

Additionally, part of the process of criminalising 'hate' involves the categorising of particularly offended or vulnerable groups who need special protection. One outcome of this is that campaigners and paid representatives of certain defined 'groups' or 'cultures' systematically attempt to prove that they are being offended. Again, a newer form of sect-like behaviour subsequently evolves as these special-interest groups clamour to demonstrate the lack of respect being shown to 'their culture'. Indeed, this was evident in the discussion stages of the Offensive Behaviour Bill and in the written submissions to the Justice Committee, with different organisations, even children's organisations, competing to illustrate the victimised nature of their 'group'.

Within the Old Firm, it is Celtic fans that are categorised by their opponents as being 'victims' – as mortally or 'forever offended' – making claims about the unfair treatment not only of Celtic Football Club but Catholics or the 'Scots Irish'. Today, however, Rangers fans are also likely to adopt a victim identity and to represent opposing sentiments as offensive to their 'culture' or 'tradition'.

On the Strathclyde Police Facebook site (http://www.facebook.com/StrathclydePolice), for example, concerns about Celtic songs have been raised by Rangers fans in an attempt to get them banned. One comment by John McDougall Senior, for instance, asked if the police would stop Celtic fans singing 'Roll of Honour' because 'it must be very upsetting for anyone who has lost a loved one'. Members of Rangers Supporters Trust made similar arguments to me about the upsetting nature of some Celtic songs for those in the crowd who had relatives killed in Northern Ireland. In a Trust statement (2008) about the 'Famine Song', it is the 'abuse' of members of the Royal Family that is discussed. Therapeutic and victim-centred language is used to explain how Celtic's offensive songs are upsetting, perhaps even traumatising. Indeed, Rangers fans' celebration of the British Army is increasingly couched in non-political, even non-nationalistic terms today (a trend seen more widely in Britain as a whole) with 'our boys' themselves being represented as hard-done-to victims rather than 'proud fighters' and defenders of Britain and British interests abroad.

Part of the shift towards a victim identity has come with the transformation of religious and political beliefs and loyalties associated with clubs like Rangers and Celtic into 'traditions' and 'cultures'. Almost any outlook or 'tradition' across the UK can now be defended through the argument that 'it's my culture'. For example, the singer Billy Bragg has suggested that left-wing people should stop challenging the anti-democratic nature of the Royal Family and respect monarchists as another aspect of multiculturalism.[15] On a Radio Four debate, discussing the Queen's Diamond Jubilee, a unionist politician from Northern Ireland put a Sinn Fein spokesperson on the defensive by demanding that he should respect his Queen – after all, it is 'my culture'.[16] Even the British National Party defend their views today by using the language of multiculturalism.

The shift towards understanding people as part of a 'culture', rather than as individuals with ideas and beliefs, has escalated in the last two decades and could potentially develop much further in Scotland – creating a new divide between the 'British Rangers' *tradition* and the 'Irish Celtic' *culture*. Discussing the 'Scots Irish', academic John Kelly describes the Catholic/Celtic part of Scotland as an 'ethnic' group, and uses analogies to equate the treatment of black people with that of the ethnic Scots Irish. Despite accepting that structurally – in terms of jobs, services, housing and so on – there is little or no discrimination against Catholics in Scotland, Kelly talks about 'attitudinal' sectarianism. Denying the ethnic identity of the 'Scots Irish' consequently becomes understood as a form of racism. Once established as a 'culture', the trend is to demand recognition for your identity and also to search for examples where this respect is not forthcoming. As a result, academics like John Kelly are keen to discover and promote examples of the mistreatment of the 'Scots Irish'.[17]

CONCLUSIONS

An important question to consider is whether the development and promotion of different 'cultures' in Scotland could encourage a more significant divide. The recent development of multiculturalism in Northern Ireland is worth noting in this respect. In the past, the British authorities would argue that there could be equality for all British citizens, including Catholics, in Northern Ireland. Irish republicans disagreed, pointing to the endemic inequality that existed in the north, and countered British claims by arguing that a united Ireland was essential for the freedom and equality for *all*, including Protestants. Today, in comparison, even the belief or aim of equality has been lost and the Northern Ireland Assembly itself embodies the need to provide specific recognition (or 'respect') for the different, separate, 'communities'. For example, no one group can hold the positions of both First Minister and Deputy First Minister and these positions must be shared between Unionist and Nationalist parties. In essence, the assembly assumes that there are two intractable communities which are and forever will need separate representation. Past political claims of universalism – or a potential common humanity (from both sides) – are thus replaced by the invention of these static, ever-lasting unionist and nationalist 'communities' which must now learn to respect each other's difference. As Kevin Rooney (2008) notes, 'Far from overcoming and dissolving differences, the peace process had encouraged us to champion them and preserve them into the future.'

Scotland is not Northern Ireland in terms of sectarianism. However, it is possible that the new sectarianism in Scotland could emerge around different 'traditions' and 'cultures'. Speculatively, it is possible to imagine a situation in Scotland where the 'celebration of difference' and the inclination to adopt cultural identities will encourage a new form of divide between some Irish-Celtic and British-Rangers fans. This is especially possible when the state encourages 'group identities' and gives support and protection to those who can act as a particular 'community'. The fact that the 'Famine Song', once sung by Rangers fans at their Celtic rivals, has already been defined as 'racist' in Scotland illustrates the acceptance and promotion of the idea of there being different peoples – different 'races' even – among the white population of Scotland.

Of course, for most Scots, life goes on, and 'cultural difference' has little or no meaning to a largely white, Scottish, secular society: Scotland is not Northern Ireland and multiculturalism will not develop here in such an obtuse separatist form.

Nevertheless, the self-indulgent narcissists and the equally chronically offended sensibility of identity-conscious individuals intermingle and provide a basis for escalating offence claims in society. This becomes all the more likely when 'tolerance' is such an important governing framework within politics and when law is underwriting the encouragement of offence claims.

Today people are being educated to be offended. Within football, as we have seen, one result of these developments is that counter-claims among football fans emerge; they 'handcuff' themselves to opposing fans, and attempt to 'pull them over the edge'. This development at Old Firm games in particular is all the more unnecessary and ridiculous given the lack of depth of the 'sectarianism' that exists today. In the past, it could be argued that 'sectarian' chants at Old Firm games had weight and significance because there was a religious and, more importantly, a political situation or background giving wider meaning to them. Today this is no longer the case, and ironically it is the anti-sectarian industry, the construction of 'cultures' and the elevation of 'offence' that give weight to words. Power is *given* to the words by the victim framework within which they are now interpreted – to words that today carry no social or political significance. These are zombie terms re-animated by the 'offence' legislation and promoted by an aggressive form of victimhood.

NOTES

1. This LexisNexis newspaper search starts in 1992 with *The Herald* and 1993 with *The Scotsman* and *Scotland on Sunday*. The search was for any article containing both the terms 'Old Firm' and 'sectarian'. A separate search of any article in these newspapers using the term 'sectarian' was also carried out.
2. The video of the debate may be viewed at http://news.bbc.co.uk/democracylive/hi/scotland/newsid_9582000/9582406.stm (last accessed 5 September 2012).
3. By 2002, 36 per cent of Scots surveyed said they were 'Church of Scotland', 14 per cent (and 24 per cent in Glasgow) identified themselves as Catholic, and the largest number of people – 37 per cent – had no religion. About half of those who identify their religion as Church of Scotland go to church less than once a year, while the same is true for 30 per cent of Catholics. Young people under the age of twenty-five are far less likely to go to church than those over fifty-five years of age and, as Bruce and his co-authors note, young Scots simply do not regard religion as important. In terms of morality, the issue of sex before marriage is not a Catholic–Protestant question but a generational one. The Catholic Church may oppose things like abortion and contraception but Catholics – especially younger Catholics – do not. The Orange Order exists but is dwindling, despite an increase in membership during the Irish troubles. It is seen as religiously intolerant by the mainstream churches and has little by way of political support (Bruce, S. et al. 2004). Three- quarters of Celtic fans are 'Catholic' but this doesn't mean they are religious. Being Catholic is arguably more culturally significant than it is religious, part of this being an association with Ireland; however, only 8 per cent of Catholics in Scotland identify themselves as Irish, even when given the opportunity to choose from a number of identities. This is a smaller number than the actual number of Irish people who have moved to and live in Scotland. Finally, when looking at the limited significance of 'sectarianism' in Scotland, in a Glasgow City Council survey of over a thousand people, it was found that religion played virtually no part in terms of who respondents would prefer to have as a neighbour. Between 1 and 2 per cent of people said

the religion of their neighbour would be of relevance; most of those who said that it mattered were elderly. It is worth bearing in mind that this was a survey of Glaswegians, the place you would expect sectarianism to be more significant than anywhere else in Scotland. Yet hardly anyone cared about the religion of their neighbour. See http://www.glasgow.gov. uk/NR/rdonlyres/DA614F81-4F1B-4452-8847-F3FDE920D550/0/sectarianism03.pdf (last accessed 5 September 2012).

4. There is still the possibility of tensions related to the newly developing cultural differences celebrated and indeed promoted by the peace process in Northern Ireland. However, these should be understood in terms of the 'new sectarianism' discussed below.

5. See http://www.scotland.gov.uk/Topics/Justice/law/sectarianism-action-1/Education (last accessed 5 September 2012).

6. An anti-sectarian industry began to grow prominently at this time, with grants being awarded to beat bigotry. Discussions started in 2001 between Celtic and Rangers about their possible involvement in the new ministerial group to tackle sectarianism. The campaign Sense over Sectarianism was launched; the public-sector trade union Unison came out in opposition to sectarianism; even former James Bond star Sean Connery came forward to oppose bigotry. Football club-based campaigns like Bhoys Against Bigotry were set up and the National Union of Students in Scotland created their own anti-sectarianism campaign. By 2006, an Action Plan on Sectarianism was set up by the Scottish Government with the aim of creating a tolerant and 'truly multicultural and multi-faith Scotland' (see Flint 2008).

7. See http://www.scotland.gov.uk/Resource/Doc/160254/0043618.pdf (last accessed 16 October 2012)

8. See Cohen, N. (2012), 'We Only Pretend to Defend Free Speech' in *Standpoint* January/ February edition, http://standpointmag.co.uk/node/4257/full (last accessed 16 October 2012).

9. See Josie Appleton's *Don't Play the Offence Card: A New Deal for Public Debate*, a Manifesto Club think piece available online at http://www.manifestoclub.com/files/Appleton0907.pdf (last accessed 16 October 2012).

10. See Waiton, S. (2012), *Snobs' Law: Criminalising Football Fans in an Age of Intolerance*, pp. 124–9. Here the argument is made that in the UK in the 1980s and into the 1990s there was a change from the more politically oriented notion of being 'black', for example, towards a newly constructed self-identification of being part of specific and indeed separate communities like the 'Muslim community'.

11. 'Celtic and Rangers must unite to beat the "Sectarian Bill"' in Take a Liberty (Scotland), http://takealiberty.blogspot.co.uk/ (last accessed 27 September 2011).

12. See http://www.followfollow.com/ (last accessed 28 September 2011).

13. See http://news.bbc.co.uk/democracylive/hi/scotland/newsid_9581000/9581000.stm (last accessed 16 October 2012).

14. Listen to the debate at http://www.battleofideas.org.uk/index.php/2011/session_detail/5736 (last accessed 16 October 2012).

15. See *The Mirror* on 3 June 2012, 'Is the future British? Or will it be English, Scottish and Welsh?', in which Billy Bragg explained that, 'I believe in a multi-cultural society that has room for the monarchists as well as the anarchists and all of the other traditions that make up our national fabric.'

16. BBC Radio Four *Any Questions* on 1 June 2012 from Belfast. On the panel, leader of the Ulster Unionist Party, Mike Nesbitt; deputy leader of the Democratic Unionist Party, Nigel Dodds; Sinn Finn representative and education minister at Stormont, John O'Dowd; and Provost of Magee Campus and Dean of Academic Development at the University of Ulster, Deirdre Heenan.

17. Hear John Kelly discussing these issues on Listen to the Debate at http://www.battleofideas. org.uk/index.php/2011/session_detail/5736 (last accessed 16 October 2012).

REFERENCES

ACPOS (2009), *Equality and Diversity Strategy 2009–2012*, Glasgow: ACPOS, http://www.acpos. police.uk/Documents/Policies/ACPOSEquDivStrategy2009.pdf (last accessed 5 September 2012).

BBC Sport (2011), 'Celtic get date for Uefa chants hearing', 14 November 2011, http://www.bbc. co.uk/sport/0/football/15706740 (last accessed 5 September 2012).

Bruce, S., Glendinning, T., Paterson, I. and Rosie, M. (2004), *Sectarianism in Scotland*, Edinburgh: Edinburgh University Press.

Flint, J. (2008), 'Governing Sectarianism in Scotland', *Scottish Affairs*, 63: Spring, 107–24.

Furedi, F. (2004), *Therapy Culture: Cultivating Vulnerability in an Uncertain Age*, London: Routledge.

Hutcheon, P. (2011), 'Parliament Staff Offered Training in How Not to Be Religious Bigots', *Sunday Herald*, 20 November 2011, http://www.heraldscotland.com/politics/political-news/ parliament-staff-offered-lessons-in-how-not-to-be-religious-bigots.15853773 (last accessed 5 September 2012).

Leader article (2011) 'Flawed Strategy', *Scotland on Sunday*, 26 June 2011.

Ramsay, P. (2012), *The Insecurity State: Vulnerable Autonomy and the Right to Security in the Criminal Law*, Oxford: Oxford University Press.

Rangers Supporters Trust (2008), *A position statement on the 'Famine Song'*, Glasgow: Rangers Supporters Trust.

Rooney, K. (2008), 'From insurgency to identity', *Spiked Review of Books*, 15: July, http://www. spiked-online.com/index.php?/site/reviewofbooks_article/5515/ (last accessed 5 September 2012).

Rooney, K. (2011), 'Turning football fans into snitches', *Spiked On-Line*, 21 April 2011, http:// www.spiked-online.com/index.php/site/article/10448/ (last accessed 5 September 2012).

Rose, G. (2011), 'Anti-sectarian jail scheme gets funding boost', *Scotland on Sunday*, 25 September 2011.

Rosie, M. (2004), *The Sectarian Myth in Scotland: Of bitter memory and bigotry*, Basingstoke: Palgrave Macmillan.

Spiers, G. (1996), 'Glasgow's sectarian image doesn't bear close scrutiny', *Scotland on Sunday*, 14 January 1996.

Waiton, S. (2012), *Snobs' Law: Criminalising Football Fans in an Age of Intolerance*, Dundee: Take a Liberty (Scotland).

Žižek, S. (2009), *Violence*, London: Profile.

8   Hegemonic Fandom and the Red Herring of Sectarianism

Paul Davis

INTRODUCTION

This chapter argues, with the help of illustrations, that football sectarianism is morally impermissible, and that its primary explanation is the dominant culture of fandom and not sectarianism in broader Scottish or Glaswegian society. Objections to the moral argument are considered and rejected. The Offensive Behaviour and Threatening Communications (Scotland) Act 2012 is endorsed. The chapter concludes with the argument that there are compelling grounds for magnanimity towards the flammable baggage carried by each half of the Old Firm.

HEGEMONIC FANDOM

Football fandom is heterogeneous. However, there remains a dominant fan culture, which may be called 'hegemonic fandom'. Hegemonic fandom is defined by spiteful aggression; an appetite for anger and pique; and petty or cultivated hostilities and grudges, typically directed with special venom at one particular rival. Football sectarianism is an illustration of this. Sectarianism, as I briefly argue later, has limited significance in present-day Scotland, including Glasgow (see the chapters in this volume by Rosie and Waiton). However, hegemonic fandom's characteristics, alongside the historical moorings of the Old Firm, sponsor its regular and luminous cultural visibility. That sectarian sentiments are only one of the regressive poisons culturally enabled is a point that bears illustration. When either of the Old Firm travels to Edinburgh, their fans are taunted with 'In my Glasgow slum . . .' (see Kelly in this volume). Celtic fans have retorted with scorn of Edinburgh's AIDS record. (As a Celtic fan, I am most familiar with Celtic fans.) Some Celtic fans were unable to celebrate Henrik Larsson without calling Alan Shearer a 'wanker'. Fans visiting Tottenham mock the Holocaust. Tottenham fans sing that Arsène Wenger is a paedophile. Cardiff City fans sing 'In my Swansea slum'. Syed (2011) also recounts the cases of Arsenal fans 'scoffing at the assassination of Togo players at the African Cup of Nations' and a Youtube video of a four-year-old boy singing lines in mockery of the Munich air disaster. The list could go on, and does in Bruce et al. (2004: 131), who comment that 'Much football fan behaviour is highly ritualised . . . Rival football supporters, who can represent different neighbourhoods, cities or countries, deliberately exaggerate their differences for the purpose of ritual insult.'

The preceding does not entail a thorough-going disconnection, which should be rejected, between hegemonic fandom and the rest of culture. First, hegemonic fandom, while not confined to Britain, is very small part apotheosis and large part travesty of a narrative of British working-class machismo, a narrative arguably heightened in Scotland. Bruce et al. (2004: 173) comment wisely that 'Urban Scotland has a problem of incivility. Too many men drink too much, take drugs, carry weapons, and regard any insult to an easily offended sense of propriety as justification for assault.' Second, it is implausible to deny that hegemonic fandom is capable of quite faithfully reflecting broader social problems, illustrated in Hibs fans' disparagement of Rudi Skacel as a 'fuckin' refugee' during an era of hostile popular discourses of immigration and asylum seekers (see Kelly's chapter). However, the cod machismo characteristic of hegemonic fandom means that it is a site for the performance of antipathies which are autonomous in at least one of two senses: (i) they no longer exist elsewhere or not at the pitch of their performances in fandom; and (ii) their performers in fandom do not feel them elsewhere, or not to the extent affected in fandom. Bruce et al. (2004: 132) are again correct that 'football rivalry is a social force in its own right that should not, without considerable scaling down, be taken to stand for anything else'. Football sectarianism illustrates the point, since its antipathies manifest points (i) and (ii) above.

SECTARIANISM IN PRESENT-DAY SCOTLAND

It is difficult to find a definition of sectarianism to please everyone – compare sexism and racism – and it might be that this particular chapter isn't desperately furthered by the effort. It might indeed be revealing that Bruce et al.'s (2004: 4) definition, 'a widespread and shared culture of *improperly* treating people in terms of their religion', is incomplete and unfaithful to their treatment, yet precedes compelling critique of the belief that sectarianism is a significant force in present-day Scotland. It might be more fruitful to propose questions – themselves contestable, naturally – putatively entailed by the enquiry, and if a definition is helped, fair enough. It is such an enterprise of territory-mapping which Bruce et al. carry out persuasively. It should be noted that the set of questions implicated in enquiry into whether sectarianism is a significant force in modern Scotland might not be the set implicated in enquiry into whether sectarianism exists in modern Scotland. Further, it might be that the definitional question is more pressing in the latter case. Space permits recognition of only a selection of those questions, one of which outruns Bruce et al. (2004), which I regard as the most important with respect to the former enquiry.

Inter-marriage and friendship

Bruce et al. (2004: 96–7) report from the 2001 Scottish Social Attitudes Survey and NFO Social Research (2003) survey that across Scotland only 3 per cent mind 'a great deal' about a relative marrying someone of a different religion and a further 7 per cent mind 'slightly', while in Glasgow over 80 per cent did not mind at all. These sentiments are reflected in action: for Scots aged 25–34, more than half the Catholics are married to non-Catholics. As Bruce et al. (2004: 97) infer, 'Young Scots no longer regard religion (or more precisely religio-ethnic identity) as an important consideration in the most important personal decision they make.' Moreover, the 'relative indifference' to religion is replicated when the question is friendship: the Glasgow survey uncovered only 6 per cent of respondents who reported religion as a consideration, a response much more common from Muslims than Catholics or Protestants.

Residential segregation: no uneasy peace[1]

'If Scotland really is endemically sectarian, we would expect this to show up in residential segregation; Protestants would want to exclude Catholics and Catholics would avoid living next to those who did not want them' (Bruce et al. 2004: 94–5). However, religious segregation seems not to show up even in Glasgow, the city where sectarianism is supposed to be worst (and which houses each of the Old Firm). The 2001 Census shows no obvious geographical pattern to Catholic residency in Glasgow and in the NFO Social Research (2003) survey, only 5 per cent of Glaswegians said they would avoid a particular part of the city because of their religion (Bruce et al. 2004: 95–6).

Employment discrimination and workplace behaviour

The picture here seems more ambiguous. Bruce et al. (2004: 156), despite recognition that Catholics have suffered discrimination, reproduce some data (2004: 78–80) that shows, for instance, that while Roman Catholics make up only 16 per cent of the Scottish population, 58 per cent of Catholics aged 18–34 and 47 per cent aged 35–54 are in non-manual occupations. Again, social category AB, which includes managerial and professional occupations, is 22 per cent Roman Catholic, and category C1, which includes supervisory, clerical and junior managerial occupations, is 27 per cent Catholic. The Census results alongside figures from the preceding surveys motivate Bruce et al. to conclude (2004: 80) that 'religious differences in social class are largely restricted to older Scots'.

However, no set of outcomes can demonstrate discrimination or its absence. For instance, if Catholics (say) were under-represented at some socio-economic level, that could be, as Bruce et al. (81, 85–6, 154–7) sketch, the result of disadvantage other than discrimination. Conversely, however well represented a group are, they might fare yet better if not victims of discrimination. The latter point dovetails with the Scottish Social Attitudes Survey findings (Bruce et al. 2004: 83) that 14 per cent of Catholics and 6 per cent of Protestants felt that religion is relevant to jobs they could apply for and that 21 per cent of 'well-educated' Glaswegian Catholics under forty-five and 8 per cent of equivalent Protestants felt likewise.

Whether the immediately preceding respondent beliefs are correct is an open question, and the Scottish Social Attitudes Survey did not probe for details of putatively prohibited jobs. However, Catholic avoidance of pitching for jobs thought out-of-bounds is one facet emphasised by Walls and Williams (2005: 764–5) in reply to Bruce et al. They interviewed seventy-two participants (Walls and Williams 2003) in the west of Scotland, thirty-three Protestants and thirty-nine Catholics, with about half the sample aged forty-six and the rest sixty-six. There were seven personal claims of discrimination made by Catholics, two made by Protestants, accounts by Protestants who had witnessed anti-Catholic discrimination and cases in which Catholics described the immediate withdrawal of a job offer once their religion became clear (Walls and Williams 2005: 762). The modesty, however, of Walls and Williams' avowed conclusions should be observed: they claim to have established the fact but not the prevalence of discrimination (ibid. 761); they conclude that large numbers of west of Scotland Catholics aged over fifty (in 2005) have lived at an economic disadvantage (ibid. 765); and they plead that 'the question of how much of the disadvantage has been caused by discrimination can no longer be baulked' (ibid. 765). The responsible inference from current evidence is that sectarian employment practice is, as Walls and Williams (2000) argue about Catholic disadvantage, going but not gone.

Purdie (1991: 78) notes, more broadly, that for generations 'sectarianism has been part of the culture of some of the most heavily industrialised and densely populated areas of Scotland'. Finn et al.'s (2009) workplace focus group findings suggest that the sectarian culture, manifested in, for instance, humour and graffiti (ibid. 53–7), has yet to disappear from the Scottish workplace, both in and beyond Glasgow. Jeremian conclusions about the scale of sectarianism in present-day Scotland might, however, be premature, on grounds which I further expound below.

The unheard voices of grown-up Scotland

Something burbles under Bruce et al.'s (2004) account and is part of the explanation for the inter-marriage, friendship, residency and even social class profiles of Scotland's population, yet demands robust articulation. Consider the following discursive formation: Catholics, Protestants, Irish, British, loyalist, unionist, Rebel, the Orange Lodge, the Hibernians, King Billy, 1690, July 12, 1916 and Irish paramilitarism. How many twenty-first-century residents of Scotland (including Glasgow) would find this discursive formation a socio-cultural, ideological and affective foreign country? It could well be a healthy majority (though see Bradley's chapter). Journalists and politicians sing the mantra – sometimes with forked tongue – of anti-sectarianism. Academics in Scotland run a cottage industry of writing on sectarianism (including this book!). Episodes such as the Old Firm match of 2 March 2011 can generate an apparent tsunami of controversy over sectarianism. But how many Scottish residents are not at any level engaged? More pointedly, how many are either mystified, bored, repulsed, nauseated or indifferent? How many are plain oblivious as they travel to and from their sectarianism-illiterate or indifferent workplaces and proceed apace with their multiple identities, their self-actualisations or ordinary suburban lives largely indistinguishable in symbolic flavour from those in the rest of Britain? How many would be agog to hear that the country in which they happily live is 'endemically sectarian'?[2] It could be that a majority of modern Scottish residents have no special love for Catholicism, Protestantism or Irishness, not because they loathe any of the three, but because they don't see any of them – much like being black, Asian or gay – as significant or interesting enough to incite feelings either way. Rather, they will find in the 'sectarianism debate' only a monumental turn-off. The size of this constituency – if only we knew – could well be the most powerful reason for affirming the limited scale of sectarianism in present-day Scotland.

THE MORALITY OF FOOTBALL SECTARIANISM

Football sectarianism has moral equivalences with sectarianism in general, football racism, racism in general, football sexism, sexism in general, and indeed much other behaviour within hegemonic fandom. Like the other -isms, it is, again, tricky to define and presumes a hierarchical dualism or set of them. Like the other -isms, it takes diffuse forms and admits of degrees of transparency and degrees of intent.

It is worth observing that Bruce et al., despite their preceding (2004: 2–3) cautionary comment about extrapolation from fandom, later characterise the sectarian repertoires within fandom as 'ritual abuse' (ibid. 130–2). If this characterisation is correct, there is sufficient reason to find football sectarianism morally problematic. Football sectarianism is morally impermissible on grounds equivalent to those on which its preceding counterparts are morally impermissible, grounds which philosophers will recognise as Kantian.[3] Football sectarianism entails the absence of due respect for the human worth of its individual victims, the failure (in more formal Kantian language) to treat the individual members of at least one group as ends-in-themselves. I now try briefly to illustrate these arguments with four putatively sectarian chants, accompanied by some reflection on taxonomic and procedural consequences.

Illustrations and taxonomic reflection

No Pope of Rome contains the lines, 'No Pope of Rome, no chapel to sadden my eye, no nuns and no priests, no rosary beads, every day is the twelfth of July.' These words denigrate key signifiers of Catholic identity; exclude, inferiorise and arguably demonise Catholicism; and privilege Orangeism. The song therefore fails to show due respect for the humanity of Catholics and arguably anyone unsympathetic to Orangeism. No definition of sectarianism is necessary for the conclusion that the song is sectarian.

The Billy Boys has the lines, 'We're up to our knees in Fenian blood, surrender or you'll die', which, in their callous celebration of 'Fenian' bloodshed, manifest indifference to the humanity of the Catholics, Irish, nationalists and republicans who are the intended victims, and involve, arguably, privileging, exclusion, inferiorisation, demonisation and symbolic annihilation. Again, no definition of sectarianism is necessary for the conclusion that the song is sectarian. Consider, by analogy, a song with the words, 'We're up to our knees in Nazi blood, surrender or you'll die', and its lusty singing at a Scotland–Germany match. This would involve a morally unthinkable disregard for Nazi humanity, even in case of just war.

The Celtic supporters' line, 'Soon there'll be no Protestants at all' (sometimes performed in preamble to *The Soldier's Song*) involves the exclusion and inferiorisation of Protestants, the privileging of Catholics, and arguably the symbolic annihilation of Protestants. It involves the absence of due respect for the human worth of Protestants. No definition of sectarianism is necessary for the conclusion that the line is sectarian.

Consider, finally, the Celtic fans' ditty, 'King Billy had an army of a hundred thousand men, and the whole fuckin' lot got shot, bang! bang! . . . Glory, glory, what a hell of a way to die, to die an Orange bastard!' This song, through its celebration of Orange bloodshed, involves a callous disregard for the humanity of Orangemen, and promulgates their exclusion, inferiorisation, demonisation and symbolic annihilation. Consider, again, the morality – in case of just war – of lusty singing of the lines, 'Hitler had an army of . . . men, and the whole fuckin' lot got shot, bang! bang! . . . What a hell of a way to die, to die a Nazi bastard!'

Before leaving the final example, the notion that it should be considered sectarian bears some defence. Finn et al. (2009: 62), for instance, propose that sectarianism is most commonly (i) anti-Catholicism or (ii) anti-Protestantism or (iii) anti-Irish racism. While the three previous examples are, by those lights, clearly sectarian, it is less obvious that this fourth one is. Anti-Protestantism is the only viable option, and many who sing the chant would claim that it is not anti-Protestant but anti-anti-Catholic–Protestant. However, even if this claim is true – something Orangemen and women might contest – I think it taxonomically and procedurally helpful to consider the chant sectarian, due to the conjunction of two features. First, Orangeism is part of the preceding discursive formation of Scottish sectarianism. Second, the chant is, for the reasons given, intrinsically immoral. It might be, however, that we should not be neurotically hung-up on distinguishing the sectarian from the non-sectarian. While there is vital insight in the counsels of Finn et al. (2009: 62) and Kelly (2011) that we seek to discipline promiscuous conceptions of the sectarian – so that simple religious differences[4] or innocuous affirmations of Irishness[5] are not deemed sectarian – we should not presume there is always an answer to the question, 'Is x sectarian?'[6]

Indeed, the prospect that such a presumption is false might be part of the explanation of the focus group confusion and contestation which Finn et al. (2009: 23, 62) diagnose in terms of the 'omnifarious' meanings of sectarianism. The optimum conception of the sectarian might be particularist, nuanced and open to the prospect of no answer to the question 'Is x sectarian?' for some values of x – the more in light of the polysemous character of symbols. Furthermore, it might be wise to drop or normatively deprioritise the concept of the sectarian in some cases. For instance, while there are, again, viable reasons for deeming the fourth of the preceding chants sectarian, its categorical moral illegitimacy is sufficient to guide response to it.

Finally, how would Irish rebel songs fare within the approach I sketch? They are, for sure, part of the said discursive formation. However, it is less than clear that they are essentially immoral in sentiment; for instance, they don't essentially revel in the blood of opponents. They are, as their name intimates, songs of rebellion against British rule in Ireland (see Bradley's chapter). There are, of course, many Irish rebel songs, and a discriminate treatment is again in order. However, it might well be unhelpful and even dangerous indiscriminately to deem them sectarian.

Objections and replies

The first objection I consider is that football sectarianism is morally permissible on freedom-of-speech grounds. An enthusiasm for free speech, for which he claims the imprimatur of Mill, plays a significant role in Waiton's (2011 and this volume) moral downplay of football sectarianism and accompanying rejection of the Offensive Behaviour at Football and Threatening Communications Act (Scotland) 2012 ('the Bill' from now). This objection could carry only insofar as football sectarianism takes the form of words, songs and chants, and it is, within these limits, yet futile. Words, including those sung or chanted, are actions and therefore subject to moral limits. We have proper moral prohibitions on what may be done with words. For instance, one is not morally permitted to spread malicious lies about the person in the job one wants or to stand outside the home of one's Asian neighbours shouting – or singing – 'Pakis go home'. A defence of such behaviour on freedom-of-speech grounds suffers from deficits of understanding about speech, morality and the ideal of free speech, which is not in any of its exponents an ideal of morality-free speech. Football sectarianism, insofar as it is manifested in words, songs or chants, needs a far stronger moral defence than waving the flag of free speech.

Before leaving this objection, it is worth registering that Waiton's (2011) claim to the illustrious sponsorship of Mill is ambitious. Mill certainly prizes free and rational discussion of political, social and religious ideas, with the robust disagreement sometimes entailed (Mill 1962: 141–83). But football sectarianism, with its dichotomising expressions of (for instance) privilege, exclusion, inferiorisation, demonisation and symbolic annihilation, is no companion of free and rational discussion. The content of football sectarianism (recall my illustrations) is sharply antithetical to both the free and rational discussion and the overlapping freedom of self-expression championed by Mill. Football sectarianism celebrates the silencing, sometimes via brutal killing, of difference – it does not tolerate difference, as Mill did indeed urge that we should. Indeed, not only are there luminously Millian reasons for moral rejection of football sectarianism and approval of the Bill (to which I return), but the latter contains a clause which could have come from Mill's pen: 'The Offence will **NOT** [emphasis in Act] restrict freedom of speech, including the right to criticise or comment on religious or non-religious beliefs, even in harsh terms' (http://www.scotland.gov.uk/Topics/Justice/law/sectarianism-action-1/football-violence/bill).

The second objection is that the football fans which are the objects of football sectarianism are not offended by it. Waiton (2011), again, tells keenly of Ibrox conversation with 'old Rangers fans' who 'simply don't understand the problem' and dismiss things shouted at them as 'water off a duck's back'. The first part of the reply is that no amount of fans at games who report non-offence yields knowledge of any fans who don't attend because they are offended by football sectarianism. The second and more substantive part is worth breaking into two related elements. First, even if it is the case that no one within or around a practice-community is offended by a certain quality of the practice, it does not follow that the quality is morally defensible. To deny this is to succumb to a relativistic appeal to the moral standards internal to a practice, standards which might be deficient. While the view from within a practice-community might be unfailingly relevant to moral evaluation of its contents, it is not incorrigible; it can be mistaken. Put bluntly, a culture can get it morally wrong. Therefore, total absence of offence at football sectarianism would not secure moral standing for such sectarianism.

Second, the absence of offence can signify, not moral legitimacy, but a morally coarsened culture; naturalisation; a certain resignation; tactical self-training; a self-respect deficit; ignorance, moral or otherwise; or inadequate moral thinking. Illustrations abound, and I offer only one. How many women have not been offended by systematic sexual harassment or broader subordination, either because of the oppressive naturalisations of gender or because of some combination of resignation and tactical self-training? Even universal non-offence yields no moral apologia and is consistent with moral bankruptcy. The moral case against football sectarianism is similarly independent of whether anyone is in fact offended by it.

The final objection I consider repays substantial elaboration and a hospitable hearing, since its two premises, and a third in cahoots with the second, have every chance of being correct. Football sectarianism is morally permissible because (i) sectarianism is relatively insignificant in present-day Scotland, and (ii) the performers of football sectarianism are typically not especially bigoted characters (I use 'bigoted' here interchangeably with 'sectarian'). Waiton (2011), invoking Bruce et al. (2004) and Rosie (2004), notes that 'some very useful work . . . has blown holes in the idea that Scotland is . . . a sectarian country'. I have myself, again, already offered some defence of premise (i) and don't return to it. The first and vital point to make in support of (ii) is that performers of football sectarianism are not homogeneous in relation to bigotry of *character*. They doubtless cover a range, disqualifying a bigoted/non-bigoted binary opposition.[7] The range includes the committed, entrenched bigot who systematically configures social reality through his bigoted template and is very difficult to change. It also includes ignorant, ethically immature and merely negligent fans who feel a mild bigotry which is activated only through football or who are liable to be swept or cajoled into inherently vicious practices of which they might have scarce comprehension.

Premise (ii) entails that few practitioners of football sectarianism come close to the area inhabited by the committed, entrenched bigot. I think the truth, conversely, is that a significant majority embody either mild, football-localised bigotry or stronger football bigotry alongside milder bigotry – if any – elsewhere. So-called religion and politics is frequently a ready-to-hand pretext for the poisons associated in hegemonic fandom with pleasure and social credentialing. Many of the Celtic fans, for instance, who perform football sectarianism go home, again, to non-Catholic or Protestant or even Orange wives, husbands or partners and even children; have – without desire to shoot, banish or ill-treat – workmates, friends and relatives who are non-Catholic, Protestant, unionist, loyalist or Orange; and support Scotland or Britain in international sport, regardless of the religious or ethnic backgrounds of their representatives (see McVey's chapter). Similarly, many of their Rangers counterparts doubtless go home, again, like former Rangers captain Barry Ferguson,[8] to Catholic (or ex-Catholic) wives, husbands or partners and even children; don't feel paroxysms of horror – or much at all – when walking past a chapel; have – without desire to shoot, banish or ill-treat – friends, relatives and workmates who are Catholic, Irish, Irish diaspora, nationalist or republican; and support Scotland or Britain in international sport, regardless of the religious or ethnic backgrounds of their representatives.

Moreover, a third premise, '(iii)', snuggles up to the immediately preceding premise (ii) and also provides a measure of (perhaps oblique) support for (i). Premise (iii) is that many performers of football sectarianism care little about religion, ethnic identity or Irish politics. It isn't the easiest for a Celtic fan (say) who performs football sectarianism to convince in his apparently ardent identifications and aversions if, as is frequently the case, he doesn't attend church; doesn't pray; couldn't name and wouldn't recognise his parish priest; does zilch for Lent; doesn't go to Confession; barely extends theologically to belief in God, let alone Jesus; pays scarce attention to Irish politics; visits Ireland less than he does the Mediterranean; and frequently behaves, by performing football sectarianism, in a way that sits uncomfortably with any kind of Christianity (as do the other ignominies of hegemonic fandom).[9] Nor is it the easiest for his Rangers counterpart to impress in his apparently ardent identifications and aversions if, as is frequently the case, he can't say confidently what kind of Protestant he is; is wholly irreligious; barely extends theologically to belief in God, let alone Jesus; pays scarce attention to Irish politics; could fit what he knows about 1690 onto the back of a postage stamp; visits Northern Ireland less often than he visits the Mediterranean; and frequently behaves, by performing football sectarianism, in a way that sits uncomfortably with any kind of Christianity.

It might be, indeed, that the most egregious facet of a discourse with several is the unabashed references to 'religious divisions' between the sectarianism performers at Ibrox and Celtic Park respectively. Given, as Bruce et al. (2004: 115) put it, 'the vast majority of Scots have no particular religion and care not at all about theological disputes', there is scarce reason to believe that football sectarianism's performers are heavily represented within the remainder. The (ethno)-religious language is, again, 'a convenient language of abuse' (Bruce et al. 2004: 143), and it is likely that the stance of a good many performers of football sectarianism is comparable to that of the two young boys in London who painted a swastika on the front door of an elderly Jewish couple without any idea of what it represented (Bruce et al. 2004: 143–4).

Would the above premises (i) and (ii) – the latter jollied along by (iii) – morally rescue football sectarianism? No. The preceding Kantian argument against football sectarianism is independent of questions about the scale of sectarianism in Scotland, the characters of football sectarianism's performers and the credentials of the latter's identity and aversion-claims. The inherent character of football sectarianism – the flouting of the human worth of some others – is sufficient for categorical moral rejection. The imperative to respect all persons as ends-in-themselves contains no clause that we may temporarily disrespect other persons. Therefore, swift return to full respect once the football context is over is irrelevant to the moral nature of the disrespect shown in the football context. Consider, by analogy, the man who tries to defend verbal abuse of his wife – including the impugning of her religious and ethnic background – by saying, 'I abuse her only on Friday night in the kitchen. I show her full human respect in all other contexts.' Is this a tenable moral defence of his weekly abuse?

Furthermore, the current objection to this (Kantian) moral case against football sectarianism is, despite the truth – as I take it – of premises (i), (ii) and (iii), possibly the most morally dangerous and ideologically regressive of all. Condoning football sectarianism in a society in which sectarianism is in decline elsewhere and in which its performers are typically not too bigoted (nor very religious, political or ethnically aware) is morally worse than condoning it in different circumstances, since the former involves the following prospectus: 'Sectarianism has limited significance nowadays. However, if you happen to be a serious bigot, you are at liberty to express and cultivate your bigotry through football for a few hours weekly and if you are not a bigot, or not much of one, you are similarly at liberty to inhabit and enjoy the bigot's mind-set of disrespect, callousness, privileging, exclusion, poison, demonisation et al. Give it a whirl!'

How much respect do we have for the social practice of football if we are willing to so morally prostitute it? How much respect do we have for ourselves as a society? What sort of society are we to extend these offers to its members, to play so fast and loose with social character and social climate? We would be, on the Kantian grounds already adduced, immoral, but we would be odiously condescending to boot, since Old Firm and other fans are capable and worthy of better of an afternoon or evening than trading barren insult supposedly over what sort of Christian one is, where one stands on the Irish Question or where one's ancestors came from. Jimmy Reid was right that nothing is too good for the working class (Kerr 2010); conversely, some things are much too bankrupt for it. Football sectarianism – alongside the rest of the detritus of hegemonic fandom – is among the latter. Take a Liberty (Scotland), under whose aegis Waiton (2011) writes, conceives itself as standing up for the ordinary fan against the pompous and self-observing posturing of the political and media classes, but it is a pseudo-radicalism (see Crawford in this volume) which condones morally squalid behaviour within any social constituency. If Take a Liberty wants to champion football fans, then it needs to crank up its conception of them from a condescending vision of moral entitlement to behave in ways off-limits for anyone else.

THE BILL

The moral–legal interface is famously hazardous, and I offer nothing approaching a thorough defence of this particular attempt at the legal enforcement of morality (see the chapters by Hamilton-Smith and McArdle and by Goodall and Malloch for discussion of the law and sectarianism). I first, contrariwise, declare a quite strong sympathy with Waiton's (2011) withering critique of the psychology of the recent anti-sectarianism repertoires of Scottish politicians, which Waiton (2011) diagnoses as expressive of a 'momentary sense of common goodness and moral purpose'. My sympathy is especially strong with respect to the fall-out of 2 March 2011. A tempestuous Old Firm meeting and a relatively insignificant managers' touchline flare-up was excuse for fabrication of a moral monster which wannabe moral gladiators could queue up to ostentatiously fight.

However, the immediately preceding truth does not disqualify the Bill. The psychology of those who draft the Bill or publicly emote over 'sectarianism' is one question, and whether there is good reason to support the Bill is another. It is consistent to hold that the public discourse since 2 March 2011 is inscribed with some shady social psychology and that there is good reason to support the Bill. Indeed, it is probably the case that most public efforts to improve moral awareness – whether aimed at legislation – entice a purer-than-thou constituency, motivated by the self-aggrandisement resulting from the parade of one's supposed moral sensibilities. Consider the moral improvements over the last century in our responses to children, women, blacks, gays and the disabled. The narrative in each case surely includes a Gadarene rush of campaigners and contributors motivated by the wish to take a gratifying view of themselves and the wish that others share this view. But that provides no objection to any argument that the changes to which they might have contributed are moral improvements which deserve support (nor does it entail that everyone contributing to the changes is egoistically motivated). Moreover, Marx (1955: 116) taught us that history progresses by its bad side. The proximate cause of the Bill might be an overreaction of Jeremiahs with moral exhibitionist predilections. Yet it might be morally salutary and deserving of support. The contours of socio-cultural life regularly show up ambiguity such as this, and a mature society is able to live with it.

I offer regrettably little legislative defence of the Bill. The moral impermissibility of, not only football sectarianism, but the catalogue of disrespect within hegemonic fandom, plays an ineliminable role. Indeed, the ultimate cause of the Bill is hegemonic fandom, even if those implicated in its proximate cause don't realise or would be reluctant to acknowledge it. There is, again, controversy about the extent to which the law should enforce morality. However, any notion that the law never does or never should enforce morality is insupportable. Laws about, for instance, assault, racism, slander and child abuse are clearly and properly motivated by the moral character of violence against the person, racism, slander and child abuse respectively, albeit the moral character of the foregoing is not the only thing for legislators to consider. There is no a priori reason why the morality of football sectarianism should not similarly legally motivate us. If football sectarianism is, as I have argued, morally impermissible, then the notion that we should have a legal right to perform it is something in need of explanation. Moreover, football is, in Scotland, a significant cultural practice, which, in common with football in many other places, is in recent decades an environment where, again, morally indefensible behaviour is routine. Attempts at change from within the culture have had limited success. Respect for football, respect for ourselves, respect for our society, respect for the football fans who properly reject hegemonic fandom, and respect, indeed, for the fans who embody hegemonic fandom together provide a robust case for legal enforcement of morality in the shape of the Bill. It might be that in ten years the Bill will be as unexceptionable as seatbelt enforcement, and that, as Tony Benn would say, you can't find anyone who didn't think it in the first place.

THE RATIONALITY OF MAGNANIMITY

I conclude by arguing that there is compelling reason for magnanimity over the flammable baggage of the Old Firm clubs. Take Rangers' former discrimination against Catholics. It is not admirable and its cessation is a robust moral improvement. Celtic fans might revile it or try their damnedest to do so. However, there are reasons why a magnanimous response behoves everyone. The first is the simple 'Let he who is without sin . . .' directive, to which I add nothing. The second involves the sympathetic historical imagination which we apply graciously elsewhere and of which we will ourselves one day stand in need. Simply, the world one hundred years ago was very different from now. Religion was far more definitive of personal and social life in Scotland than it now is. Scotland had, like the rest of Britain, histories of anti-Catholicism and anti-Irishness,[10] and had to reckon with an Irish Catholic football club whose team threatened to show the natives how to play. Factor in Rangers' proximity to the Protestant stronghold of the shipyards,[11] and the anti-Catholicism which inscribed Rangers is quite intelligible – if not justifiable – against their socio-cultural backdrop. Furthermore, change is tricky when habit and structures of feeling have taken hold, the more in the football world of a city and country in ways conservative. To consider Rangers' former discrimination an index to the entire character of the club, with its many and varied fans, is harsh and mistaken (see McKillop in this volume), and that despite the malaise which has seen liquidation and reinvention in the bottom tier of the Scottish senior game.

Exactly the same applies regarding the flammable motives involved in Celtic's founding. One objective was to prevent Catholics courting apostasy by mingling with Protestants.[12] This is hard to imagine in present-day Scotland, and Rangers fans might similarly strive to revile it. But, again, we need to get inside the skin of Celtic's founders, an effort which should yield a more generous verdict. The mutual magnanimity proposed is reinforced by the fact that each club has evolved considerably. Catholic players are now commonplace at Ibrox, Rangers have had a Catholic manager too, and Celtic has long since grown into a more pluralist ideology than that of their founding. In an era in which Ian Paisley and Martin McGuinness have sat together in government, in which Peter Robinson has attended a GAA match amid low-key security and a warm reception (BBC News 2012), and in which Sinn

Féin representatives have met the Queen, it should not be beyond Old Firm fans to show magnanimity to the other side, warts and all. The dastardly snag, again, is hegemonic fandom, which is not primed for generosity, least of all towards mandatorily hated rivals.

The third reason overlaps with the second. If we were to subject our socio-cultural lives to an ideological-cum-moral boil wash, what would not fall out tattered and fit only for the bin? If churchy roots, for instance, are indicting, then Celtic has companions in guilt, including Aston Villa, Wolves, Birmingham City, Hibernian, Everton and Bolton, with religious solidarity, again, probably among the founding motivations in each case.[13] Should non-Christians and the wrong kinds of Christian therefore not support any of these clubs? More generally, don't we all sup with the devil in engaging with a social practice – sport – suffused with narratives of class, gender, race and colonialism? Away from sport, some of our canonical fairy-tales, for example *Cinderella*, have dubious ideological encodings. Are they to be binned? Should women refuse the 'caring' qualities because they have been ideologically encouraged in them for oppressive reasons? Should men refuse authority on equivalent grounds? Rangers and Celtic might not survive boil wash, but so little would that there would be precious little value in being any longer alive. Suniti Namjoshi (Warner 1994: Epigraph) wrote:

And all the little monsters said in a chorus:
You must kiss us . . .

. . . But the evil you do,
The endless ado.
Why bless you?
You are composed of such shameful stuff.

Because, said the monsters, beginning to laugh,
Because, they said, cheering up.
You might as well. You are part of us.
(emphasis in text)

Namjoshi's merry gang rudely alert us that there is no prelapsarian state on offer. Our *selves* are indelibly inscribed with moral and ideological ambiguity[14] – and even sub-Faustian pacts – which we accept alongside our perpetual and routinely challenging moral and ideological evolution. Old Firm fans don't tend to click to boil wash elsewhere, and it is only the ugly frissons of hegemonic fandom which so enthuse them to do so with the club their counterparts hold dear.

CONCLUSION

We do not need to choose between the Bill and the extension to fandom of the foregoing generosity. The remaking of football's social world can use both. The remaking has begun, and needs to continue in order that football sectarianism disappears – hammering another nail into the coffin of Scottish sectarianism – with the other carbuncles on the face of fandom. If that is agreed, we can switch to something more inspiring, and then, as the legendary James Sanderson oft-implored, get out to a game . . .

NOTES

1. This is an allusion to Gallagher (1987).
2. This expression is a paraphrase of views expressed by commentators such as MacMillan and O'Hagan. See Bruce et al. (2004: 1, 169).
3. This element of my treatment is influenced by Dixon's (2007) excellent treatment of on-field trash talking.
4. See Finn et al. (2009: 62).
5. See also Kelly (2007) for some exposé of the 'sectarianising' of the Irish identity.
6. For compelling critique of the dichotomising impulse in general, see Kretchmar (2007) and Prokhovnik (1999: 20–49).
7. My treatment at this point is indebted to Jones and Fleming (2007) and McNamee (2010).
8. See Bruce et al. (2004: 130). For a first-person account of Kenny Dalglish's religious indifference, see Dalglish (1996: 5–6).
9. The Kirk's Edinburgh Presbytery, responding in 1935 to Protestant Action Society violence, condemned 'all methods of violence, all interference with personal freedom, and every word and action which expressed the spirit of hatred' as 'fundamentally unchristian' (Bruce et al. 2004: 55).
10. For brief exposé of Britain's historical anti-Irishness, see Curtis (1984).
11. See Murray (1984: 84–5).
12. See Murray (ibid.: 60).
13. See Goldblatt (2006: 40).
14. Terry Eagleton (2011: 12) has written: 'Lots of men and women in the West are fervent supporters of bloodstained setups. Christians, for example. Nor is it unknown for decent, compassionate types to support whole civilisations steeped in blood. Liberals and conservatives, among others. Modern capitalist nations are the fruit of a history of slavery, genocide, violence and exploitation every bit as abhorrent as Mao's China or Stalin's Soviet Union.'

REFERENCES

BBC News (2012), 'Gregory Campbell supports Robinson's attendance of GAA match', 30 January 2012, http://www.bbc.co.uk/news/uk-northern-ireland-16777870 (last accessed 15 June 2012).

Bruce, S., Glendinning, T., Paterson, I. and Rosie, M. (2004), *Sectarianism in Scotland*, Edinburgh: Edinburgh University Press.

Curtis, L. (1984), *Nothing but the Same Old Story: The Roots of Anti-Irish Racism*, London: London Against Racism.

Dalglish, K. (1996), *Dalglish: My Autobiography* with Henry Winter, London: Hodder and Stoughton.

Devine, T. (ed.) (2000), *Scotland's Shame? Bigotry and Sectarianism in Modern Scotland*, Edinburgh: Mainstream.

Dixon, N. (2007), 'Trash talking, respect for opponents and good competition', *Sport, Ethics and Philosophy*, 1: 1, 96–106.

Eagleton, T. (2011), *Why Marx Was Right*, New Haven: Yale University Press.

Finn, G., Uygun, F. and Johnson, A. (2009), *Sectarianism and the work place: report to the Scottish Trades Union Congress and the Scottish Government*, Glasgow: Scottish Trades Union Congress.

Gallagher, T. (1987), *Glasgow: The Uneasy Peace*, Manchester: Manchester University Press.

Goldblatt, D. (2006), *The Ball is Round: A Global History of Football*, London: Penguin.

Jones, C. and Fleming, S. (2007), '"I'd rather wear a turban than a rose": a case study of the ethics of chanting', *Race, Ethnicity and Education*, 10: 4, 404–14.

Kelly, J. (2007), 'Hibernian Football Club: the forgotten Irish?', *Sport in Society*, 10: 3, 514–36.

Kelly, J. (2011), '"Sectarianism" and Scottish football: critical reflections on dominant discourse and press commentary', *International Review for the Sociology of Sport*, 46: 4, 418–35.

Kerr, H. (2010), Letters: Jimmy Reid obituary, *The Guardian* [online], 15 August 2010, http://www.guardian.co.uk/theguardian/2010/aug15/letters-jimmy-reid-obituary (last accessed 15 June 2012).

Kretchmar, R. S. (2007), 'Dualisms, dichotomies and dead ends: limitations of analytic thinking about sport', *Sport, Ethics and Philosophy*, 1: 3, 266–80.

McNamee, M. (2010), 'Racism, racist acts and courageous role models', in M. McNamee (ed.), *The Ethics of Sports*, Abingdon: Routledge, pp. 286–99.

Marx, K. (1955), *The Poverty of Philosophy*, trans. Institute of Marxism Leninism. Moscow: Progress Publishers.

Mill, J. S. (1962), *Utilitarianism*, ed. Mary Warnock, Glasgow: William Collins Sons & Co. Ltd.

Murray, B. (1984), *The Old Firm: Sport, Sectarianism and Society in Scotland*, Edinburgh: John Donald.

NFO Social Research (2003), *Sectarianism in Glasgow*, Glasgow: Glasgow City Council.

Offensive Behaviour at Football and Threatening Communications (Scotland) Act 2012, http://www.scotland.gov.uk/Topics/Justice/law/sectarianism-action-1/football-violence/bill (last accessed 9 March 2012).

Prokhovnik, R. (1999), *Rational Woman: A Feminist Critique of Dichotomy*, London: Routledge.

Purdie, B. (1991), 'The lessons of Ireland for the SNP', in T. Gallagher (ed.), *Nationalism in the Nineties*, Edinburgh: Polygon, pp. 66–83.

Rosie, M. (2004), *The Sectarian Myth in Scotland: Of bitter memory and bigotry*, Basingstoke: Palgrave Macmillan.

Syed, M. (2011), 'Vile chants born of hatred at the heart of football', *The Times*, 5 October 2011, p. 79.

Waiton, S. (2011), 'The rise and rise of intolerant tolerance', *Spiked*, 5 December 2011, http://www.spiked-online.com/index.php/essays/article/11866 (last accessed 9 March 2012).

Walls, P. and Williams, R. (2000), 'Going but not gone: Catholic Disadvantage in Scotland', in T. Devine (ed.), *Scotland's Shame? Bigotry and Sectarianism in Modern Scotland*, Edinburgh: Mainstream, pp. 231–52.

Walls, P. and Williams, R. (2003), 'Sectarianism at work: accounts of employment discrimination against Irish Catholics in Scotland', *Ethnic and Racial Studies*, 26: 4, 632–61.

Walls, P. and Williams, R. (2005), 'Religious discrimination in Scotland: a rebuttal of Bruce et al.'s claim that sectarianism is a myth', *Ethnic and Racial Studies*, 28: 4, 759–67.

Warner, M. (1994), *Managing Monsters: The 1994 Reith Lectures*, London: Vintage.

9 England's Act, Scotland's Shame and the Limits of Law

Niall Hamilton-Smith and David McArdle

INTRODUCTION

For over a century, sectarianism and Scottish football have, in the minds of many commentators, been locked in a poisonous embrace (Flint and Powell 2011). Fixtures between the 'Old Firm' of Rangers and Celtic have long been associated with incidents of sectarian abuse and violence (Bradley 1995), to be discussed and recycled at length by Scotland's football-obsessed media (see Reid in this volume). However, until relatively recently the widespread perception that sectarianism was a 'problem' within Scottish football was not matched by any notable attempts on the part of government to deal with the issue directly, and only in the past twenty years has there been meaningful academic and policy debate about the issue (Kelly 2011). After the creation of the Scottish Parliament this debate culminated in legislation which sought to address the problem directly and, tentative though these measures were, they stood in marked contrast to a pre-Devolution policy best described as one of wilful denial rather than mere ignorance. As late as 1977 the McElhone Report on football crowd disorder, commissioned by the Secretary of State for Scotland, made no mention of sectarianism at all (Scottish Education Department 1977), even though sectarian disorder would have been manifestly apparent to anyone attending Old Firm games in the 1970s.

Such a startling oversight requires explanation. Some commentators have argued that football policy at this time was largely dictated by the priorities of the English game (Bebber 2012) and that the media-exaggerated figure of the English hooligan (Poulton 2005) drove security policies both north and south of the border which ignored the important particularities of context (Coalter 1985); an alternative explanation is that the issue was historically perceived as nothing more than a formulaic fan rivalry that bore no relationship to any 'real' discrimination or prejudice extant in wider Scottish society (Bruce et al. 2004). Both explanations have merit and have helped inform this research into the authors' underlying argument: that taking legislation which proved an effective, but by no means unproblematic (Pearson 2012), response to a peculiarly English 'problem' and parachuting it into

Scots law was always destined to create at least as many problems as it solved. The perception of sectarian behaviour as the province of the 'ninety minute bigots' who (to quote a former head of security at Rangers FC) 'shout something loud, but don't really mean it'[1] is still a view that is promulgated, albeit in a more refined form, by those who argue that legal responses to sectarian chants and epithets equates essentially to the criminalisation of harmless working-class banter (Waiton 2012 and in this volume). Others have argued that the banter is not merely 'harmless' but positively beneficial, acting as a putative safety valve or a 'release' for the sectarian tension and rivalries that exist outside football (Davies 2006 and this volume). A third group perceive in the political and media discourse a deliberate attempt to simplify sectarianism, characterising it as offensive behaviour that is confined to loutish football fans and otherwise alien to the values of Scottish people (Kelly 2011). Kelly argues, however, that this construction conveniently ignores the real basis of sectarian friction in the widespread and systemic discrimination experienced by Scots of Irish-Catholic descent – discrimination which, in the opinion of one of the Sheriffs interviewed in November 2010 as part of the authors' recent research (Hamilton-Smith et al. 2011), cannot be simply dismissed as football men behaving badly:

> [The response to] sectarianism in football is against a backcloth of the discrimination against Catholics in Glasgow, even in the legal profession. Lots of Catholics went into public sector work because they couldn't get jobs in the law firms, or worked in obviously Catholic firms. If you're my age and you grew up in Glasgow you'd still have a chip on your shoulder about all of that.

'THE ENGLISH DISEASE' MEETS 'SCOTLAND'S SHAME'

Regardless of one's perceptions of the history, the reasons for the sudden change of focus at the turn of the new century can be more readily explained by a number of parallel but ultimately converging developments. These have been persuasively unpicked elsewhere (Kelly 2003), but broadly the mix of Scottish devolution and the flexing of 'executive' political power in Scotland have increased attention on the sectarian behaviours that are associated with the Old Firm; the attendant media publicity and the emergence of more vocal anti-sectarianism campaigners helped transform how sectarianism in football was publicly debated and officially addressed; and a very public academic debate (culminating in a controversial and high-profile collection of essays provocatively entitled *Scotland's Shame* (Devine 2000)) contributed to the mix. The political class in Edinburgh responded to this growing debate, with the then First Minister, Jack McConnell, convening a National Summit on Sectarianism in early 2005 (Flint 2008). From this, the Scottish Executive developed an 'Action Plan on Tackling Sectarianism in Scotland' (Scottish Executive 2006) which included an explicit commitment to tackling sectarian disorder in football. However, while the Action Plan was full of promising 'actions', its Achilles' heel, to which we will return, was that it largely ignored all the preceding tensions, disagreements and debates surrounding the nature, seriousness – and indeed the

very existence – of sectarianism and sectarian disorder, preferring to treat these phenomena as self-evident in both meaning and gravity without ever establishing that
sectarian 'disorder' genuinely amounted to something more than low-level drunken
posturing that came to an end when the final whistle blew.

The most prominent commitment in the Action Plan for dealing with the perceived problems in Scottish football involved transferring an English legislative
initiative into Scotland with the avowed expectation that it would address sectarianism, and to that end the Police, Public Order and Criminal Justice (Scotland) Act
of 2006 ss. 51–66 introduced Football Banning Orders (FBOs) into Scotland some
six years after they had been promulgated in England and Wales. FBOs are court-
imposed orders that ban individuals for a specified period of time from attending
designated football matches and, in principle, other specified match-related locations such as railway stations or bars near to football stadia (Stott and Pearson 2006,
2008). Failure to abide by the conditions of these bans can be punished by imprisonment, but FBOs themselves are not conceived as a punitive aspect of sentencing in
their own right – they are ostensibly a preventative measure that can be imposed
in addition to any conventional criminal justice sanction. As they are putatively a
preventative measure they can also be imposed on individuals who have not been
convicted of any criminal offence at all, in circumstances where there is sufficient
evidence – based on a civil standard of proof (that is, on the balance of probabili-
ties) – to demonstrate that there is a risk that an individual *might* be involved in
some form of football-related violence or disorder in the future. In this respect, FBOs
belong to that area of law that mixes civil and criminal powers and is often classed as
'hybrid' legislation, the most notable example being Anti-Social Behaviour Orders
(Squires 2008). But in Scotland, applications for FBOs have almost always been
made in the immediate wake of a criminal conviction; the number of civil applications made in respect of those who have not been convicted of a football-related
offence is in single figures and, in Scotland at least, that aspect of the legislation can
almost be regarded as 'dead law' (Redhead 1995).

In the criminal context, FBOs are ordinarily requested by the police and that
request is pursued by the prosecution in court; in both Scotland and in England and
Wales, it falls to senior police officers in charge of match day operations to determine
whether individuals who are to be prosecuted for match day offences should also be
the target of an FBO. Outside of immediate match day policing operations Football
Intelligence Officers (FIOs) have a key role in identifying individuals who should be
targeted for FBOs, including proactively targeting individuals involved in football-
related violence that occurs away from the confines of football stadia. Typically,
FIOs direct intelligence-gathering efforts to build cases in support of applications
and have a role in screening arrests generally to spot football-related prosecutions
that other officers might have missed, or particular incidents that might have fallen
outside the 'ambit' of match day policing operations (for example, violence that
might occur sometime after the game, in a bar or on public transport) but which
might still merit an FBO. While the wording of the FBO legislation in Scotland is
virtually identical to that of the Football Spectators Act 1989, s 14B (which applies
only to England and Wales), the subsequent use and uptake of FBOs in Scotland has

been markedly different and by mid-2010 – nearly four years after the enactment of the legislation – the low number of banning orders being issued had become a cause for political concern, and something of an embarrassment. An FBO evaluation was commissioned by the Scottish Government in summer 2010 to examine the reasons for this ostensible lack of progress in the use of FBOs (Hamilton-Smith et al. 2011), the working hypothesis at the outset being that applications for orders were being made but – for reasons unknown – not being granted by the courts.[2] The evaluation therefore adopted a research design that primarily focused on tracking cases from the point of arrest to the point of court judgements to assess where attrition in the 'pipeline' of FBO applications was occurring.

FOOTBALL BANNING ORDERS IN SCOTLAND

Comparing FBO rates between the two jurisdictions was destined to be problematic because the contexts were so very different, but differences in how the legislation was framed and implemented provided at least a partial explanation for the greater numbers of FBOs in England and Wales. Superficially at least, a key departure in the drafting of the Scottish version of the legislation was the omission of the require-ment, present in England and Wales, for the judiciary to explain why they chose *not* to impose an FBO on the back of a football-related conviction, when prosecutors had requested such an order. This appears to have communicated a clear expecta-tion to the magistrates in England and Wales that granting an FBO in such cases was the desired and default position. No such expectation existed in Scotland or, if it did, it was never communicated to the Sheriffs (Hamilton-Smith et al. 2011).

Another key point of departure concerns how the legislation was resourced and implemented. The English legislation was supported by resources allocated to the UK Football Policing Unit, within which was embedded the Football Banning Authority.[3] The Unit's remit included providing guidance and best practice advice on matters relating to the policing of football and the issuing of FBOs, as well as acting as a central hub for sharing and disseminating relevant police intelligence (Hamilton-Smith and Hopkins 2012). In Scotland a considerably more limited level of resource (one civilian post) was available to support Scottish police forces. Of equal influence was the use of pump-priming monies in England and Wales, again administered through the Football Banning Authority, *to directly fund* – and in effect significantly incentivise[4] – individual police forces to pursue civil applications for FBOs. Such applications typically necessitated the collection and development of evidence to demonstrate that an individual merited the imposition of an order in the absence of a criminal conviction. Again, no such resources were available in Scotland and, as alluded to above, civil applications (the costs of which would need to be met by whichever constabulary was making the application) were not routinely pursued.

While the volume of FBOs may have differed, the way in which FBOs were tar-geted did not. In both jurisdictions FBOs have predominantly been targeted at two overlapping types of cases: serious incidents occurring within stadia, usually involv-ing violence or pitch invasions; and individuals who are involved in organising or engaging in acts of group violence and disorder against other 'risk supporters', whether in football stadia or not (Hamilton-Smith et al. 2011). Beyond that, the focus has consistently been on the more 'serious' offences, with 'seriousness' being defined by levels of violence and repeat offending. This seems proportionate, but it is problematic in the Scottish context because, let us remember, the focus of the legislation was originally sectarianism – and individuals convicted of sectarian offences have been far less likely to have a banning order imposed on them. Indeed, sectarian offences accounted for over 40 per cent of 300-plus convictions that were analysed because FBOs were sought, but they accounted for only 19 per cent of the cases where an FBO was actually granted (Hamilton-Smith et al. 2011: 14): legislation that had been specifically introduced to tackle sectarian disorder at football has not primarily been used for the purpose intended.

A more detailed examination of a small random sample of sixty-one cases provides some insight into these figures. Twenty-six cases involved offences that had some clear sectarian element but only nine of them led to an FBO on conviction. All but two of the twenty-six sectarian cases involved fans of one or other of the Old Firm clubs but only nine took place within the context of an Old Firm match (which leads us to believe that Rangers' demotion in 2012–13 will not, of itself, impact on the number of FBO applications). In all the cases where an FBO was granted the relevant offence took place in, or immediately outside, a football ground (compared to just over half of cases where an FBO was not granted). Furthermore, twenty-one of the twenty-six convictions involved police being proximate to the accused at the time of the offence, with only one conviction resulting from a club steward reporting, or directing police to, an offender. The majority of these sectarian cases, regardless of whether an FBO was issued or not, could not be characterised as being generally 'serious' in conventional terms (that is, they did not involve violence or particularly reckless conduct[5]). This might account for the low number of FBOs issued on the back of sectarian convictions, and would give succour to the contention that the policing of football in Scotland is framed and problematised within the framework of English-style 'hooliganism'. While media and political coverage of sectarian disorder in Scotland often gives the impression that the 'disorder' is similar to the equivalent 'disorder' targeted by the FBO legislation in England, most sectarian 'disorder' does not in fact involve violence at all but rather consists of offensive 'utterances' and gestures. However, this cannot entirely explain the patterns observed here because some sectarian offences which lacked any particularly aggravating features *did* attract banning orders, while two of the more serious sectarian cases in this sample (one involving the assault of a police officer, the other involving multiple sexual assaults) did not attract FBOs.

LOST IN TRANSLATION?

It appeared that decisions made in courts, including Sheriffs' opinions on the appropriateness of using FBOs in respect of sectarian offences, provided some explanation for the limited and rather confused use of banning orders. But there was also a perception that, somewhere along the criminal justice 'pipeline', sectarian incidents were 'filtered out' and did not lead to an arrest or a criminal charge, so that the potential imposition of an FBO was never even considered by the court. Three possible explanations may be identified (see Hamilton-Smith et al. 2011 for further details):

Identifying and recognising the offence: Match day operations focus on travel routes and the area immediately around a football stadium within a limited time encompassing pre- and post-match fan movements. Outside that timeframe there was much less likelihood that incidents of disorder would be directly linked to football – and even if they were, it was less likely that the arresting officer would consider that an FBO application might be appropriate. In any event, attempting to impose FBOs against 'one of the herd' does not usually pass muster in the Scottish courts for the reasons explained below, and even if a ringleader can be identified, much sectarian abuse is framed by a full awareness on the part of fans as to what does or does not constitute a phrase, banner or gesture that will be regarded as sectarian (Howe 2010). Consequently, insults are carefully crafted either by dropping the insult in quickly at the end of an otherwise 'innocuous' song or piece of banter, or trying to 'tip-toe round' the law by conveying coded or oblique insults which do not contravene the law but are clearly understood by well-informed rivals.

Deciding whether to act (or not): Even if a clear sectarian offence was spotted, the interest in securing a conviction needs to be weighed against the risks entailed by making an arrest. As one prosecution lawyer interviewed in November 2010 noted:

> They talk about zero tolerance in relation to sectarian issues, but I don't know that's enforceable. When you go Parkhead or Ibrox and you hear on the terraces the bile and just the pure utter sectarianism, there is very little you can do to enforce the legislation; you've got five thousand folk singing some of these songs [. . .] It would cause a riot if you arrested some of these individuals.

This perception was substantiated by a number of the Sheriffs, police officers and club security managers who were interviewed. CCTV evidence could assist here, allowing officers to identify ringleaders after the conclusion of a match, though this depended not only on the appropriate use of the cameras, but also on an individual being easily identifiable. This could be straightforward if a club season ticket holder was sitting in their designated seat, but as season ticket membership was steeply in decline during the 2010–11 football season, this was becoming less certain. The decline in season ticket sales was also considered by some respondents to 'dampen' the enthusiasm of clubs to ban fans themselves,[6] but it would be crass to simply characterise clubs as ignoring sectarian behaviour in favour of maximising their commercial returns. Overt displays of sectarian behaviour by large numbers of fans have led to clubs suffering adverse commercial and reputational consequences, with sponsors, TV broadcasters and international football governing bodies all taking a dim view of such incidents.[7]

Clubs are also increasingly responsible for the majority of in-stadia security in the form of stewarding. However, here clubs operate with limited capabilities. Stewards are usually employed by clubs themselves – many being drawn from their own fan base – and while a small minority are professionally trained, the majority are employed on a casual basis. Consistent with Moorehouse's (2006) previous research, there was a perception that these stewards had a limited stake in confronting sectarian disorder. One Football Intelligence Officer interviewed in October 2010 illustrated these tensions:

> You are getting guys who might be being paid thirty pounds a game, and they are [. . .] supporters, and are they going to stick their neck out if someone's singing a sectarian song? And if the same steward patrols the same part of the ground week after week, which they do, and if they are seen to arrest someone what the reaction to them will be, I don't know. There is a level of tolerance about it.

This reliance on stewards has recently been increasing, as pressure on police resources has caused a reconfiguration in how matches are policed: officers have been moved away from policing in the stadia and either been held back outside the stadia or located in stadia concourses ready to be called on by stewards if trouble occurs.

Effectively presenting the offence: If an offence was spotted, and if action were taken, weaknesses in process impacted negatively on FBO requests. Sectarian offences require careful documentation and effective communication because they are not usually characterised by a clear physical act of violence or the threat of it. A 'typical' sectarian offence may be a sudden gesture, a turn of words, a form of display or some other provocation, the offensiveness of which may be highly contextual and subjective; but it rarely amounts to a real or even a perceived threat of violence. Indeed, what might be characterised as 'criminal sectarianism' by one observer might be regarded by others as either just another example of the industrial banter inevitably attending the match day pageant or (in the opinion of the defendant in *Walls* v. *Brown*) an entirely proper means of expressing a perfectly legitimate political opinion. If one accepts (in the words of one of the Sheriffs interviewed in November 2010) that 'as an Old Firm fan your behaviour has to be pretty bloody dreadful before the police will feel the need to do something about it', it becomes critical that the *actus reus* of the offence, and the impact of it, is properly evidenced in police reports and court papers so that Sheriffs know why this particular individual's behaviour was so beyond the Pale and why an FBO might therefore be appropriate. But the limited resources available to facilitate and scrutinise FBO applications meant that many of these applications were in fact poorly evidenced, so that the full meaning and significance of sectarian offences was often not apparent to the prosecution, let alone to the court. When these weaknesses are allied to the enduring disagreements and ambiguities regarding what exactly constitutes a sectarian crime, conveying the 'full meaning and significance' of an offence is always contingent on the steward or frontline officer's immediate perception of its severity and, thereafter, on how that narrative is conveyed to other decision-makers – up to and including the Sheriff – who will have their own opinions and will need to be clearly persuaded as to why this incident was so egregious as to merit prosecution and an FBO application.

JUDICIAL PERCEPTIONS OF THE FBO REGIME

While these difficulties may have accounted for some requests either being overlooked in court or never getting to that stage in the first years of the FBO regime, significant steps were taken during the 2010–11 football season to improve police and prosecutors' awareness of the procedures and the quality of reporting, and by no means could all of those early failures in court be simply attributed to poor paperwork or shoddy prosecution. Research interviews with the judiciary suggested that the very wording of the legislation proved most problematic in persuading them to impose FBOs, and no amount of prosecutor training or awareness-raising had altered that state of affairs. There is no requirement under the Scottish legislation that reasons have to be given for not imposing an FBO and the Sheriffs (unlike most of their counterparts in the English magistracy) are professional criminal lawyers rather than lay people. Most gained over thirty years' experience in criminal prosecution or defence work before their elevation to the bench, and that experience has clearly informed their approach to the FBO regime.

Defending the indefensible

That said, not all situations where a Sheriff has refused to grant an FBO can be attributed to their difficulties with the wording of the legislation, and the case which most gives the impression that individual Sheriffs were not playing ball with the regime has become notorious in Scottish criminal justice circles and serves as a reminder that there will always be examples of judicial decision-making that defy explanation.

This case arose from an incident in which one fan set fire to another who was wearing an inflammable fancy-dress costume, to his severe injury. The men had been returning to Aberdeen by train after watching their team play in Edinburgh and the defendant, one Peter Wallace, had been 'mucking about' by flicking a cigarette lighter in the vicinity of the victim. His victim's costume caught light and caused him serious burns which required extensive medical treatment.[8] The case was heard in August 2010. The Sheriff did not impose a custodial sentence (Wallace was admonished and ordered to pay compensation of £25,000) and also did not impose an FBO, despite Wallace having a previous football-related conviction and thus seemingly deserving of an FBO under s. 51(3) of the 2006 Act. It is an extreme case, both in terms of the incident's severity and the perceived illogicality of the Sheriff's ruling, but it served to reinforce the generally held misconception at that time that Sheriffs in general were resisting FBOs even where the circumstances cried out for one.

But can *Wallace* really be explained in such simplistic terms? To recap, the relevant legislation is a *mutatis mutandis* application of the analogous Act of England

and Wales and provides that before a court can impose an FBO, it must be satisfied that there are reasonable grounds to believe that doing so would help to prevent violence or disorder at or in conjunction with any football matches (2006 Act, S.51(3)).[9] When proper weight is given to the language of s. 51(3) then maybe that helps to explain both the decision in *Wallace* and the Sheriffs' apparent reticence to grant FBOs; but a still-finer grasp of the significance of the Act's language is available through consideration of the High Court's judgment in *Walls* v. *Brown* [2009] HCJAC 59, which was the first occasion where a conviction leading to the imposition of a FBO (although not the imposition of the banning order itself) has been appealed in Scotland.

Here, in the course of a match between Kilmarnock and Rangers, the appellant Walls (a Rangers fan) had repeatedly sung one particular line from the infamous 'Famine Song' and had shouted sectarian abuse. For many, the mere singing of the 'Famine Song' of itself merits both a conviction and an FBO, but so far as the sentence in this case is concerned it is likely that his making 'gestures' in the direction of the home supporters, his inciting of other fans, ignoring repeated requests from stewards that he sit down and refusing to leave the ground when they asked him to do so were far more important than his sectarian singing. The totality of his actions led to a breach of the peace conviction, aggravated by religious prejudice under s. 74(2) of the Criminal Justice (Scotland) Act 2003[10] and by racial prejudice under s. 96(2) of the Crime and Disorder Act 1998.[11] He was placed on probation for eighteen months and given a two-year FBO.

Walls appealed by way of stated case, but the High Court of Justiciary upheld the conviction and confirmed that the Sheriff had been correct in her assertion that a breach of the peace may occur where the conduct complained of is 'severe enough to cause alarm to ordinary people and threaten serious disturbance to the community'. The conduct of the appellant did amount to a breach of the peace because:

> Even in the context of a football match . . . presence inside a football stadium does not give a spectator a free hand to behave as he pleases. There are limits and the appellant's conduct went well beyond those limits. . . . It is a legitimate inference that persons in the crowd are likely to be alarmed and disturbed by such behaviour and that it does have the potential to cause or threaten serious disturbance. (*Walls* v. *Brown*, paras 18–20)

Walls is notable in part for the significant role played by the wider actors – especially the stewards – in successfully securing both the conviction and the FBO, and echoes the need for coherent thinking. The testimony of a police superintendent to the effect that he, like most fans, knew the words of the rest of the 'Famine Song' (which had not been sung by Walls), that he found those words offensive and that 'sectarian and bigoted chants could have an impact on parts of a football crowd . . . were they to take offence' (para 2) were combined with evidence from a Kilmarnock FC steward and a Rangers FC steward to the effect that they were 'bothered' by the potential for an adverse reaction from the crowd around him. There had in fact been no such adverse reaction – to the contrary, Walls had successfully exhorted some of them to join his refrain and the Kilmarnock fans were ensconced at the other end of the ground; but the stewards' evidence as to the totality of his behaviour took him comfortably beyond the bounds of what was acceptable, even in 'the context of a football match'. It was clearly sufficient in law for the Sheriff to convict and for the High Court to uphold her decision.

In addition to the contribution of the police and the stewards, the Crown's being able to adduce evidence that Walls successfully encouraged others to follow suit would have been an important aspect of the FBO application because the s. 51(3) requirement that a banning order would 'help to prevent violence or disorder at or in connection with any football matches' will always be met if it can be established that the defendant was a ringleader, and on this occasion Walls clearly had been a ring-leader of sorts. However, he also had a long list of convictions for violent offences, which included at least one football-related offence, and he had served a period of imprisonment for possessing a knife. That prior history alone could have also sufficed for s. 51(3) purposes, even if he had not actually incited anyone successfully. In that regard the Sheriffs' approach in *Walls* reflected what other Sheriffs repeatedly indicated during the interviews: the phrasing of s. 51(3) means that strong arguments for imposing a banning order will always arise where a defendant has prior relevant convictions and any behaviour which carries even a threat of violence is also likely to attract an FBO; and in the absence of those features the prosecution may still be able to adduce cogent evidence of a clear link between the defendant's activities on the day and the s. 51(3) requirements that removing him from grounds is likely to contribute to a reduction in offences relating to football matches.

Walls' conviction for breach of the peace reflected his sectarian bile, his conduct towards the stewards and his repeated gesturing and posturing towards the other fans, while the consequences of what he specifically said were his 'aggravated' convictions under the 1998 and 2003 Acts. Thereafter, the two-year FBO was appropriate given his extensive criminal history and his attempts to incite his fellows; but his singing of the 'Famine Song' was probably the least significant aspect of the case and, contrary to the media's reporting of it,[12] probably had no bearing on the Sheriff's decision to impose a FBO.

Both at first instance and on appeal, *Walls* is a case which pays due heed to the limitations of s. 51(3) and the difficulties it presents for those who would routinely seek banning orders for sectarian offences, but as an example of clear judicial thinking it stands in marked contrast to the decision in *Wallace* and some of the key banning order judgments from England (*Gough v. Chief Constable of Derbyshire* [2002] QB 1213; Pearson 2002). That certainly does not mean the Scottish judiciary regards sectarianism as an insignificant issue, but it is difficult to convince them that granting a FBO against a particular individual who uses sectarian language will be appropriate when they are surrounded by up to fifty thousand other people who know what they are going to hear when they choose to attend the carnival (Vice 1997) that is Scottish football. That does not mean that no offence has been committed in those circumstances, but it does mean that a FBO cannot be easily reconciled with the phrasing of the legislation in the absence of other factors.

In reading *Walls* one also gets the impression that this was a case in which the police, the stewards, the club and the prosecution had worked closely together in order to present a coherent argument for an FBO in respect of a repeat offender who merited little sympathy.

This need for appropriate liaison should be considered in the light of the Association of Chief Police Officers in Scotland's assertion that approximately seventy Sheriffs (out of about 150 across Scotland) had attended one of two FBO training events for Sheriffs which had been held since the 2006 Act came into force. If those figures are correct, and if the Sheriffs' recollection of those training events (as recounted to the authors) is accurate, it means that almost half of Scotland's Sheriffs had been explicitly advised to expect a clear steer from the Crown if it considered a FBO to be appropriate. If that perception has thereafter been communicated to other Sheriffs it should be held even more widely. One can therefore understand why Sheriffs are not more easily disposed to grant an FBO in circumstances where the anticipated degree of robustness has not been forthcoming. Certainly there have been occasions where they have been granted *ex proprio motu*, but one Sheriff interviewed in December 2010 indicated that 'if you're suddenly confronted by one of these [FBO] applications in a busy court, well, a bit of guidance wouldn't go amiss'. The absence of joined-up thinking on the part of the police and the Crown is more likely to strike the court as an indication that an FBO is not considered necessary by them, rather than act as an incentive to act unilaterally.

The court's unwillingness to impose an FBO in *Wallace* remains difficult to reconcile with the requirements of s. 51(3) and the *Walls* guidance, but the following argument can be advanced: in *Wallace*, the Crown had accepted there had been no intent to injure (although the defendant's behaviour was clearly culpable and reckless) and a £25,000 compensation order clearly reflects the severity of the incident because a custodial sentence would have been the only realistic alternative. But the guilty plea had been tendered, and accepted, on the basis that there had been no intent to injure. In those circumstances, perhaps the Sheriff was of the opinion that a FBO imposed in response to a fleeting act of stupidity, no matter how breathtaking the act or how serious its consequences, could not help reduce football-related violence or disorder as s. 51(3) demands. But that said, Peter Wallace had a previous conviction for a football-related offence, and in the light of *Walls* his previous conviction alone should have established the link between the offence and the s. 51(3) requirement. Perhaps the fact that the incident took place some time after the match, on public transport and a considerable distance from the ground, weighed more heavily on the Sheriff's mind than it should; but even allowing for the benefit of post-*Walls* hindsight and the most generous interpretation of the law and the facts, it is not an easy decision to explain.

CONCLUSIONS

While legal practitioners and football officials may hold conflicting views as to the substance of sectarian conflict and discrimination in broader Scottish society, they have all acknowledged the need to prevent sectarian disorder within the specific confines of Scottish football. Given that degree of common ground, the failure to successfully progress sectarian-related FBO applications clearly had more to do with weaknesses in how the legislation was phrased, or how it was implemented and resourced, than with outright hostility or misunderstanding. The lack of attempts to adapt the legislation to the particularities of the Scottish context meant that it was predominantly concerned with the folk-devil of the violent 'English-style' football hooligan rather than the ninety-minute bigot. When applications did reach the courtroom, there was no evidence to suggest that any unwillingness on the part of the Sheriffs to grant FBOs can be definitively ascribed either to inadequate judicial training or judicial resistance. Rather, there was a widely held perception that the language of the law had to be approached with caution in the context of what was a draconian sanction. A measure which smacked of an obligatory punishment would never pass muster with the Scottish judiciary (for whom the concept of mandatory sentencing is entirely alien); and the slippery English judicial logic of *Gough* and other cases – to the effect that hybrid sanctions are not punishments at all but merely preventative measures that can be imposed without a great deal of reflection – would always excite suspicion among those wary of anything which smacked of 'an English Act with a kilt on' (to quote one of the Sheriffs interviewed in February 2011). Faced with the judicial obligation to do justice on the merits in every individual case, those who would advocate the widespread imposition of FBOs in Scotland are likely to remain disappointed and, at a time when there is support for a Europe-wide approach to the exclusion of 'known or potential trouble-makers' (Council of Europe 1985: Article 3(4)(d)), the risks of adopting a one-size-fits-all approach to superficially similar offences that occur in jurisdictions with their own sporting cultures and judicial thinking should not be disregarded.

The March 2011 match between Celtic and Rangers[13] precipitated yet more media comment and political debate and the knee-jerk passing of the Offensive Behaviour at Football and Threatening Communications (Scotland) Act 2012,[14] which added nothing new to the existing law on offences committed at football grounds but led to more resources being invested in policing and the preparation of FBO applications. In the immediate aftermath of that game, there were several occasions when banning orders were imposed, and imposed for longer, in circumstances where, prior to March 2011, they might not have been imposed at all or would have been of much shorter duration.[15] As a harbinger of that development, one of the Sheriffs interviewed in January 2011 had commented that:

> We're not like academics – we don't live in ivory towers. We read the papers and we know what goes on in the real world. If something were to happen which made us feel there was a greater urgency for banning orders, you would see more of them.

That match may turn out to be the 'something happening' that the proponents of banning orders must have longed for – a one-off event, perhaps akin to the England riots of August 2011, which prompted a sea-change in judicial thinking and, just as the England riots precipitated sentences comfortably outside the definitive guideline ranges (Roberts 2012), led the Sheriffs to see beyond the legislation's drafting even to the extent of imposing FBOs in cases where their use was not merely unexpected but was manifestly inappropriate and needed to be rectified on appeal.[16] Maybe judicial responses to 'that' match will ultimately be seen as far more significant than the new legislation, the increased resources for the banning order industry, the more robust requests for FBOs in those cases that did reach the courts or Rangers' well-documented demotion to the lowest level of the Scottish professional game; and while those recent cases are no more than *sotto voce* indications of the judiciary responding differently in the wake of this particularly discrediting incident, when there are more decisions to analyse there will certainly be merit in considering whether this was indeed just a passing judicial phase. If it was not, there will be a need to reconsider our understanding of how popular and political discourse – which in this case emanated from what was a largely media-driven debate – is capable of influencing the juridical field's collective interpretations of the language of law.

NOTES

1. BBC *Panorama* programme, 'Scotland's Secret Shame', broadcast 27 February 2005. Transcript available at http://news.bbc.co.uk/nol/shared/spl/hi/programmes/panorama/ transcripts/scotlandssecretshame.txt (last accessed 16 October 2012).
2. This hypothesis was fairly public, with for instance *The Scotsman* reporting on 13 April 2009 that nine out of ten FBO applications made by the police were being turned down by the courts ('Nine in ten thugs dodge stadium ban').
3. In spite of its name, the UK Football Policing Unit only supports police forces in England and Wales.
4. James and Pearson (2006) would argue that these arrangements artificially inflate the number of FBOs issued in England and Wales and led to the widespread application of FBOs on the basis of flimsy and circumstantial evidence.
5. Though one might legitimately argue that sectarian provocation within the context of a heated Old Firm encounter should be categorised as 'reckless conduct'.
6. In addition to legally enforceable FBOs, clubs could themselves issue their own club bans preventing fans from attending games played at home, and these could range from a single-match ban to a lifetime ban.
7. For example, in December 2011 UEFA fined Celtic £12,700 for its fans' pro-IRA chants at a Europa League match (http://www.bbc.co.uk/sport/0/football/16137728, last accessed 28 October 2012). One month later, fans displayed a banner critical of the governing body ('Fuck UEFA') at another Europa League match, resulting in a further fine. That first fine was roughly in line with those imposed by UEFA in respect of racist chanting, but (as a useful indicator of where UEFA's priorities lie) it was less than half that imposed on a club whose players had returned to the pitch thirty seconds late after the half-time interval (http://www.bbc.co.uk/sport/0/football/19975032, last accessed 28 October 2012).
8. See http://www.bbc.co.uk/news/uk-scotland-north-east-orkney-shetland-11084526 (last accessed 16 October 2012).
9. (2) Instead of or in addition to any sentence which it could impose, the court . . . may, if satisfied as to the matters mentioned in subsection (3), make a football banning order against the person.
   (3) Those matters are—
   (a) that the offence was one to which subsection (4) applies; and

(b) that there are reasonable grounds to believe that making the football banning order would help to prevent violence or disorder at or in connection with any football matches.

(4) This subsection applies to an offence if—

(a) the offence involved the person who committed it engaging in violence or disorder; and

(b) the offence related to a football match.

. . .

(6) For the purpose of subsection (4)(b), an offence relates to a football match if it is committed—

(a) at a football match or while the person committing it is entering or leaving (or trying to enter or leave) the ground;

(b) on a journey to or from a football match; or

(c) otherwise, where it appears to the court from all the circumstances that the offence is motivated (wholly or partly) by a football match.

10. For the purposes of this section, an offence is aggravated by religious prejudice if—

(a) at the time of committing the offence or immediately before or after doing so, the offender evinces towards the victim (if any) of the offence malice and ill-will based on the victim's membership (or presumed membership) of a religious group, or of a social or cultural group with a perceived religious affiliation; or

(b) the offence is motivated (wholly or partly) by malice and ill-will towards members of a religious group, or of a social or cultural group with a perceived religious affiliation, based on their membership of that group.

(3) Where this section applies, the court must take the aggravation into account in determining the appropriate sentence . . .

11. An offence is racially aggravated for the purposes of this section if—

(a) at the time of committing the offence, or immediately before or after doing so, the offender evinces towards the victim (if any) of the offence malice and ill-will based on the victim's membership (or presumed membership) of a racial group; or

(b) the offence is motivated (wholly or partly) by malice and ill-will towards members of a racial group based on their membership of that group.

12. http://news.bbc.co.uk/1/hi/scotland/glasgow_and_west/7786133.stm (last accessed 16 October 2012).

13. See http://www.bbc.co.uk/news/uk-scotland-glasgow-west-12664550 (last accessed 16 October 2012).

14. For full details of the bill, see http://www.scottish.parliament.uk/parliamentarybusiness/Bills/29678.aspx (last accessed 24 January 2013).

15. See, for example, http://www.bbc.co.uk/news/uk-scotland-glasgow-west-13361478 and http://www.bbc.co.uk/news/uk-scotland-glasgow-west-15333744 (last accessed 16 October 2012).

16. See http://www.bbc.co.uk/news/uk-scotland-north-east-orkney-shetland-20094243 (last accessed 28 October 2012).

REFERENCES

Bebber, B. (2012), *Violence and Racism in Football: Politics and Cultural Conflict in British Society 1968–1998*, London: Pickering and Chatto.

Bradley, J. M. (1995), *Ethnic and Religious Identity in Modern Scotland: Culture, Politics and Football*, Aldershot: Avebury.

Bruce, S., Glendinning, A., Paterson, I. and Rosie, M. (2004), *Sectarianism in Scotland*, Edinburgh: Edinburgh University Press.

Coalter, F. (1985), 'Crowd behaviour at football matches: a study in Scotland', *Leisure Studies*, 4: 1, 111–17.

Council of Europe (1985), *European Convention on Spectator Violence and Misbehaviour at Football Sports Events and in Particular at Football Matches*, http://www.coe.int/t/dg4/sport/Source/CONV_2009_120_EN.pdf (last accessed 16 October 2012).

Davies, A. (2006), 'Football and Sectarianism in Glasgow during the 1920s and 1930s', *Irish Historical Studies*, 35: 138, 200–19.

Devine, T. M. (ed.) (2000), *Scotland's Shame: bigotry and sectarianism in modern Scotland*, Edinburgh: Mainstream.

Flint, J. (2008), 'Governing Sectarianism in Scotland', *Scottish Affairs*, 63: Spring, 107–24.

Flint, J. and Powell, R. (2011), '"They Sing That Song": Sectarianism and Conduct in the Informalised Spaces of Scottish Football', in D. Bursey (ed.), *Race, Ethnicity and Football: Persistent Debates and Emerging Issues*, London: Routledge, pp. 191–204.

Gough v. The Chief Constable of Derbyshire [2002] QB 1213.

Hamilton-Smith, N., Bradford, B., Hopkins, M., Kurland, J., Lightowler, C., McArdle, D. and Tilley, N. (2011), *An Evaluation of Football Banning Orders in Scotland*, Edinburgh: Scottish Government, http://www.scotland.gov.uk/Resource/Doc/354566/0119713.pdf (last accessed 16 October 2012).

Hamilton-Smith, N. and Hopkins, M. (2012), 'The transfer of English legislation to the Scottish context: Lessons from the implementation of the Football Banning Order in Scotland', *Criminology and Criminal Justice*. Advance publication 13 June 2012, doi: 10.1177/1748895812447083.

Howe, R. (2010), 'Sectarianism': Presentation to the ACPOS Match Commander Training Course, Scottish Police College, 21 August 2010.

James, M. and Pearson, G. (2006), 'Football Banning Orders: Analysing Their Use in Court', *Journal of Criminal Law*, 70: 6, 509–30.

Kelly, E. (2003), 'Challenging Sectarianism in Scotland: The Prism of Racism', *Scottish Affairs*, 42: Winter, 35–56.

Kelly, J. (2011), '"Sectarianism" and Scottish Football: Critical Reflections on Dominant Discourse and Media Commentary', *International Review for the Sociology of Sport*, 46: 4, 418–35.

Moorehouse, H. F. (2006), *Consultation with Football Supporters on Problems of Sectarianism within Scottish Football: A Report to the Scottish Executive*, Glasgow: University of Glasgow.

Pearson, G. (2002), 'A Cure Worse than the Disease?', *Entertainment Law*, 1: 2, 92–102.

Pearson, G. (2012), *An Ethnography of Football Fans*, Manchester: Manchester University Press.

Poulton, E. (2007), 'English Media Representation of Football-related Disorder: "Brutal, Short-hand and Simplifying"?', *Sport in Society: Cultures, Commerce, Media, Politics*, 8: 1, 27–47.

Redhead, S. (1995), *Unpopular Cultures: The Birth of Law and Popular Culture*, Manchester: Manchester University Press.

Roberts, J. (2012), 'Points of Departure: Reflections on Sentencing outside the Definitive Guidelines Ranges', *Criminal Law Review*, 6, 439–48.

Scottish Education Department (1977), *Report of the Working Group on Football Crowd Behaviour*, Edinburgh: HMSO.

Scottish Executive (2006), *Sectarianism: Action Plan on Tackling Sectarianism in Scotland*, Edinburgh: Scottish Executive.

Stott, C. and Pearson, G. (2006), 'Football Banning Orders: Proportionality and Public Order', *Howard Journal of Criminal Justice*, 40: 3, 241–54.

Stott, C. and Pearson, G. (2008), *Football Hooliganism: Policing and the War on the 'English Disease'*, London: Pennant Books.

Squires, P. (ed.) (2008), *ASBO Nation: the criminalisation of nuisance*, Bristol: Policy Press.

Vice, S. (1998), *Introducing Bakhtin*, Manchester: Manchester University Press.

Waiton, S. (2012), *Snobs' Law: Criminalising Football Fans in an Age of Intolerance*, Take A Liberty (Scotland).

10 He's Back! But Scotland's National Demon Never Left: Revisiting Media Representations of Neil Lennon and Narratives of Bigotry

Irene A. Reid

INTRODUCTION: REVISITING NARRATIVES OF A SCOTTISH SOCCER VILLAIN

The 2010–11 Scottish football season attracted considerable attention among policy-makers and a range of civic organisations in Scotland. Some of the issues that emerged during the season provided the catalyst for the Scottish Government's decision to introduce the Offensive Behaviour at Football and Threatening Communications (Scotland) Act 2012, considered elsewhere in this collection. This chapter concentrates on a different aspect of the public discourse associated with some of these football-related incidents. Specifically, it explores how some media narratives may be partially culpable in contributing to particular manifestations of the ethno-religious bigotry that is Scotland's national demon.

Neil Lennon, manager of Celtic FC, was the prominent figure from the football community who featured in media accounts of a number of incidents that cast a shadow over Scotland during 2010–11. These included incidents where Lennon was critical of match referees and was in turn criticised for becoming involved in bellicose confrontations with match officials and the coaching staff and players of other clubs. Lennon himself, however, was the target of verbal abuse, physical intimidation and death threats underscored by ethno-religious intolerance. Additionally, between January and May 2011 Lennon was the intended recipient of packages that contained either bullets or explosive devices, although the vigilance of postal staff ensured these packages were not delivered. The perpetrators of this abuse and violent intimidation were condemned from across the spectrum of political and civic society in Scotland. The prejudice directed towards Lennon and others connected to Celtic FC led to the acknowledgement that 'Sectarian bigotry remains in Scottish society, even if it is mostly confined to certain areas and social classes' (Leader column, *The Express*, 19 May 2011: 12).

These were not new experiences for Neil Lennon in Scotland. As a player with Celtic FC between 2000 and 2007, Lennon was the target of sectarian abuse at football grounds around the country; he had also been verbally abused and physically attacked while undertaking his domestic and social routines in Glasgow. A critique of media representations of Neil Lennon during his playing career with Celtic FC recognised the complexity of the narratives that depicted Lennon as a soccer villain (Reid 2006, 2008). This critique also argued that representations of Lennon in these narratives revealed to Scotland its national demon: the persistence of an underlying intolerance towards ethno-religious difference, directed against those in Scotland who have Irishness and Catholic faith as part of their different identity and which coalesce around Celtic FC. This, of course, was not a new argument. A number of academics and various social and political commentators have raised concerns about the bigotry experienced by many of the Irish Catholic diaspora in Scotland (Bradley 2004, 2006a, 2006b, 2009; Finn 1991, 1999; Kelly 2011).

This chapter develops this critique of media discourses that fuse around Lennon, Celtic FC and Irishness in Scotland. In particular, it probes coverage of Lennon's return to Celtic as a coach in April 2008, reports concerning his involvement in an angry confrontation with Rangers' then assistant manager Ally McCoist, and representations of Lennon relating to certain sectarian-fuelled events during the early months of 2011. Two familiar themes re-emerged: first, Lennon was portrayed as the villain of Scottish football; and second, in some sections of the press, a veil of insensibility was cast over the problem of ethnic and religious intolerance in Scottish society.

READING SPORT CRITICALLY

This chapter is grounded in a conceptual framework that underpins discourse analysis. Scholars who conduct critical sociological analysis of media sport often employ this approach, highlighting how ideologies concerning gender, nationhood, racism and ethnicity embedded in wider society are manifest through sport (Bruce 2004; Bolsmann and Parker 2007; Falcous 2007; Jackson 1998; Spencer 2004). An important principle underpins this approach: the narratives that surround sport 'offer unique points of access to the constitutive meanings and power relations of the larger worlds we inhabit' (McDonald and Birrell 1999: 283). In critical discourse analysis, all narratives are inter-textual, therefore the communication of a particular event is constructed, interpreted, given meaning and understood in the context of pre-existing narratives, experiences and knowledge (Fairclough 1995; Riggins 1997). This is important, as McDonald and Birrell (1999: 293) attest:

> History does not start with the incident, although narratives of it might. An incident is often the effect of pre-existing discourses even while it shapes and

continues new ones. It is impossible to demarcate the incident (in which something 'happened') from narratives (versions or accounts of 'what happened').

In critical discourse analysis, observations of journalists and the views of other contributors to media narratives are understood not to be neutral. That is not to say that media creates the bigotry or other forms of intolerance, or that media personnel deliberately promote intolerant views in society. However, as Kelly (2011: 425) contends, 'a dysconscious sectarianism' embedded in the codes and meanings of a society means 'many . . . press actors may be consciously unaware of the ideologically laden nature' of their constructed narratives concerning football, ethnicity and religion. As a social institution the media communicates the 'social and cultural goings-on' (Fairclough 1995: 57) of the society and cultural practices such as football that are part of it. The media therefore reinforces dominant ideologies through 'the sets of practices and discourses by which knowledge is constructed in the media not the personal inclinations of media workers' (Bruce 2004: 863; see also Crawford in this volume). The knowledge, language and tone used and the presence or absence of alternative perspectives are crucial elements in communicating particular events, and in accepting – or denying – the persistence of racism and other forms of discrimination (Drew 2011).

HE'S BACK! LENNON RETURNS TO PARADISE

Neil Lennon played for Celtic FC between December 2000 and May 2007. In June 2007 he joined Nottingham Forest as a player, then in January 2008 he moved to Wycombe Wanderers where another former Celtic player, Paul Lambert, was manager. Aged thirty-six in June 2007, Lennon was in the twilight of his career as a professional footballer, and had spoken of his interest in coaching or management when he retired as a player. Lennon returned to Celtic on 3 April 2008 as a coach within the management team headed by Gordon Strachan. This was unexpected, but the club and the press emphasised he was there in a 'looking, learning and advisory capacity' (Cully 2008: 58).

Media reaction to Lennon's unexpected return to Celtic FC was generally positive. Four themes dominated the reports: Lennon's standing among supporters and within the club marked him as a Celtic man, one of the Bhoys; his charismatic personality and leadership qualities; his controversial status as soccer's villain; and his potential as a future manager of the club. The narrative reminded readers that Celtic was the 'one true love' of the Irishman (Wilson 2008: 99); *The Herald* noted Lennon was 'steeped in success and Celtic tradition' (Broadfoot 2008: 4) and many newspapers picked up his quote that Celtic was the place 'where my heart lies' (Hannah 2008). Cutting through these themes, certain media rituals and stylistic norms of production around Scottish football were evident such as contrived headlines, hyperbole, and the views and opinions of players (former and current) and the cadre of football journalists who pronounced on the reasons for and merits of the return of 'Lenny . . . a Sellick Mind Reader' (Waddell 2008: 70).

Woven through the narratives were media allusions to public perceptions of the former player's aggressive and provocative personality and someone who courted trouble – Scottish football's villain. Lennon was the 'fiery Irishman' who was never far from controversy (McConnell 2008: 58), and 'a man who could not have avoided the thick of the action if he tried' (Broadfoot 2008: 4; also Campbell 2008: 53; Leckie 2008). As the next section demonstrates, old narratives of Lennon as an aggressive and provocative character featured prominently in Scottish press coverage of one incident in 2011 where Lennon and McCoist were central.

LENNON: THE RETURN OF SOCCER'S VILLAIN?

In March 2010, twenty months after returning to Celtic, Neil Lennon became manager of the club. His first full season as manager proved turbulent. Through the media, football journalists and some of his fellow managers rebuked Lennon and his club for their public disapprobation of Scottish football authorities. On some occasions, Lennon's animated behaviour on the touchline during matches was also criticised, particularly an angry but brief altercation with Rangers' assistant coach Ally McCoist at the end of a match between Celtic and Rangers.

On Wednesday, 2 March 2011 Celtic FC and Glasgow Rangers met at Celtic Park in a replay of their fifth round tie in the Scottish Cup. The match, the fifth between the two clubs since the season began in August 2010, was the fourth fixture between the clubs in an eight-week period that started on 2 January. The concentration of fixtures between the clubs in a short period was unusual even with the limited number of teams in the top tier of Scottish football. Strathclyde Police, the force responsible for policing the fixtures, had made known some of its concerns about increasing incidents of public disorder and domestic violence that appeared to coincide with the fixtures.

Between each match, the press followed its ritual pattern of amplifying incidents that occurred during matches. Two issues received particular attention: the friction developing between Celtic's captain Scott Brown and Rangers' new loan signing El-Hadji Diouf (Keevins 2011a: 8; Wilson 2011a: 4); and a claim by Diouf that Lennon had verbally abused him (Jackson 2011a: 52, 51; Jordan 2011: 67). However, some papers hinted at a growing tension between the management and coaching teams of the two clubs. Offering his verdict on the Scottish Cup tie at Ibrox (6 February), *Daily Record* journalist David McCarthy (2011: 2–3) compared the reactions during the match of McCoist and Lennon. He noted that with McCoist poised to become Rangers' manager at the end of the season, 'next term it promises to be some battle between two men who live and breathe their clubs'. The anticipated battle may have referred to tactics, team formations and game strategies but it took a literal form three weeks later when the teams met at Celtic Park in the Cup-tie replay.

Celtic won the Scottish Cup replay (1–0) on 2 March. A variety of heated incidents punctuated the match, but the confrontation between Lennon and McCoist dominated newspapers for several days after the match. Both men had been involved in heated exchanges during the game, notably during the first half when Diouf had remonstrated aggressively with the fourth official and then with the Celtic manager (McGowan 2011: 78, 79; Grant 2011a: 2; Jackson 2011b: 70–1). At the end of the match, Lennon and McCoist approached each other to shake hands as is customary in sports contests. The scene showed both men initially in an amicable interaction but this changed suddenly; McCoist leaned forward and said something to Lennon, whose facial expression and body language turned to anger. Lennon pulled back from the handshake, and there followed some animated gesticulating and bellicose verbal interaction. As was the case during the first-half touchline incident, other members of each club's coaching staff intervened to ensure the incident did not become more serious; the confrontation was over in a few seconds, and as one journalist reported, 'No punches were thrown between Lennon and McCoist' (Grant 2011b: 2).

The reaction in the press was in part understandable, but also predictable. The Chief Executive of the Scottish Football Association Stewart Regan condemned the 'inflammatory and irresponsible behaviour' of players and members of both clubs' management teams (cited in Campsie 2011: 1). Newspapers reproduced still images of the confrontation in the main news sections and sports section for several days after the match. The images served to reinforce the pejorative narrative that developed over several days in which the Celtic manager was depicted less favourably than McCoist. Although not included here, it is worth noting that in each reproduction cameras captured Neil Lennon's face, while McCoist was pictured from behind. The repetitive reproduction of this image over a number of days supported the media-constructed narrative that Lennon was more culpable than Rangers' assistant manager. Under images of the incident in the *Daily Record* the back page referred to 'a furious reaction' from Lennon (Ralston 2011: 71), while its front page claimed 'words were exchanged and Lennon suddenly snarled and launched himself at McCoist' (McGivern 2011: 1, 7). The *Daily Mail* referred to 'a brawl' (Sports Mail Comment, 2011: 80), and in *The Herald* Michael Grant opined that Lennon 'reacted venomously' (2011c: 2). One newspaper in particular, the tabloid *Daily Record*, ran a series of sensational headlines that framed a narrative of 'BENCH WARFARE' between the two clubs. In this framework it was alleged 'the REAL reason McCoist lost the plot' was because of alleged verbal attacks by the Celtic manager on certain Rangers' players' (Jackson 2011c: 78).

A central technique in constructing Lennon as the villain is the incorporation of other football people whose views are deemed 'rational' while others' views are constructed as irrational by decontextualising the information offered (Finn 2000). For instance, Rangers manager Walter Smith was represented as a voice of reason and rationality, claiming McCoist 'felt Neil Lennon was being a bit aggressive with a Rangers player' (cited in McGowan 2011: 79). In another example, former Celtic player and manager Murdo MacLeod (2011: 75) suggested Lennon 'still possesses a player mentality' but 'he has to learn to calm down, stop getting involved and keep his emotions in check'. Others shared MacLeod's view and they may have been legitimate. However, in the corresponding column former Rangers and England player Mark Hateley (2011: 74) was more critical of Lennon. Despite his opening caveat his comments contributed to the evolving media narrative that cast Lennon as the villain:

> What I'm about to say has nothing to do with my previous playing partnership with Alistair [McCoist] or my past association with Rangers as one of Walter Smith's squad. Neil Lennon's actions continue to leave me gobsmacked. He appears not to have learned from previous touchline confrontations . . . Alistair must have been incensed about something to react the way he did. I've always known him to be cool, calm and focused. And I can never remember him confronting anyone in the manner he was adopting with Neil.

A feature of the media's constructed narratives about sports people is its capacity to 'prioritize, personalize and sensationalize characters' and events associated with them (Lines 2001: 285). This was evident in the press accounts surrounding the altercation between Lennon and McCoist in March 2011. Indeed, some sports journalists in Scotland are aware of the potential power of the media in this respect; as Hugh MacDonald (2011: 4) noted, 'there is a danger that sports writers can be pious when addressing matters that arise out of an atmosphere they are not blameless in creating'. This potential to influence tensions that persist around the Old Firm was also acknowledged by James Traynor who briefly reflected on the hypocrisy of the media craving 'controversy' but then condemning it 'when the Old Firm deliver' (2011: 50, 51). The purpose of this media technique may be to maximise audience attention, but this process is neither neutral nor without potentially serious consequences.

SCOTLAND'S NATIONAL DEMON NEVER LEFT

One issue was largely absent from media narratives about Neil Lennon's return to Glasgow in 2008 and subsequently his appointment as manager; his recurring experience of abuse – verbal and physical – fuelled by ethno-religious intolerance during his time as a Celtic player (Lennon 2006a). It is, however, apposite to revisit Neil Lennon's own reflections about the bigotry he experienced in Scotland as a Celtic player:

> Now the bigotry thing is not going to go away it's going to be here a long time after I'm gone but what I have been is an Irish Catholic who has been very, very high profile . . .
>   Some people say I bring it on myself, it's the image I portray on the pitch. Maybe it is to a certain extent but to me that's cowardly journalism and they're not getting to the root of the problem really. If I go away they'll just sweep it under the carpet and carry on as if I didn't play here for the last 5 years, but it'll stay with me. (Lennon, 2006b)[1]

One report from 3 April 2008, the day Celtic announced Lennon's return to the club, did highlight the problem. In *The Herald*, political editor Douglas Fraser (2008:

7) reported that 'former Labour First Minister' Jack McConnell had criticised his successor Alex Salmond (Scottish National Party) for complacency about sectarianism (Fraser 2008: 7). McConnell raised the matter 'in the Scottish Parliament' after 'Celtic coach Neil Lennon was knocked unconscious by attackers in Glasgow after the Old Firm match at the weekend', and 'Rangers player Nacho Novo had a guard placed on his home after critics posted his address on an internet site, as an incitement to others'.[2] The attack on Lennon was mentioned by Spiers (April 2011) but other Scottish newspapers did not comment on McConnell's criticism of Salmond, nor the incident involving Lennon.

It is worth noting that Neil Lennon's experience of bigotry in Scotland is not an isolated problem for one individual. Two young footballers, Aiden McGeady and James McCarthy (formerly of Celtic and Hamilton respectively), were verbally abused at football grounds around Scotland after each confirmed his decision to play international football for Ireland, rather than Scotland; both were Scots-born third-generation Irish (Bradley 2009, 2011). In April 2011, packages containing viable explosive devices addressed to Paul McBride QC and Trish Godman, a Labour Member of the Scottish Parliament between 1999 and 2011, and Glasgow-based republican organisation *Cairde na hÉireann* were intercepted by mail staff (Forsyth 2011: 7; Marshall 2011: 9; Wilson 2011b). Godman, a Celtic supporter, had worn a Celtic top on her last day as an MSP; McBride, a Catholic, who also supported the club, had represented Celtic FC and some of its staff, including Lennon, in relation to SFA disciplinary matters. During this period the press also reported a live bullet was sent to Cardinal Keith O'Brien, Archbishop of St Andrews and Edinburgh, at the time of the Papal visit to Scotland and England in September 2010 (Hamilton 2011). Others who do not have a public profile but whose Irish ethnicity and Catholic religion marks their social identity have also reflected on their experience of bigotry in Scotland (see, for example, Bradley 2006b; Ferns 2004; Ferrie 2004; Minogue 2009; Walls and Williams 2003). The incidents raise the question of whether Celtic, Irishness, Catholicism or republicanism or a combination of some of these is the target of hatred. They also reveal that bigotry 'is more than a football issue' (Wilson 2011b: 2). The intolerance is a manifestation of a particular social malaise that is 'Scotland's shame' (MacMillan 2000). As James MacMillan attests, 'even when it is not particularly malign' this remains 'a significant element of Scottish culture' (2000: 15, 16; see the chapters by Rosie and Waiton for a counter-argument).

We might presume that in reflecting on his previous experiences in 2006, Neil Lennon did not have some prophetic vision of the future. Rather, in considering how media narratives had represented him and the abuse he had encountered as a player and private citizen in Scotland Lennon pointed to two mechanisms that contribute to the processes by which the media can be culpable in reproducing discourses that sustain 'sleep-walking bigotry' (MacMillan 2000: 15). Specifically, Lennon noted how the media blamed him – at least in part – for the abuse and ethno-religious intolerance he received, and he suggested the underlying issue was taboo. These rituals of media coverage illustrate two mechanisms in public discourse that reinforce and naturalise dominant ideological systems of 'othering' to sustain intolerance. They are part of the process by which certain meanings and knowledge associated with certain social groups and ideas become dominant and natural, while alternative explanations are marginalised and undermined (Riggins 1997).

IT'S NOT OUR PROBLEM: TECHNIQUES TO DENY AND DEFLECT BIGOTRY

Previous analyses have highlighted the presence of at least four techniques in public discourses associated with bigotry in Scotland (Bradley 2009, 2011; Gallagher 2000; Finn 2000; Kelly 2011; Reid 2008). These are particularly apparent when the issue of ethno-religious bigotry against the Irish Catholic diaspora coalesces around football, notably individuals and communities associated with Celtic FC. First, the narratives simply deny or ignore the problem. Second, the prejudice is acknowledged but its presence is contained by suggesting that perpetrators of such prejudice are aberrant individuals who are part of a minority in the west of Scotland. This includes the assertion that bigotry in Scotland is football's problem, and in particular restricted to the Old Firm. Third, the narratives acknowledge the intolerance but deflect blame back to the individual and to others who speak out. Fourth, accusations of intolerance are rejected, but complainants and accusers are themselves accused of intolerance. These techniques are not particular to public discourses denying intolerance in Scotland. They are embedded in discourses associated with forms of racism and othering in many other nations (Jackson 1998; King 1997; Spencer 2004). They operate 'subtly, covertly and insidiously' (Levine 1988: 8, cited in Jackson 2001: 128) in conjunction with a whole system of ideas, values, myths and practices to deflect and neutralise allegations of racism and sustain the social power of a particular community. Collectively they contribute to the operation of an anti-sociological imagination within media reporting that denies the problems encountered by particular individuals are evidence of a wider social issue.

During spring 2011 some of these techniques were evident once again in press reports that Lennon was the target of verbal abuse and death threats. These incidents often arose soon after the controversial Old Firm matches of the period, and therefore the media was able to deflect attention and contain the problem as one particular to football, or associated with other communities. For example, in January 2011 mail staff in Northern Ireland intercepted three packages containing bullets. One package was addressed to Neil Lennon, and each of the other two to Niall McGinn and Paddy McCourt, Celtic players also from Northern Ireland and Catholic (Wilkie 2011: 4; Brown 2011: 23). Although the main news pages of newspapers deplored the incidents, some of the sports pages countered their revulsion with what appeared to be an attempt to play down the matter. One journalist referred to this as 'the darker side of being an Old Firm figure' (MacFarlane 2011: 62), implying it was expected, and a supporters' hotline column suggested, 'The best antidote is humour' since this was the behaviour of 'idiots' who were 'fellow countrymen' of the three Celtic employees (Keevins 2011b: 46).

There was also some suggestion in the media narratives that Lennon himself was to blame: 'a magnet' for aggravation because he chose to live and socialise in Glasgow (Alexander 2011: 6) and 'thrives on confrontation' (Clark 2011: 63). The *News of the World* provided a more irresponsible piece of journalism concerning the incident. It claimed the bullets were sent by members of the Ulster Defence Association (UDA) because through the modern social communication forum 'Twitter' Lennon allegedly called Rangers' Kyle Lafferty 'a lump of wood' after the Old Firm match at Ibrox on 2 January (McKendry 2011a: 10–11). In January 2011, since the packages were sent from and intercepted in Northern Ireland, the media narratives deflected the problem from Scotland. This particular sensationalised report perhaps overlooked what would evolve and escalate.

Throughout January and February reports emerged in the press of other abuse and violent threats. Hate-fuelled social network groups appeared on the Facebook site where anonymous individuals expressed their objective to 'Kill Neil' (Carson 2011: 20; Dickson 2011: 18) or branded him 'dead man walking' (Silvester 2011: 1, 4). The sites were closed after politicians and ordinary Celtic supporters complained. However, Facebook's owners initially rejected calls to remove these communication groups because in their view 'the comments do not represent a credible intention to kill Lennon' and dismissed them as 'nothing more than "jokey" and "pub talk"' (Rainey 2011: 16). Other reported incidents included verbal abuse from two adult men directed at Lennon, his partner and son as they left a Glasgow theatre (Duffy 2011: 1, 12), and it was reported their Glasgow home was placed under police security on the day of the Scottish Cup tie at Ibrox (McKendry 2011b: 7; McAulay 2011: 9). In February, reports appeared once again of alleged death threats issued by the UDA (Beattie 2011: 15; McGinty 2011: 9).

It was against this context that Lennon and his Rangers counterpart Ally McCoist had their public but brief altercation at Celtic Park on 2 March. Two days after the match, news emerged of 'A fresh threat' when staff at a postal sorting office in Ayrshire discovered 'a suspect package' addressed to Lennon (Grant 2011d: 1; Musson 2011: 1, 5). It was reported that the package was 'a hoax', but Celtic's Chief Executive Peter Lawwell confirmed the pressure the manager lived under, adding: 'No one in any walk of life should have to live their life in this way' (cited in Musson 2011: 5).

The violent threats and intimidation were condemned in the press in Scotland, but comment on the issues remained part of a muddling narrative. Ethno-religious bigotry was still contained within a discourse that framed it as a problem for the west of Scotland and football. To illustrate, one sports journalist suggested problems associated with policing and modifying behaviour at Old Firm games could be resolved more easily than the 'challenge' of 'tackling ubiquitous central belt bigotry and ignorance' (Grant 2011e: 20). At the same time, contributors to some sports pages persisted with a line that linked the Lennon–McCoist confrontation and blamed the Celtic manager for the ethno-religious bigotry. One contributor to a newspaper phone-column opined, 'Lennon has brought a large amount of hate back into Scottish football', while another criticised his 'venomous attitude' (cited Parks 2011: 49).

Journalists also reworked the narrative patterns that meld the offences with suggestions that the Celtic manager is, in part, to blame. In *Scotland on Sunday* Tom English (2011: 10) acknowledged 'the hateful sentiment' behind the saga of 'bullets in the post . . . the apparent UDA death threats' and the suspect package. He continued, 'We have an image of Lennon as a street-fighter, as a guy who is unmoved by the sectarianism directed at him, who in some instances actually revels in it all.' Of course, it would be wrong to assert that any individual is without flaws, and Graham Spiers and Bill Edgar (2011: 10–11) pointed out that 'Lennon is no innocent'. They are, however, correct that 'something, surely, is amiss when a football figure' experiences what 'Lennon has suffered'. This begins to identify an important issue; that media narratives associated with football in Scotland can be a mirror to society.

CONCLUSIONS

A central element of Scotland's national myth is that it is inherently tolerant and egalitarian. The point argued here is that in certain circumstances the fusion of Irish ethnicity, religion and Celtic FC reflects to Scotland its national demon of intolerance. The official public discourse deplored the explicit intimidation of Neil Lennon in spring 2011. However, newspapers' sensationalised reporting of events and the use of certain common techniques to deny intolerance contain and limit knowledge and understanding of the deeper malaise. Once again a critique of the public narratives in 2011 has shown that while many in Scotland acknowledge the problem of ethno-religious bigotry, the media represented the issues in ways that personalise, demonise and sensationalise.

The centrality of Neil Lennon to incidents during the 2010–11 football season were in part the catalyst for anti-sectarian legislation in Scotland; this may be instructive. Journalist Andrew Smith pointed out the inadequacy of excuses that Neil Lennon's personality and identity are the cause of the abuse and intimidation he receives. Smith (2011: 19) asserted, 'This is baloney that deliberately fuses and confuses two separate issues.' He is, of course, correct, but in explaining his assertion Smith reiterates some of the same techniques used by other journalists by containing the problem in relation to particular groups and sections of society. The resurgence of explicit displays of ethno-religious bigotry confirmed that this particular form of racism, including denial of its presence, survives partially hidden from and unspoken of in public discourse

Reflecting on some of the events that occurred between January and March 2011, Spiers and Edgar (2011) asked Scotland an important question: 'What can be done to cure the prejudice and bigotry in our midst?' The answer, however, is complex, and although timely, revisiting narratives that pull together media representations of Neil Lennon and ethno-religious bigotry will not resolve this conundrum. The evidence considered here highlights once again that bigotry continues to exercise debate under certain circumstances. This of course is necessary if, as many hope, Scotland is to 'project an image of a bright, modern 21st century' society 'which has left the old days of sectarian division far behind' (McMillan 2011: 31; see Flint and Powell in this volume).

Hilliard (1994, cited in Kennedy and Hills 2009: 3) suggested there is an anti-sociological imagination in some media sports reporting. He asserted this protects 'the interests of those in power' and 'deflects attention away from political and social issues' (ibid., see a similar argument in Crawford's chapter). A sociological imagination is one that 'enables us to grasp history and biography and the relations between the two within society' (Mills 1959: 4). It is therefore important to be mindful in considering media narratives associated with Neil Lennon, Celtic FC and the Irish in Scotland, that the tribulations of one individual are not simply personal problems but a manifestation of a wider social malaise. If this sociological imagination is absent from media reporting of football-related events in Scotland, academic scholarship must continue to interrogate media narratives where the rituals and patterns of reporting conceal Scotland's ethno-religious demon.

NOTES

1. The series *A Tough Call*, BBC Radio Scotland, was presented by sports journalist Graham Spiers. At the time Spiers also worked for *The Herald* newspaper; the interview was the basis for an article published in *The Herald* on Saturday, 8 April 2006, the day before the radio programme was broadcast.
2. Spaniard Nacho Novo signed for Rangers from Dundee in July 2004, a few weeks after he failed to agree terms with Celtic. In October 2008 Novo spoke about death threats and malicious damage to his car and home and receiving threatening letters 'every time I face Celtic' (*Daily Telegraph* 2008). Neil Lennon stated 'everybody knows Nacho Novo's home came under attack and was patrolled by security guards' (Grant 2010; Keevins 2010). It is unclear why Novo was targeted; it is unlikely the abuse was due to ethno-religious prejudice comparable to Lennon's experience but there is no justifiable excuse for the intimidation of anyone.

REFERENCES

Alexander, D. (2011), 'Another charge is just a day in the life for Lennon; Aggravation has an odd way of finding Celtic manager', *The Sunday Times* Sport, 16 January.

Beattie, J. (2011), 'Lennon in death threat UDA in Lennon threats', *Daily Record*, 19 February.

Bolsmann, A. and Parker, A. (2007), 'Soccer, South Africa and celebrity status: Mark Fish, popular culture and the post-Apartheid state', *Soccer and Society*, 8: 1, 109–24.

Bradley, J. M. (ed.) (2004), *Celtic Minded: Essays on Religion, Politics, Society, Identity and Football*, Glendaruel: Argyll Publishing.

Bradley, J. M. (ed.) (2006a), *Celtic Minded 2: Essays on Celtic Football Culture and Identity*, Glendaruel: Argyll Publishing.

Bradley, J. M. (2006b), 'Sport and the contestation of ethnic identity: Football and Irishness in Scotland', *Journal of Ethnic and Migration Studies*, 32: 7, 1189–1208.

Bradley, J. M. (2009), 'The Great Irish Hunger, Celtic FC and Celtic supporters', in J. M. Bradley (ed.), *Celtic Minded 3: Essays on Religion, Politics, Society, Identity and Football*, Glendaruel: Argyll Publishing, pp. 9–50.

Bradley, J. M. (2011), 'In-groups, out-groups and contested identities in Scottish international football', *Sport in Society*, 14: 6, 818–32.

Broadfoot, D. (2008), 'Celtic insist it's no short-term fix as Lennon returns: Former captain all set for a new era at Celtic', *The Herald* Sport, 5 April.

Brown, C. (2011), 'Police confirm third suspect package sent to Celtic', *The Scotsman*, 12 January.

Bruce, T. (2004), 'Marking the boundaries of the "normal" in televised sports: the play-by-play of race', *Media, Culture & Society*, 26: 6, 861–79.

Campbell, I. (2008), 'Lenny: make a fight of it', *The Mirror*, 5 April.

Campsie, A. (2011), 'Call for Old Firm alcohol cup mayhem', *The Herald*, 4 March.

Carson, A. (2011), 'Vile yobs start 2nd Lennon death site', *The Sun*, 19 January, http://www. thesun.co.uk/sol/homepage/news/scottishnews/3359161/.html (last accessed 5 November 2012).

Clark, G. (2011), 'Factor or fiction? Lennon thrives on confrontation . . . but only because the man's such a perfectionist says Mjallby', *Scottish Star*, 16 January.

Cully, R (2008), 'Talking Celtic: Gordon Strachan reveals reasons behind the sensational homecoming of former Hoops captain Neil Lennon', *Evening Times*, 5 April.

Daily Record.co.uk (2011), 'Celtic manager Neil Lennon recieves [sic] death threat from loyalist paramilitaries', 19 February 2011, http://www.dailyrecord.co.uk/news/scottish-news/celtic-manager-neil-lennon-recieves-1095434 (last accessed 24 January 2013).

Daily Telegraph (2008), 'Rangers' Nacho Novo has received death threats from fans of Old Firm rivals Celtic', 5 October, http://www.telegraph.co.uk/sport/football/teams/rangers/3139867/ Rangers-Nacho-Novo-has-received-death-threats-from-fans-of-Old-Firm-rivals-Celtic-Football.html (last accessed 5 November 2012).

Dickson, B. (2011), 'Kill Neil facebook jibe; sick web threats to Celtic coach Lennon', *The Sun*, 17 January.

Drew, E. M. (2011), '"Coming to terms with our own racism": journalists grapple with the racialization of their news', *Critical Studies in Media Communications*, 28: 4, 353–73.

Duffy, G. (2011), 'Lenny's livid lover snaps at vile yobs; Lennon's girl lashes thugs', *The Sun*, 22 February.

English, T. (2011), 'It all comes to a head: Neil Lennon deals with constant intimidation, but he must also learn to control his temper', *Scotland on Sunday* Sport, 6 March.

Fairclough, N. (1995), *Media Discourse*, London: Hodder Education.

Falcous, M. (2007), 'The decolonizing national imaginary: promotional media constructions during the 2005 Lions Tour of Aotearoa New Zealand', *Journal of Sport & Social Issues*, 31: 4, 374–93.

Ferns, P. (2004), 'Let the people sing', in J. M. Bradley (ed.), *Celtic Minded: Essays on Religion, Politics, Society, Identity . . . and Football*, Glendaruel: Argyll Publishing, pp. 173–80.

Ferrie, S. (2004), 'The wearing of the green', in J. M. Bradley (ed.), *Celtic Minded: Essays on Religion, Politics, Society, Identity and Football*, Glendaruel: Argyll Publishing, pp. 181–8.

Finn, G. P. T. (1991), 'Racism, religion and social prejudice: Irish Catholic clubs, soccer and Scottish society – II social identities and conspiracy theories', *The International Journal of the History of Sport*, 8: 1, 370–91.

Finn, G. P. T. (1999), 'Scottish myopia and global prejudices, *Culture, Sport, Society*, 2: 3. 54–99.

Finn, G. P. T. (2000), 'A culture of prejudice: Promoting pluralism in Education for a change', in T. M. Devine (ed.), *Scotland's Shame: Bigotry and Sectarianism in Modern Scotland*, Edinburgh: Mainstream, pp. 53–88.

Forsyth, R. (2011), 'Lennon sent a "viable" explosive device; Police lift news blackout after packages were sent to Celtic manager, prominent QC and female MSP', *The Daily Telegraph (Scotland)*, 20 April 2011.

Fraser, D. (2008), 'McConnell blasts "weak" Salmond over sectarianism', *The Herald*, 3 April.

Gallagher, T. (2000), 'Holding a mirror to Scotia's face: Religious anxieties and their capacity to shake a post-unionist Scotland', in T. M. Devine (ed.), *Scotland's Shame: Bigotry and Sectarianism in Modern Scotland*, Edinburgh: Mainstream, pp. 41–52.

Grant, M. (2010), 'Morons, masochists and mistakes – just another day in the Old Firm madhouse for Neil Lennon', *The Herald* Sport, 27 October, http://www.heraldscotland.com/

sport/spl/celtic/morons-masochists-and-mistakes-just-another-day-in-the-old-firm-madhouse-for-neil-lennon-1.1064037 (last accessed 5 November 2012).

Grant, M. (2011a), 'Celtic follow script as Rangers lose plot', *The Herald* Sport, 3 March, http://www.heraldscotland.com/sport/spl/rangers/celtic-1-rangers-o-celtic-follow-script-as-rangers-lose-plot-1.1088218 (last accessed 5 November 2012).

Grant, M. (2011b), 'Grim repercussions from Parkhead's nuclear fall-out', *The Herald* Sport, 4 March 2011.

Grant, M. (2011c), 'After feeding frenzy, tentative steps are taken towards peace', *The Herald* Sport, 5 March, http://www.heraldscotland.com/sport/spl/celtic/after-feeding-frenzy-tentative-steps-are-taken-towards-peace-1.1088710 (last accessed 5 November 2012).

Grant, M. (2011d), 'Threats could force Lennon to quit in the summer, says Thompson', *The Herald* Sport, 5 March, http://www.heraldscotland.com/sport/spl/celtic/threats-could-force-lennon-to-quit-in-the-summer-says-thompson-1.1088713 (last accessed 5 November 2012).

Grant, M. (2011e), 'Taxpayers entitled to expect politicians to address Old Firm problem', *The Herald* Sport, 7 March.

Hateley, M. (2011), 'Everyone must calm down and start to show some respect for dugout rivals', *Daily Record*, 4 March.

Hamilton, T. (2011), 'Cardinal Keith O'Brien sent a live bullet in the post', *Daily Record*, 21 April.

Hannah, R. (2008), 'Coach Lenny', *The Scottish Sun*, 4 April.

Jackson, K. (2011a), 'Diouf: Lennon hurled abuse at me in half-time tunnel bust-up', *Daily Record*, 8 February.

Jackson, K. (2011b), 'Best of enemies', *Daily Record*, 3 March.

Jackson, K. (2011c), 'Bench warfare', *Daily Record*, 4 March 2011.

Jackson, S. J. (1998), 'A twist of race: Ben Johnson and the Canadian crisis of racial and national identity', *Sociology of Sport Journal*, 15: 1, 21–40.

Jackson. S. J. (2001), 'Exorcizing the ghost: Donovan Bailey, Ben Johnson and the politics of Canadian identity', *Media, Culture & Society*, 26: 1, 121–41.

Jordan, T. (2011), 'Scott ups the ante as Diouf hits out', *Evening Times*, 8 February.

Keevins, H. (2010), 'Madness and mayhem', *Daily Record*, 27 October.

Keevins, H. (2011a), 'Now for something completely Dioufrent', *Daily Record* The Winner, 7 February.

Keevins, H. (2011b), 'Hugh's Hotline', *Daily Record*, 11 January.

Kelly, J. (2011), '"Sectarianism" and Scottish football: Critical reflections on dominant discourse and press commentary', *International Review for the Sociology of Sport*, 46: 4, 418–35.

Kennedy, E. and Hills, L. (2009), *Sport Media and Society*, Oxford: Berg.

King, J. E. (1997), 'Dysconscious racism: ideology, identity and miseducation', in R. Delgado and J. Stefancic (eds), *Critical White Studies: Looking Behind the Mirror*, Philadelphia: Temple University Press, pp. 128–32.

Leckie, B. (2008), 'Neil Lennon', *The Scottish Sun*, 5 April.

Lennon, N. with M. Hannan (2006a), *Neil Lennon Man and Bhoy*, London: Harper Sport.

Lennon, N. (2006b), *A Tough Call: Neil Lennon*, BBC Radio Scotland, first broadcast on Sunday, 9 April 2006.

Leader column (2011), 'Society demands an end to religious hate crimes', *The Express*, 19 May.

Lines, G. (2001), 'Villains, fools or heroes? Sports stars as role models for young people', *Leisure Studies*, 20: 4, 285–303.

McAulay, R. (2011), 'Cop watch foils Lenny plot', *The Sun*, 7 February.

McCarthy, D. (2011), 'Coisty v Lenny promises to be a roller coaster ride', *Daily Record* The Winner, 7 February.

McConnell, A. (2008), 'I'll be on my best behaviour as coach promises Neil', *Evening Times*, 5 April.

MacDonald, H. (2011), 'Football the loser amid March madness', *The Herald* Sport, 3 March.

McDonald, M. G. and Birrell, S. (1999), 'Reading sport critically: A methodology for interrogating power', *Sociology of Sport Journal*, 16: 4, 283–300.

MacFarlane, I. (2011), 'I won't go down in mail of bullets', *Daily Star*, 14 January.

McGinty, S. (2011), 'Loyalists in death threat to Celtic manager', *Scotland on Sunday*, 20 February.

McGivern, M. (2011), 'Mayhem', *Daily Record*, 3 March.

McGowan, S. (2011), 'Accusations and acrimony', *Daily Mail*, 3 March.

McKendry, G. (2011a), 'Flashpoint; three Old Firm exclusives terror group sent bullets to Celts', *News of the World*, 16 January.

McKendry, G. (2011b), 'Lennon under terror guard', *News of the World*, 6 February.

MacLeod, M. (2011), 'Lenny's touchline antics threaten to put his good work with team in shade', *Daily Record*, 4 March.

MacMillan, J. (2000), 'Scotland's shame', in T. M. Devine (ed.), *Scotland's Shame: Bigotry and Sectarianism in Modern Scotland*, Edinburgh: Mainstream, pp. 13–24.

McMillan, J. (2011), 'Scottish perspective: Unionism fades, with explosive effect', *The Scotsman*, 22 April.

Marshall, A. (2011), 'Anguish is all too familiar', *Daily Record*, 21 April.

Mills, C. Wright (1959), *The Sociological Imagination*, Oxford: Oxford University Press.

Minogue, T. (2009), 'The elephant in the room', in J. M. Bradley (ed.), *Celtic Minded 3: Essays on Religion, Politics, Society, Identity . . . and Football*, Glendaruel: Argyll Publishing, pp.157–69.

Musson, C. (2011), 'Lennon's 24-hour guard', *Daily Record*, 5 March.

Parks, G. (2011), 'Hotline', *Daily Record*, 7 March.

Rainey, S. (2011), 'Facebook won't close Lennon threat site', *Belfast Telegraph*, 19 January.

Ralston, G. (2011), 'We won It . . . Diouf Lost It', *Daily Record*, 3 April.

Reid, I. A. (2006), 'Scotland's demon? A critique of the media discourse of Neil Lennon and Celtic', in J. M. Bradley (ed.), *Celtic Minded 2: Essays on Celtic Football Culture and Identity*, Glendaruel, Argyll Publishing, pp. 233–56.

Reid, I. A. (2008), '"An outsider in our midst". narratives of Neil Lennon, soccer & ethno-religious bigotry in the Scottish press', *Soccer & Society*, 9: 1, 64–80.

Riggins, S. H. (1997), 'The rhetoric of othering', in S. H. Riggins (ed.), *The Language and Politics of Exclusion: Others in Discourse*, London: Sage, pp. 1–30.

Silvester, N. (2011), 'Facebook bans Celts boss death page', *Sunday Mail*, 27 February.

Smith, A. (2011), 'Time to bite the bullet: Scotland must ask itself why it seems to tolerate the campaign of hatred against Neil Lennon', *Scotland on Sunday* Sport, 13 March.

Spencer, N. E. (2004), 'Sister Act VI: Venus and Serena Williams at Indian Wells: "sincere fictions" and white racism', *Journal of Sport & Social Issues*, 28: 2, 115–35.

Spiers, G. (2011), 'Lennon a marked man solely because of his upbringing and old prejudices', *The Times (Scotland)*, 21 April.

Spiers, G. and Edgar, B. (2011), 'One man's troubles in a divided city where the bigots still rule; Neil Lennon risks attack every day as Celtic manager', *The Times (Scotland)*, 19 March.

Sports Mail Comment (2011), 'Shameful! Lennon and McCoist brawl spells new low for Old Firm', *Daily Mail*, 3 March.

Traynor, J. (2011), 'Pious and bovril', *Daily Record*, 7 March.

Waddell, G. (2008), 'Lenny will be a Sellick mind reader; He's on the right wavelength', *Sunday Mail*, 6 April.

Walls. P. and Williams, R. (2003), 'Sectarianism at work: Accounts of employment discrimination against Irish Catholics in Scotland', *Ethnic and Racial Studies*, 26: 4, 632–62.

Wilkie, S. (2011), 'Celtic duo sent Bullets in post', *Daily Star*, 10 January.

Wilson, M. (2008), 'Parkhead hero Neil delighted at chance of a return to his one true love', *Daily Mail*, 4 April.

Wilson, R. (2011a), 'Private battle central to the war', *The Herald* Sport, 7 February.

Wilson, R. (2011b), 'Lennon would be better served if more were revealed than the raw figure on the touchline', *The Herald* Sport, 12 May, http://www.heraldscotland.com/sport/football/lennon-would-be-better-served-if-more-were-revealed-than-the-raw-figure-on-the-touchline.13663343 (last accessed 5 November 2012).

Neglected Perspectives: Class, Gender and Football Supporters

11 Women, Football and Communities: Gendered Conceptualisations of 'Sectarianism'

Kay Goodall and Margaret Malloch

INTRODUCTION

There have been significant advances in understanding bigotry in Scottish football. In particular, analyses of law and masculinity in the context of Scottish history and current affairs are opening new avenues of research (Hopkins 2009; Abrams 1999; Collier 1997). However, there has been a very limited focus on the less visible impact that experiences of bigotry have on women in local communities. This chapter explores three key areas. Firstly, the current legal framework, including the failings and the merits of the Offensive Behaviour at Football and Threatening Communications (Scotland) Act 2012. This section examines public order law and how concepts of racism and religious prejudice have been judicially considered through their English equivalents (see the chapter by Hamilton-Smith and McArdle), incitement to hatred law, and conceptions of sectarianism in Northern Irish law. It will consider how these concepts impact on women's experiences. Secondly, the chapter presents findings and photographs from the authors' exploratory photography and discussion project, carried out alongside a two photographers and aimed at documenting women's views and experiences of sectarianism in Scotland. Thirdly, the chapter concludes by examining how past and current law impacts on the relationship between gendered experiences within communities.

The recent attention to football and bigotry in Scotland has been conducted within a largely male and masculine context. With few exceptions, the debates have been led by men and the attention given to 'football' and 'violence', which are often uncritically connected to 'sectarianism', have been presented within a predominantly male arena. Although establishing a wide scope which included interfaith work, education, sport, football matches and parades (One Scotland 2005), recent media coverage and policy attention (One Scotland 2006) has focused predominantly on the issues surrounding events related to football matches. The Scottish Government (One Scotland 2005: 5) acknowledged that:

> There was a danger in over-associating Scottish football with bigoted sectar-
> ian behaviour . . . there was no doubt that people perceived sectarianism to be
> associated with sport and football. However, sectarianism was not caused by
> football nor was it just a problem for football.

However, as Flint (2008) notes, an audit of religiously aggravated crimes revealed
that 33 per cent of reported incidents related to football or football teams, in comparison to 12 per cent related to 'religious' marches (see further analysis of these and
more recent figures in the chapters by Rosie and Waiton in this volume). Attention
to football increased following the events which took place during the 2011–12
football season resulting in the introduction of the Offensive Behaviour at Football
and Threatening Communications (Scotland) Act 2012.

When gender is discussed in relation to football or 'sectarianism' it has tended
to focus on problematic images of masculinity (for example, Williams and Taylor
1994). Our intention was to consider the impact of recent debates on football
and its relationship to 'sectarianism' in terms of women's views of this issue and of
these recent discussions. This chapter sets out to recontextualise this debate. It is
based on an exploratory project conducted by the authors (Goodall and Malloch,
forthcoming), alongside photographers (Mary Gordon and Craig MacInnes), which
set out to highlight gendered conceptualisations of 'sectarianism' as experienced
through a visual lens alongside an analytical examination. Our aim was to develop
a critical analysis of understandings and experiences of 'sectarianism' as experienced
by women and understood within the contexts of football and communities. In
particular, we hoped to set out a new approach to understanding 'sectarianism' in
Scotland, providing an opportunity to present new forms of methodological and
analytical approaches.

PUBLIC ORDER LAW AND CONCEPTS OF RACISM AND RELIGIOUS PREJUDICE

Offences with a sectarian element have been problematic for Scottish legislators
for some time. Anything close to a legal definition, never mind a legal concept, has
been near-impossible to formulate. This is not for lack of drafting skill or ingenuity,
but because sectarianism itself in Scotland is nebulous: multi-faceted and poorly
understood. In practice, the courts have implicitly developed a conception of it
through the criminal law of offences racially or religiously aggravated. Northern
Ireland has come close to a definition of sectarianism in criminal law as a matter of
religious belief or political opinion.[1] In Scotland, however, there remains no mainstream political party affiliated with what is popularly conceived as sectarian interests. Nonetheless, many people in Scotland continue to have ideologically polarised
interests in the political business and status of Ireland, particularly its relationship
with Britain and the United Kingdom – and so a political element remains, yet there
is no hook to hang it on in law.

One Scots appeal case considered the relationship between religious prejudice and an expression of political loyalty. The assumption was that if political opposition to supporters of the Fenian Brotherhood could be proved, this would be a defence or a mitigation when the offender had been charged with a religiously aggravated public order offence.[2] Likewise in another Scottish case, it appears that chanting pro-IRA songs could not by itself be defined as religious prejudice (Scotsman 2011). In contrast, in Northern Ireland, it can be the opposite: evidence of hostility towards the Fenian Brotherhood would be regarded as strong evidence of religious prejudice. This was made clear in 2011 in a debate about the definition of 'sectarian chanting' in a bill placed before the Northern Ireland Parliament. This was that 'it consists of or includes matter which is threatening, abusive or insulting to a person by reason of that person's religious belief *or political opinion* or against an individual as a member of such a group' (Northern Ireland Assembly 2011, emphasis added). The definition had been drawn up by the NI Human Rights Commission and was opposed only by the Ulster Unionist Party (which thus prevented it from becoming part of Northern Irish law).

The case law has revolved around male-identified behaviours. In 2006, the Scottish Government produced an analysis of the religiously aggravated cases reported to the Procurator Fiscal Service over a period of eighteen months between 2004 and 2005 (Doyle 2006). Nearly half took place either in the street or in football stadia. The great majority were cases of Breach of the Peace. Nearly half involved alcohol (this is probably an underestimate) and nearly all of the perpetrators were male, typically aged somewhere between sixteen and thirty. Nearly all the cases involved what typically would be seen as 'sectarianism' associated with the two mainstream Christian denominations, rather than behaviour derogatory towards people associated by the perpetrator with other religious groups (64 per cent of incidents were identified as directed towards Roman Catholicism and 31 per cent towards Protestantism). 'Directed towards' does not necessarily mean that this was directed at a particular person seen to be Roman Catholic or Protestant: it can include an indiscriminate display of prejudice. The researchers also did not distinguish between these and incidents seen as linked to anti-loyalist/Orange and anti-republican motivations or behaviour. Placing these together substantially affects the proportions (see Rosie in this volume).

The typical criminal profile, then, is of a particular type of sectarian behaviour: public disorder engaged in by drunk young men. We are not told what proportion of victims are women. All we know is that women are almost entirely absent from the officially recorded body of perpetrators. The typical offence often involves football and disorder in the street, as a province of men rather than women, young men rather than older men, and men who are publicly drunk. Such scenarios have also been predominantly associated with being working class.[3]

An important point to be aware of here is that Scots law is capable of treating almost any offence as racially or religiously aggravated, so it is not the law which leads actors through the criminal justice process to single out as sectarian these sorts of male-identified activities. The absence of gender-related data, however, is also seen in independent social research, something we discuss in the next section. Another important element, of which people are often unaware, is that the law requires that there first be a basic offence. Its ambit is limited to *aggravation* of the kinds of offences that are already known to Scots law. These aggravated cases are dealt with primarily by sentence enhancement. Commentators often argue, for instance, that sectarian speech alone amounts to a crime in Scots law (see Waiton in this volume): in fact, we require more than that. There can be no conviction unless the person has also committed an offence. This is as it should be; no offence punishing speech alone could survive a human rights challenge. Equally, though, it explains why the experiences of sectarianism we discuss later are rarely seen as matters for criminal law.

'Racial' aggravation is defined by section 96 of the Crime and Disorder Act 1998. Almost any offence can be treated as racially aggravated if it is proved that the offender evinced, or was motivated by, 'malice and ill-will'[4] on the ground of the victim's membership (or presumed membership) of a 'racial group'. This includes Irish identity. A 'religiously' aggravated offence is defined in section 74 of the Criminal Justice (Scotland) Act 2003. This has a particularly sophisticated formulation, different from that elsewhere in the UK. Here, the ground is the victim's membership (or presumed membership) of a religious group, or of a social or cultural group with a perceived religious affiliation.

What amounts to a religious group is particularly broad. It is a group of persons defined by reference to their (a) religious belief or lack of religious belief; (b) membership of or adherence to a church or religious organisation; (c) support for the culture and traditions of a church or religious organisation; or (d) participation in activities associated with such a culture or such traditions. There is a reason for such a long-winded formulation. The legislation followed a parliamentary debate about tackling sectarianism: that is primarily what lay behind creating this provision in the statute.[5] The problem is that sectarianism in particular in Scotland is often far removed from its religious roots. The provision was meant to capture as much of the variety of sectarianism as possible, while not losing all sight of boundaries to judicial discretion.

THE 2012 ACT

The latest legislative response to what is seen as football-related sectarian crime is the Offensive Behaviour at Football and Threatening Communications (Scotland) Act 2012. A bill was introduced to the Scottish Parliament after an exceptionally bad season of football-related disorder, ranging from widely televised sectarian chanting to abuse of, death threats towards, and the sending of pseudo-incendiary devices to football professionals and others associated (some, albeit loosely) with Celtic Football Club, which is popularly (if misleadingly) regarded as being identified with Roman Catholicism.

The statute in fact focuses on much more than football sectarianism (which is implicitly and mistakenly reduced in most public debates to a problem of religious prejudice rather than encompassing anti-Irish racism). It lays out what are described as two offences, although in practice it creates what legal observers might regard as rather more than that (Goodall 2011b). The first of the two offences, section 1, is intended to capture 'the full range'[6] of behaviour which is (a) likely to incite public disorder and expresses, stirs up, or is motivated by religious hatred, or (b) is threatening, or (c) would be likely to be considered offensive by a reasonable person, when any of these take place at or in relation to regulated football matches. These include, but are not confined to, behaviour seen as sectarian.

The threatening or offensive behaviour is not confined to any particular type of prejudice, and when it involves expressing hatred this may be towards a person or group of persons because of their religious affiliation, race, nationality, ethnic or national origins, sexual orientation, transgender identity or disability. The offence is intended to combat other forms of prejudiced expression which have been highlighted in Scottish football, such as those which have gained most attention: racism and homophobia.

Most of this is already provided for under Scots criminal law, and is less novel than it looks. There are, however, two specific concerns that will surely continue to cause worry. Expressing hatred which is or would be 'likely to incite public disorder' is very wide and perilously close to the UK's long-standing conceptions of incitement to hatred or inciting another to commit an offence. In England and Wales, incitement to religious hatred, for instance, requires that the person intends to stir up religious hatred by his/her actions.[7] The section 1 provision does not require that the person intend this. Although there is the extra element of public disorder, it does not require that public disorder is actually stirred up by his/her expression of hatred. It does not even require the presence of enough people to be likely to result in public disorder. It is easy to see why this wording is there: it would be frustrating if a person could not be prosecuted simply because it was heard by a small group of people or because there were enough police officers present to control trouble. However, the ambit of the offence will raise concern.

An extra provision, section 7, which emphasises the right to freedom of religious expression, was added in an amendment to the Bill before enactment. However, this section applies only to the second offence in section 6 – not to the expressing hatred etc. offence in section 1. Crucially, a conditional right to freedom of expression is already protected in Scotland under, among other things, section 1 of the Human Rights Act 1998. Nonetheless, given the extent to which public and press debate has exaggerated the extent of the Act, this should have been made clearer.

Behaviour that is offensive to a reasonable person is also a formulation so wide that it will need to be reined in by prosecutorial policy and the exercise of judicial discretion.[8] We could have a long wait before cases go to appeal and lead to authoritative judicial precedent which throws some light on this. Few appeal cases on interpreting racial or religious aggravation have ever reached a Scottish court and when they have, the judiciary has not taken the opportunity to expound at length on the law (see Hamilton-Smith and McArdle in this volume). This has been very unhelpful and the result is that for interpretation we need to look at the body of related English law. Although it can be argued that the Scottish legal system does not need the level of detail and fine precision that English law does, because it does not have the volume of near-identical cases which need to be meticulously differentiated (Goodall 2000), the result is that we should not rely on the hope that case law will help us understand the legal meaning of terms in the 2012 Act any time soon. Yet, because this is missing, the risk is that too much attention is given to those who argue that such law is inherently illiberal, as Stuart Waiton does in this volume. That would further exclude the voices of those who argue that such law has a valuable, protective function – in particular, the voices of the women heard in our research.

The second offence, section 6, deals with communication of threatening material. It is not restricted to behaviour related to football (unlike the expressing hatred offence in section 1). It focuses on cases where someone 'communicates material' to at least one other person (so this includes, for instance, someone sending a message through a private e-mail and not on a public webpage). This is an offence if it happens in one of two ways. First, if the person intentionally or recklessly communicates material which threatens (in several possible ways), or incites, a seriously violent act which would be likely to cause fear or alarm to the person or group targeted. The other way the offence can be committed is if the offender communicates to another person threatening material which is intended to stir up religious hatred.

The first way covers not just religious hatred: it refers to any act targeted at a person 'of a particular description' – a term which is not defined. We might assume it is aimed at problems such as homophobia, hatred on the grounds of disability and so on, but the Act does not tell us. Section 9 of the Act requires that the Scottish Government reviews how the two offences have operated and report on this by the start of August 2014. This is a sensible provision but it is not a substitute for making the law as clear as possible.

Nonetheless, the concentration by commentators on the breadth and clarity of the 2012 Act has skewed the debate. It has become an argument over the freedom of young men to engage in what one side refers to as banter. Some commentators claim that such law is an assault on the freedoms of the socially excluded, yet ignore the confidence and safety of groups of people who already suffer from long-standing, widespread discrimination.[9] The very poorest Scots originate from ethnic minorities rather than the majority white working class.[10]

What is interesting here is the focus on typically masculine expressions of sectarian public disorder. A late addition to the debate has turned to the roles of women, but only in the context of women as victims of domestic abuse which is said to be caused by the problems of disorder which surround football. This tells us little about how women see sectarianism, how they are affected by it and how they are actively involved in it. The next section addresses the context of this gap.

WOMEN'S PERSPECTIVES AND EXPERIENCES OF SECTARIANISM IN SCOTLAND

Our project set out to explore gendered conceptualisations of 'sectarianism' as experienced by women and understood within the contexts of football and communities. Our explorations took a number of forms, including photographic work which attempted to capture images which symbolised women's roles within communities; and the intersection of collective identity formation with the commercialisation of football. We accessed local community areas and specific events, including republican and Protestant-affiliated parades, to obtain visual depictions. We also spoke with ten women to obtain their views on these issues and discussed these issues in informal interviews with key stakeholders from a range of organisations. Our study aims to combine visual and discursive aspects of this issue, and the exploratory nature of this work is emphasised (Goodall and Malloch, forthcoming).

Recent discussions of 'sectarianism' have not been unusual in omitting any consideration of women (see Rooney 2006). When women have been referred to in these discussions, they are depicted as potential supporters (for example, more women at games being thought to improve male behaviour)[11] and potential victims (consideration of the relationship between football violence and domestic abuse). Few of the studies carried out into 'sectarianism' and Scottish society refer to women other than in the context of 'mixed marriages' (for example, NFO Social Research 2003; McAspurren 2005). Similarly, football inquiries have also focused predominantly on men (for example, Working Group 1977).

Increases in the number of women attending football matches (BBC News 2010) have been linked to changes in football stadia and attempts to make football more 'family friendly' with the introduction of all-seater stadia, and free-market influences which emerged alongside the changing perceptions of football fandom after the Hillsborough disaster (Malcolm et al. 2007). Marketing strategies have become increasingly geared towards the football 'consumer', moving away from the working-class traditional supporter to target the middle-class fan (see Crawford's chapter). The number of women attending games in Scotland has increased, as it has elsewhere in the UK, with women apparently making up almost one-quarter of fans at English Premier League games (Premier League 2011), and there is more effort made by clubs to encourage women to attend, with fans reporting feeling safe both inside and outside the stadium before and after matches.

Pope (2010) highlights the perceptions that the changing basis of football support from traditionally working class to the middle classes' 'gentrification' of football coincided with a perception that growing female support also heralds the 'feminisation' of football. As Pope (2010: 473) describes, this has led to something of a 'backlash' against the 'new female fan', with views that they are 'inauthentic' fans (see also SIRC 2008). It is interesting to note that despite the importance of team colours, most major clubs provide a range of merchandise in pink – presumably for the girls!

There is something of a dichotomy about the way in which the broader issues of sectarianism and its relationship to football are presented. Women have been largely ignored as active participants in the coverage of these issues, as players (see Macbeth 2008) or supporters (Pope 2010); a situation replicated across Europe (SIRC, 2008) where they are not generally involved in any football-related disorder.

Although there has been a great deal of recent attention to offensive behaviour and its policing (in terms of racism in the English Premier League with the

Figure 11.1 Hanging out to dry. Rangers and Celtic sell a range of children's clothing. Shown here are two girls' babygros, which are both sold in pink.
Photograph: Mary Gordon

prosecution and subsequent acquittal of John Terry; in Scotland in terms of the criminalisation of 'sectarian' chanting and offensive behaviour), little has been done to address the ongoing use of sexist and misogynistic language (see also Williams and Taylor 1994 and an example of sexism in football 'banter' cited by Rosie in this volume) in such contexts.[12] Similarly, Hickman and Walter (1995) draw attention to the failure to address anti-Irish racism within the UK.

Debates surrounding the appropriateness (or not) of criminalising so-called 'offensive' behaviour have been ongoing within feminist academic and activist communities (Hanmer and Saunders 1984; Kelly and Radford 1990). Feminists have campaigned against sexual harassment (physical and verbal) while at the same time staunchly defending the importance of 'free speech' and rights to self-expression (evidenced particularly in debates around censorship and pornography, Rodgerson and Wilson 1991; MacKinnon 2006). However, the cumulative effects of demeaning and threatening acts have been shown to impact significantly on experiences of safety by individuals and groups. This insight should not be lost when we consider the debates around young men's freedom in public spaces in the context of public order and sectarianism.

Figure 11.2 Pretty in pink. Rangers and Celtic have produced a range of women's merchandise in shades of pink, instead of the traditional blue and green team colours. Photograph: Craig MacInnes

Women's views

Our discussions with women highlighted their ambivalence about the association between football and 'sectarianism'. Some of the women we spoke with enjoyed football; others did not take an interest in the game itself. Similarly, they indicated that 'religion' was not something they generally spoke about, and many had 'mixed' marriages. Indeed, there was some initial reluctance to discuss these wider issues, and often it took time before the women chose to engage with the question of whether sectarianism was of any relevance in their lives or if, instead, it was something they felt able to fence off by using avoidance strategies. Hence, extended interviewing or focus groups would be a method appropriate to this field of research. Early in a conversation, one woman exclaimed: 'Can you not ask us about sex? You'll get a lot more answers.' The predominant view was that the issue of 'sectarianism' as reported in the media was 'hyped up', although there was a perception that young people and men were increasingly violent, both in the home and in the public sphere. Women who spoke of personal experiences of sectarianism gave examples of egregious bigotry seen in their personal lives, which some saw as a societal problem and others saw as anomalous and reflecting the perpetrator's personality flaws. One woman identified the link between football rivalry and the underpinning basis of religion:

> Certainly you hear them saying that when there is an Old Firm game on, certain pubs become battle grounds. It can be quite bad at times. But again, no one says it is about religion, it's 'he's a Rangers supporter', 'he's a Celtic supporter' . . . but it's the same old thing. People say to me, 'How come your son is a Rangers supporter when you are all Celtic?' In other words, how come your son is a Rangers supporter when you are all Catholics?

Women and victimisation

Attention has, however, been directed to women, in the Scottish Government's contextualisation of these issues, as victims of domestic abuse. The potential for increased victimisation following major football matches has been considered a cause for concern (Palmer 2010). In Scotland this has been particularly linked with Old Firm games[13] (Cavanagh 2011). Calculations based on Strathclyde Police statistical data indicated that recorded incidents of disorder/anti-social behaviour, violence, domestic abuse and bigotry showed some increase on days when an Old Firm game took place. In particular, it would appear that there were 31 per cent more recorded incidents of domestic abuse on Saturdays when Celtic and Rangers played each other (98 incidents on an 'average' Saturday and 128 on Old Firm Saturdays) and a 34 per cent increase (from 97 to 130) on Sundays when Old Firm games took place, with a 13 per cent increase on Tuesday/Wednesday games (from 58 to 65). Although similar increases in reported incidents of domestic abuse can be seen on public holidays – notably Easter Monday and early May holidays – the levels of domestic abuse incidents recorded on New Year's Day are significantly higher (between 147 and 279 in the last five years in Strathclyde, and over twice as high as an 'average' Saturday).

Cavanagh (2011: 6), however, highlights a number of caveats regarding the statistical data presented. The figures consist of police recorded incidents so include detected as well as reported incidents – this may be affected by higher numbers of police officers working on these days. It is also impossible to extrapolate any causal factors associated with these increases; some minor variations may be the result of 'normal statistical fluctuations'.

Our women respondents stated that men who were violent in the home were likely to be violent regardless of football. This is in line with research on the behaviour of violent men where antecedents of violence are often random and serve to justify violence in the aftermath of abusive and/or violent incidents, rather than working as a 'causal' factor (Cavanagh et al. 2001; Dobash and Dobash 1983, 1984). Indeed, the women suggested that some men were likely to use football as an excuse to be violent (that is, if their team lost). One respondent from a women's support project with involvement in the recent discussions in Scotland surrounding football and violence commented:

In a nutshell, we do not consider football or sectarianism (or alcohol) to be a cause of domestic abuse. Domestic abuse is much more than violence, but even the connections between incidents of violence occurring within domestic abuse and these issues are rather more complicated than the simplistic story of cause and effect. Co-occurrence is not causality. These issues and many, many more may provide an excuse used by the perpetrator. A discourse that links the two may also provide a conducive context for continued abuse and excuse-making.

Similarly, trouble at marches and parades was seen as often caused by over-consumption of alcohol among the bystanders and onlookers at such events rather than the marchers themselves (also noted by NFO Social Research 2003 and One Scotland 2005). Kelly (2003: 46) argues that the annual Orange parades in Scotland are often underpinned by 'the possibility of public disorder. That is why many Catholics simply leave town during the parades; that is why there is such a massive police presence, especially around Catholic churches, schools, halls and pubs. Sectarian hostility simmers throughout the marches . . .'

Although this may be indicative of the problems of identifying and collating incidents of sectarian or 'hate' crime (for example, Green et al. 2001; Kelly 2003), like the broader nature of violence against women and its general invisibility (Hanmer and Saunders 1984), capturing changes in reported incidents of domestic abuse may say something about football-related violence, but only indirectly. What is of much more importance is what this says about male violence towards women more generally. Studies of 'hate crime' tend to highlight a correlation between bigoted attitudes and behaviour. Similarly, studies of domestic violence perpetrators indicate significantly entrenched views about authority and entitlement. This is often manifested in personal relationships where male power is exerted and where the woman's resistance may result in intimidation, threats and/or violence (Dobash and Dobash 1983; Seidler 1994).

Women, as part of the wider community, may also be subjected to wider displays of problematic behaviour within local communities, as passengers on public transport and in the wider public arena. More broadly, concerns surrounding prostitution and potential trafficking for the purpose of sexual exploitation at major sporting events have been noted (Palmer 2010).

NFO Social Research (2003) conducted a study (based on a representative sample of 1,000 adults) to determine the scale, nature and impact of sectarianism in the city of Glasgow. Both men and women took part in the research, but there is no indication of any differences in response, or level of participation, by gender. In terms of findings, respondents' experiences of crime were differentiated by age, social group, religion and ethnicity but not by gender. Although gender is considered in relation to 'perceived motivation for crime' (NFO Social Research 2003, Table D-3: 29), even in these cases where gender is identified as a motivating factor for crime, the report does not indicate if this is reported by men or women. Gender is reported in relation to perceived motivation for discrimination experiences within the workplace, where 13 out of 54 respondents who believed they had received unfair treatment within the workplace believed this was due to their gender; again, however, there is no indication if the respondents were male or female and therefore believed that the unfair treatment they had received was due to being a man or a woman.

In the NFO Social Research report, consideration is given to experiences of social exclusion and concerns by respondents about personal safety. This may be an area where issues of gender could be expected to be particularly pertinent: however, without the statistical breakdown of the gender ratio of respondents, this is difficult to untangle. Twenty-five per cent of respondents indicated that there were particular places in Glasgow they would avoid due to fear about their personal safety. In relation to use of public transport, women were more likely than men to report having avoided using public transport at some point in the past due to concerns about their safety – 22 per cent compared to 11 per cent of men (NFO Social Research 2003: 35).

Women and safety strategies

During most of the discussions with women, when asked about the effect of 'sectarianism' on their lives, initial reactions were often to say that it had no effect.[14] However, when asked if they would go about their business as usual, for example on the day of an Old Firm game, typically women immediately responded that they would make plans to avoid the football crowds. Women also spoke of the precautionary measures they would be likely to take to avoid getting caught up in football crowds, commenting that they would 'avoid town when there is a game on' or 'work around it': for example, avoiding times when football supporters were going to or from matches. One woman, encapsulating the views of other respondents, commented: 'I wouldn't go out! . . . you think you aren't affected, but you're not affected because you try and get yourself out of the firing line.' When asked what she would be avoiding, one woman replied that she would not want to get caught up in any potential 'trouble' surrounding an Old Firm game, or 'men fighting or shouting, because it does intimidate you'. By contrast, women indicated they would not have the same concerns about other football team matches; the rivalry of the Old Firm resulted in deliberate and strategic avoidance behaviour.

This form of avoidance behaviour/strategy means that the impact of 'sectarianism' is hidden. Strategies of self-management and avoidance of risk in leisure spaces have also been examined by feminist scholars (Skeggs 1999; Green and Singleton 2006; Brooks 2011). Kelly and Radford (1990: 40) consider the dual phenomena of the minimising and silencing of women's experiences (in relation to male violence) and note: 'In order to be able to speak about something, one must first be able to name and define it.' The current emphasis on football and, in particular, conceptions of 'sectarianism' may serve to exclude and invalidate women's experiences of concerns about wider social issues.

Women also spoke of the concerns they had for the safety of partners or sons, with one woman indicating that she and her friends (all of whom enjoyed watching football) would try to ensure that their menfolk were in a 'safe' place to enjoy the Old Firm game:

I'll say to my son and his pals to get a few drinks and watch the game in the house so that I know he will be safe, like bringing them in. And I think women do that, say the older generation who have got sons, they are trying to protect them. They don't know that they are being kept in . . . I always find myself saying, 'Where are you going after the game?' . . . 'Don't go into the town [Glasgow].' And I know my friend does the same by making a big meal to provide the temptation of food and a good atmosphere. And I can think then, 'Fine, I don't care what the score is', you know they are going to be OK.

Such communal, private strategies seem linked to a perception that such events are a site of physical danger, and connect women's own avoidance behaviour and personal unease with those forms of violent expression more easily recognised by criminal law. The women's hidden experiences are communal both in a private sense and as part of the public arena of popular debates about 'sectarianism'. One is not clearly understood without the other.

CONCLUSIONS

This chapter has presented some of the findings from an exploratory study of sectarianism in Scotland, examined through the perceptions and experiences of women. Our findings raise a number of interesting issues but the next step is to clarify the existing complexities surrounding definitions and meanings of sectarianism. The views of women do, however, add an important viewpoint to existing debates and highlight the ways in which 'sectarian' divisions sustain 'patriarchal structures' by maintaining control over public space and social, structural hierarchies of power (see also Aretxaga 1997; Roulston and Davies 2000).

Our examination of women's experiences highlights the failure to include a gendered perspective in the debate about developing and enforcing criminal law. Offensive behaviour legislation is not likely to tackle the ongoing and enduring problem of misogynist behaviour (see an example cited by Rosie in this volume), nor will it always increase the safety of women. Similarly, debates about offensive behaviour, criminalising of football fans and concerns about a 'lack of tolerance' (Waiton 2012) fail to take into account the reality of gendered abuse (along with homophobic, racist or disablist intimidation).

As with 'sectarianism', there is a very real challenge surrounding the 'naming' of particular forms of behaviour. Although the Scottish Government and other agencies have drawn attention to the incidence of recorded incidents of domestic abuse surrounding particular events, this can ignore the ongoing process of violence which characterises abusive relationships. It thereby fails to address the underpinning concerns that women express with regard to feelings of safety and security. Similarly, a focus on football can lead to a disconnection from wider social issues by concentrating attention on men (notably working-class football fans) 'behaving badly' while failing to acknowledge the impact of ongoing intimidation that women are often required to manage.

This is also reflected in the suggested consensus that the motivation for sectarianism is ethno-religious. This may fail to recognise an imbalance of power between the larger group of mostly Scottish-originating Protestants and the smaller group of Scottish and Irish Catholics. This issue is most visibly captured in the context of the Old Firm: however, given Rangers' current location in the Third Division, the forthcoming football season may be somewhat quieter than recent ones.

NOTES

1. Northern Ireland Assembly, Official Report, amendment 9, tabled 3 March 2011 (emphasis added); see also Goodall (2011a).
2. *Walls* v. *Brown* [2009] HCJAC 59, 2009 JC 375.
3. On public perceptions of 'street crimes' in Scotland and the 'ned/chav phenomenon', see Young (2012). Research regularly finds men, particularly young men, to be the agents of such crimes: see Heidensohn and Silvestri (2011: 348). As regards social class in particular, the young and socially disadvantaged have less autonomous private space of their own, so their social encounters are more likely to take place in spaces defined as public and more open to policing (Muncie 2009: 254).
4. This probably means the same as 'hostility' in the English equivalent. See the parliamentary debates on the Crime and Disorder Bill: Lord Monson, HL Deb vol. 585 col. 1277, 12 February 1998 and Lord Hardie, HL Deb vol. 585 col. 1305, 12 February 1998.
5. On this, see in particular the focus of the key report which led to the introduction of the provision (Scottish Executive 2002).
6. Offensive Behaviour in Football and Threatening Communications (Scotland) Bill (SP Bill 1), Policy Memorandum, TSO 2011, p. 3.
7. Public Order Act 1986, Part 3A.
8. For further discussion, see Goodall (2011a, 2011b).
9. See for instance the comments and submissions by Findlay, Rooney, Taylor and Waiton in Scottish Parliament (2012).
10. See the analysis in Netto, Sosenko and Bramley (2011).
11. This appears to be an international phenomenon. Following problematic behaviour at football matches, the Turkish Football Association made a decision to ban men from stadia. Initially deciding that the Istanbul side was to play two home matches behind closed doors after a violent pitch invasion in a previous European game, the association conceded that women and children under twelve could watch the games. Forty-one thousand women and children attended the first game against Manisapor and players from both teams threw flowers to the fans before kick-off. A distinctly changed atmosphere was noted by players and fans with both sides applauded (Aljazeera.net 2001; Fogg 2011; Lewis 2011).
12. The offence that John Terry was accused of related to his alleged racist act in the use of 'black' to insult an opposing player. His alleged use of the word 'cunt' did not, however, attract further discussion beyond the court. In a similar vein, the routine 'banter' in football talk-shows on both television and radio (for example, Radio Scotland's *Off the Ball*, http://www.bbc.co.uk/podcasts/series/otb) frequently contains innuendo-filled material as part of their discussion of football action.
13. This refers to games between Celtic and Rangers. In the last five seasons (between 2006–7 and 2010–11), twenty-four matches took place between these two teams (Cavanagh 2011: 2). In the forthcoming season (2012–13) this may be less of a problem given the current difficulties facing Rangers. Levels of recorded offending at these matches are low (with

fifty-five recorded incidents of antisocial behaviour/disorder, fifteen recorded incidents of violence and twenty-seven recorded incidents of bigotry at these games) (Cavanagh 2011: 3). However, wider concerns relate to incidents which take place outside stadia and in the wider communities.

14. It may be of interest, however, that when interviews took place in summer 2012, we were given several examples of situations where men had used their savings, unbeknown to their wives/partners, to support the Rangers Fighting Fund in face of potential liquidation. These examples were given as potential financial repercussions for women.

REFERENCES

Abrams, L. (1999), '"There was nobody like my Daddy": Fathers, the Family and the Marginalisation of Men in Modern Scotland', *The Scottish Historical Review*, 78: 206, Part 2, 219–42.

Aljazeera.net (2011), 'Women and children to watch football for free', http://www.aljazeera.com/sport/football/2011/09/2011930124257543150.html (last accessed 15 November 2011).

Aretxaga, B. (1997), *Shattering Silence*, Princeton: Princeton University Press.

BBC News (2010), '"More Diverse" crowds at Premier League Football', 25 August 2010, http://www.bbc.co.uk/news/uk-11079597 (last accessed 14 June 2012).

Brooks, O. (2011), 'Guys! Stop Doing It!', *British Journal of Criminology*, 51: 4, 621–34.

Cavanagh, B. (2011), *Analysis of Police Incident Statistics on Days of Major Events (Draft)*, Unpublished paper: Edinburgh: Scottish Government Justice Analytical Services.

Cavanagh, K., Dobash, R., Dobash, R. and Lewis, R. (2001), '"Remedial Work": Men's Strategic Responses to their Violence against Intimate Female Partners', *Sociology*, 35: 3, 695–714.

Collier, R. (1997), 'After Dunblane: Corporeality and the (Hetero) Sexing of the Bodies of Men', *Journal of Law and Society*, 24: 2, 177–98.

Dobash, R. and Dobash, R. (1983), *Violence Against Wives*, New York, NY: Free Press.

Dobash, R. and Dobash, R. (1984), 'The Nature and Antecedents of Violent Events', *British Journal of Criminology*, 24: 3, 269–88.

Doyle, K. (2006), *Use of Section 74 of the Criminal Justice (Scotland) Act 2003 – Religiously Aggravated Reported Crime: an 18 Month Review*, Edinburgh: Justice Department Analytical Services Division Scottish Executive.

Flint, J. (2008), 'Governing Sectarianism in Scotland', *Scottish Affairs*, 63: Spring, 120–37.

Fogg, A. (2011), 'Why Turkey's women and children directive is good for football', *The Guardian*, 23 September 2011, http://www.guardian.co.uk/commentisfree/2011/sep/23/fenerbahce-women (last accessed 15 November 2011).

Goodall, K. (2000), 'What defines the Roles of a Judge? First Steps towards the Construction of a Comparative Method', *Northern Ireland Legal Quarterly*, 51: 4, 535.

Goodall, K. (2011a), 'Tackling sectarianism through Criminal Law', *Edinburgh Law Review*, 15: 3, 423.

Goodall, K. (2011b), Written submission to the Justice Committee, Offensive Behaviour at Football and Threatening Communications (Scotland) Bill, OB65, 26 August 2011, p. 1. Available from the author at https://dspace.stir.ac.uk/handle/1893/3338.

Goodall, K. and Malloch, M. (forthcoming), *Women and Communities: Gendered conceptualisations of 'sectarianism'*, Stirling: Scottish Centre for Crime and Justice Research.

Green, D., McFalls, L. and Smith, J. (2001), 'Hate Crime: An Emergent Research Agenda', *Annual Review of Sociology*, 27, 479–504.

Green, E. and Singleton, C. (2006), 'Risky Bodies at Leisure: Young Women Negotiating Space and Place', *Sociology*, 40: 5, 853–71.

Hanmer, J. and Saunders, S. (1984), *Well-Founded Fear: A Community Study of Violence to Women*, London: Hutchinson.

Heidensohn, F. and Silvestri, M. (2012), 'Gender and Crime', in Maguire, M., Morgan, R. and Reiner, R. (eds), *The Oxford Handbook of Criminology* (5th edn), Oxford: Oxford University Press, pp. 381–420.

Hickman, M. and Walter, B. (1995), 'Deconstructing Whiteness: Irish Women in Britain', *Feminist Review*, 50, 5–19.

Hopkins, P. (2009), 'Responding to the "crisis of masculinity": the perspectives of young Muslim men from Glasgow and Edinburgh, Scotland', *Gender, Place and Culture*, 16: 3, 299–312.

Kelly, E. (2003), 'Challenging Sectarianism in Scotland: The Prism of Racism', *Scottish Affairs*, 42: 32–56.

Kelly, L. and Radford, J. (1990), '"Nothing Really happened": the invalidation of women's experiences of sexual violence', *Critical Social Policy*, 10: 39, 39–53.

Lewis, J. (2011), 'What, a football match with only women spectators?' *The Guardian*, 21 September 2011, http://www.guardian.co.uk/football/2011/sep/21/football-match-only-women-spectators (last accessed 15 November 2011).

McAspurren, L. (2005), *Religious Discrimination and Sectarianism in Scotland: A brief review of evidence (2002–2004)*, Edinburgh: Scottish Executive.

Macbeth, J. (2008), 'Attitudes towards women's football in Scottish society', *Scottish Affairs*, 63: Spring, 89–119.

MacKinnon, C. (2006), *Are Women Human? And other international dialogues*, Cambridge, MA: Harvard University Press.

Malcolm, D., Jones, I. and Waddington, I. (2000), 'The people's game? Football spectatorship and demographic change', *Soccer and Society*, 1: 1, 129–43.

Muncie, J. (2009), *Youth and Crime* (3rd edn), London: Sage.

Netto, G., Sosenko, F. and Bramley, G. (2011), *Poverty and Ethnicity in Scotland: Review of the literature and datasets*, York: Joseph Rowntree Foundation, http://www.jrf.org.uk/sites/files/jrf/poverty-ethnicity-Scotland-full.pdf (last accessed 30 October 2012).

NFO Social Research (2003), *Sectarianism in Glasgow – Final Report*, Glasgow: Glasgow City Council.

Northern Ireland Assembly (2011), *Official Report, amendment 9, tabled 3 Mar 2011*, Belfast: Northern Ireland Assembly. This was debated on 7 March 2011, http://archive.niassembly.gov.uk/record/reports2010/110307.htm (last accessed 30 October 2012).

One Scotland (2005), *Record of the summit on sectarianism 14 February 2005*, Edinburgh: Scottish Executive.

One Scotland (2006), *Calling Full Time on Sectarianism*, Edinburgh: Scottish Executive, http://www.scotland.gov.uk/Resource/Doc/90629/0021809.pdf (last accessed 5 November 2012).

Palmer, C. (2010), *Violence against women and sport: A literature review*, London: Trust for London.

Pope, S. (2010), '"Like pulling down Durham Cathedral and building a brothel": Women as "new consumer" fans', *International Review for the Sociology of Sport*, 46: 4, 471–87.

Premier League (2011), *A Growing Fan Base*, www.premierleague.com/en-gb/about/a-growing-fan-base.html (last accessed 18 June 2012).

Rodgerson, G. and Wilson, E. (eds), (1991), *Pornography and Feminism: the case against censorship*, London: Lawrence and Wishart.

Rooney, E. (2006), 'Women's Equality in Northern Ireland's Transition', *Feminist Legal Studies*, 14, 353–75.

Roulston, C. and Davies, C. (eds) (2000), *Gender, Democracy and Inclusion in Northern Ireland*, Basingstoke: Palgrave.

Scotsman (2011), 'Sheriff right to dismiss case against man singing IRA songs, says expert', *The*

Scotsman, 30 March 2011, http://www.scotsman.com/news/sheriff-right-to-dismiss-case-against-man-singing-ira-songs-says-expert-1-1560025 (last accessed 5 September 2012).

Scottish Executive (2002), *Tackling Religious Hatred: Report of Cross-Party Working Group on Religious Hatred*, Edinburgh: Scottish Executive.

Scottish Parliament (2012), *Passage of the Offensive Behaviour at Football and Threatening Communications (Scotland) Bill 2011, SPPB 170*, Scottish Parliamentary Corporate Body, http://tinyurl.com/8ndd686 (last accessed 30 October 2012).

SIRC (2008), *Football Passions*, Oxford: Social Issues Research Centre.

Seidler, V. (1994), *Unreasonable Men: Masculinity and Social Theory*, London: Routledge.

Skeggs, B. (1999), 'Matter out of place: visibility and sexuality in leisure spaces', *Leisure Studies*, 18: 3, 213–32.

Waiton, S. (2012), 'Anti-Racism is now just official etiquette', *The Scotsman*, 16 July 2012, http://www.scotsman.com/news/stuart-waiton-anti-racism-is-now-just-official-etiquette-1-2413963 (last accessed 24 January 2013).

Williams, J. and Taylor, R. (1994), 'Boys keep swinging: Masculinity and football culture in England', in T. Newburn and E. Stanko (eds), *Just Boys Doing Business? Men, Masculinities and Crime*, London: Routledge, pp. 214–33.

Working Group (1977), *Football Crowd Behaviour*, Edinburgh: Scottish Education Department.

Young, R. (2012), 'Can Neds (or Chavs) Be Non-delinquent, Educated or Even Middle Class? Contrasting Empirical Findings with Cultural Stereotypes', *Sociology*, OnlineFirst Version of Record, 10 September 2012.

12 The Politics of Anti-sectarianism

Joe Crawford

INTRODUCTION

> In today's era, which proclaims itself post-ideological, ideology is thus, more than ever, a field of struggle – among other things, the struggle for appropriating past traditions. (Žižek 2011: 100)

The enactment, on 1 March 2012, of The Offensive Behaviour at Football Matches and Threatening Communications (Scotland) Act 2012, by the Scottish National Party (SNP) administration has generated a great deal of criticism from a wide range of individuals and groups. Stuart Waiton, academic and founder of the pressure group Take a Liberty, has been one of the most vociferous opponents of the Act (see Waiton's chapter in this volume). Waiton's position on current issues surrounding the debate is that the actual problem, rather than being 'sectarianism', is indeed 'anti-sectarianism'; itself a form of political pragmatism, enacted by 'new tolerant elites desperate to hold on to an issue that gives them a momentary sense of common goodness and moral purpose' (Waiton 2011: 1).

This chapter explores the reasons why anti-sectarianism and its complementary set of offended individuals have not only become an issue for the SNP Government but have led to the implementation of such a controversial Act. In doing so, this chapter will attempt to extend the debate around sectarianism, or in this case, the politics of anti-sectarianism, by making two broad but inter-related points. Firstly, it will be argued that the very existence of offended elites (Waiton 2011) owes its genesis to the fact that the 'legitimate' right to have the monopoly over the definition of sectarianism is the very stake in the struggle between various groups, a process which is highly political insofar as it operates within 'commonsense' or 'mainstream' discursive tropes, which ultimately result in the universalisation of the dominant institutional order (Hall et al. 1978). To name the world is to make the world (Bourdieu 1991), an assertion which invites an analytical approach associated with untangling a social world which is not only defined by certain groups, but which is embedded within the very state which these groups dominate. The second point is that the punitive process of legislating in order to impose the legitimate definition of the problem has other, wider political motives, with the pressing question being not one of criminal justice, but of who gets to decide what constitutes a crime and of whose interests this definition ultimately serves. These political motives, it will be argued, are firmly rooted in the foundations of the neoliberal Leviathan, not as an economic system, but as a political project of state-crafting which exists to create the social conditions for the formation and reproduction of 'a Centaur-state that practices liberalism at the top of the class structure and punitive paternalism at the bottom' (Wacquant 2012: 66).

LANGUAGE AND SYMBOLIC POWER

In a world where reality is socially constructed (Berger and Luckman 1966), the hidden dimensions of the debate around football bigotry are made all the more pernicious by social processes which obscure the fact that its very definition is, itself, a stake in the struggle between competing sections of society. This approach highlights that the class-based nature of the problem is obfuscated through the practices of various powerful groups (Bourdieu 1991), their success dependent on their ability to gain and maintain positions in social space, in order to hold the 'symbolic' authority over how issues are defined, in what terms, and with what consequences. Bourdieu's elaboration on this process makes the point as follows: 'Symbolic power is the power to make things with words . . . In this sense, *symbolic power is a power of consecration or revelation*, the power to consecrate or to reveal things that are already there' (Bourdieu 2003: 23, emphasis in the original).

The recent interest in the issue of sectarianism by various groups illustrates the point further. This specific political 'field' on which the game of anti-sectarianism is played out is made up of the football clubs themselves, politicians, the police, media pundits, academics and, as Waiton highlights, a wide array of 'minority groups' (Waiton 2011) united under the banner of victims of intolerance, all of whom are involved in the struggle for recognition at various levels of governance, depending on their particular agendas and political ambitions. What becomes evident on critical examination is that these so-called 'offended elites' are merely political actors, utilising contemporary tactics best suited to their position within the game, in order to win the struggle for the monopoly over the legitimate right to define the problem of sectarianism, a feat of consecration that is, in itself, an embodiment of power (Bourdieu 1991).

Two questions require to be simultaneously addressed from the outset; firstly, why legislate against sectarianism and, secondly, after four years of almost complete silence from the SNP on the issue, why now?

It can be argued that, in addition to a number of high-profile attacks and threats on leading figures who could perhaps be deemed to have had some connection (however spurious) to Celtic Football Club in 2011, there were three other contributory factors which helped facilitate the passing of legislation on sectarianism. Firstly, the corporatisation of sport, football in particular, witnessed a repositioning of the political positions of many fans, evident in the shift from historical identities to more bourgeois forms of leisure consumption as the fanbase has morphed considerably over the last few decades from one which was dominated by working-class men and involving the continued projection of certain forms of masculinity (see Williams and Taylor 1994) to something more akin to a middle-class spectacle (Hayes 2006). The second point is that opinion poll data, presented by the Scottish Government on their online introduction to the Offensive Behaviour at Football and Threatening Communications (Scotland) Act 2012, showed that the 'general public' had, at that particular time, a healthy appetite for measures to tackle sectarianism. Thirdly, that the unprecedented levels of political capital held by the SNP Government were enough to give them the edge in the struggle to define the 'problem' at precisely the time when the political stakes were purposefully 'raised' in the midst of talk of an independence referendum.

FROM COLLECTIVE IDENTITY TO INDIVIDUALISTIC FORMS OF LEISURE CONSUMPTION

Given that the problems associated with sectarianism have a firm historical foundation and given that the interpretation of this history is the very stake in the struggle between groups, any shift in position in the political field can, according to Bourdieu (1984), result in opportunities to impose new, or at least alternative, meanings and definitions of past traditions. Arguably it was the epochal changes in employment practices caused by wholesale de-industrialisation over the last forty years which created the material conditions for a splitting of what was previously a working class divided between religious or ethnic background (Irish Catholic or Scottish Protestant) into what can arguably be divided into two broad groups which have themselves been fractured and splintered many times over; namely those of the working class in more secure forms of employment and those situated in a more precarious economic position on the margins of the employment sphere (Wacquant 2012). As Jones (2011) points out, this process, spanning decades, saw the British working classes make the transition from 'salt of the earth' to 'scum of the earth', as widespread stigmatisation of class was taken to new levels. This demonisation of the working classes has been accompanied by the dismantling of 'institutional social capital' (Wacquant 2008) across the most deprived areas of the UK, which has seen forms of public assistance, such as social housing, and welfare services change from being institutions which provide social protection to become mechanisms for the surveillance and punishment of marginalised groups (Wacquant 2009, 2012).

It has been argued that the football club and the tribalism connecting people to it and to each other, although often seen as problematic, is the only form of social solidarity and community cohesion that many people, particularly those who lack the necessary forms of capital to participate in wider society, can realistically hope to engage with (Hayes 2006). However, as the consumer side of football rose to dominate the sport in the last twenty years (Finn and Guilianotti 2000), what was once the cohesive glue that bound the fans to their club has begun to show signs of becoming an impediment to other objectives, namely the pursuit of commercial exploitation. As the more traditional working-class fans, particularly those on the periphery of the labour market, were further marginalised by 'increased admissions and the plan to convert the game into a television controlled, integrated leisure package for middle-class "family" consumers' (Williams and Taylor 1994: 233), the game's symbolic order was set to alter both inside and outside the sporting arena.

A useful illustration of the effects of commercialisation in sport on the politics of identity is the fall-out from the Tiger Woods scandal May 2009 where the alleged infidelities of one of America's most clean-cut sports personalities led to the cancellation of tens of millions of dollars of sponsorship deals. Henry Giroux (2009: 1) draws attention to the fact that the tragedy of the celebrity endorser scandal is that it detracts from Woods' image as 'wonderfully dull', an image that 'didn't distract consumers from the products he pitched . . . earning him $100 million annually'. Giroux concludes, 'the more he obliterated his own personality, the more successful he was as a brand and commodity in selling not just products but a lifestyle, desire and commodity-driven dream machine' (Giroux 2009: 1). There is a strong argument to be made that the commercialisation of Scottish football has added to the pressures on clubs to address the issues perpetrated by those whose politically motivated behaviour is deemed to be 'offensive and threatening', that is to say, offensive to market ideology and threatening to corporate profits.

The processes of commodification and marginalisation of 'difference' is the subject of an article by Houck (2006), imaginatively titled 'Crouching Tiger, Hidden Blackness; Tiger Woods and the Disappearance of Race', which illustrates the relentless drive not only to obliterate specific identities in sport, but to create the perfect conditions for passive spectatorship, dressed up in market-friendly tropes which focus on the material and commercial aspect of the game, celebrating wealthy owners and board members, exorbitant weekly wages for star players, lucrative sponsorship deals, TV rights, etc. Another example of the de-politicising effects of the corporatisation of sport is Michael Jordon, who when asked why he refused to endorse the African-American Democrat candidate standing against Jesse Helm replied, 'Republicans buy sneakers too', a far cry indeed from the political convictions of the man he replaced as the world's most famous sports icon, Muhammad Ali.

For Kellner (2001: 25, quoting Dubord 1970), the de-politicisation of sport is not only the inevitable means by which to optimise merchandising revenue through the creation of spectacle, but is also a tool for the pacification of the sports fan: 'The concept of the spectacle is integrally connected to the concept of separation and passivity, for in passively consuming spectacles, one is separated from actively producing one's life.' Kellner goes on to point out that the 'correlative to the spectacle is the spectator, the passive viewer and consumer of a social system predicated on submission, conformity and the cultivation of marketable difference' (Kellner 2001: 40).

It can therefore be argued that increasing social differentiation and the resulting demographic changes in the type of supporters who can afford to be avid football fans has not only had a major impact on the modern game of football but has encouraged many Old Firm fans in Scotland to a move away from more traditional forms of antagonism embodied by open support for either side of the republican/unionist divide. The closer a person moves, in social space, towards powerful groups and individuals, the more their political views are inclined to reflect those of the 'legitimate' view, embodied by the dominant discourse (Savage 1991; Bourdieu 1984, 1991). In the case of those making the transition from a working-class to a more middle-class lifestyle, socialised through the division of labour, the 'habitus'[1] (see Bourdieu 1984) evolves by making transitional changes in preferences and classifications; as people make the transitory journeys required in meeting the aspirations of their perceived social trajectory. The process involves a transformation in the mundane practices of a day-to-day existence where gains in distinction[2] are sought and to which newly occupied positions in social space are added to their corresponding lifestyle choices, that is, from beer to wine, from chip shops to restaurants, from a sedentary lifestyle to regular exercise, from class-based politics (often synonymous with republican and unionist fervour in Scotland and Northern Ireland) to a more 'mainstream', liberal worldview (which rejects political partisanship in favour of the status quo). As Giulianotti (2004: 19), states:

> In football terms, a sizeable middle class audience is financially enfranchised to consume . . . [the] club[s]' products and gain access to prestige fixtures. The habitus of this social class, it might appear, would more readily see the club as a 'lifestyle' interest rather than as a core cultural resource of a socially excluded community.

This, of course, leaves fans vulnerable to division through 'official' government intervention, as upwardly mobile supporters will tend to lean towards more official discourses, while more excluded or marginalised groups will be more likely to turn towards historical or political community values to create the necessary social solidarity to participate in the struggle to define their collective history. Karl Mannheim (1954: 8) offers a useful description of what happens to traditional values during the transition from a working-class to a more middle-class lifestyle, through mobility in the unequal distribution of labour:

> Only when horizontal mobility is accompanied by intensive vertical mobility, i.e. rapid movement between strata in the sense of social ascent and descent, is the belief in the general and eternal validity of one's own thought forms shaken. Vertical mobility is the decisive factor in making persons uncertain and skeptical of their traditional view of the world.

It is, therefore, easy to observe the ways in which *nemos* (the power of vision and division, see Bourdieu 1994) can split those whose identities are linked to more traditional notions of, say, republicanism or loyalism, with all the incumbent trappings (open support for paramilitary groups such as the IRA or the UDA and Orange Order marches or the much less frequent republican marches) and internal logic of practice, from those who see themselves as occupying a distinctively superior position in social space. The first point being made here is that the 'legitimate' or 'mainstream' position promoted by dominant social groups is not imposed on the dominated, but rather presents itself as an aspirational goal (Eagleton 1991) which comes with all the trappings of respectability (Elias 2000) and which certain dominated sections of society might strive towards. The second point is that, on top of the fact that 'sectarianism' in Scotland has been steadily decreasing (Rosie 2004; Bruce et al. 2004, 2006; Raab and Holligan 2011), the stratification of the working classes, which accompanied the de-socialisation of labour caused by the dismantling of the Fordist–Keynesian compact, would most probably have resulted in a further decline in the attachment of Old Firm fans to political causes seen as both outdated and, for some of the more affluent sections, unbecoming of their social status, without legislation being implemented to foster such a shift.

A PROBLEM OF PERCEPTION, OR THE PERCEPTION OF A PROBLEM?

Another factor which assisted the choice of prioritising anti-sectarianism as a policy target was the promotion of statistical data which alluded to the (ironic) growth in levels of intolerance to various forms of intolerance by the Scottish public, evidenced as follows (Scottish Government 2012):

- 89% of Scots agree that sectarianism is offensive
- 89% of Scots agree that sectarianism is unacceptable in Scottish football
- 85% of Scots agree that sectarianism should be a criminal offence
- 91% agree that stronger action needs to be taken to tackle sectarianism and offensive behaviour associated with football in Scotland

These factors, coupled with the remarkable victory of the SNP in a democratic system which was set up to preclude the overall majority of any one single party, gave the SNP Government unprecedented levels of political capital, which they pragmatically put to use by deciding to implement an Act of the Scottish Parliament, in a highly problematic area, previously thought to be insoluble.

That there were so many dissenting voices, from practically all quarters during the legislative phase, offers an insight into the nature of the struggle which had, until the SNP triumphed through the imposition of the Offensive Behaviour at Football and Threatening Communications (Scotland) Act 2012, displaced the power relations which lent previous definitions their legitimacy. Through the enactment of statutory provisions, the SNP Government succeeded in winning the war over the legitimate right to define the problem of sectarianism, as well as the solution, while raising the stakes and forging the kind of profile necessary to create political competence (Flint 2008) through what it promoted as the forward thinking and ambitious objective of eradicating sectarianism.

The fact that the discourse around the issue of sectarianism in Scotland is largely determined by powerful groups explains why the issue mostly exists without reference to the historical context in Ireland, or at least, when the historical context is raised, it is done so in a way in which words such as 'imperialism', 'military occupation', 'oppression', 'internment' and 'economic exploitation' are conspicuous by their absence. These selective omissions, which require an approach seeking to question the assumptions that underpin many of our everyday orthodoxies, are essential if we are to break free from 'a false critical thought which, under cover of apparently progressive tropes celebrating the "subject," "identity," "multiculturalism," "diversity," and "globalization," invites us to submit to the prevailing forces of the world, and in particular to market forces' (Wacquant 2004: 1).

When placed in comparison with other intellectual traditions, particularly the more critical schools of thought found in France and Germany, the problems associated with 'commonsense' thought are over-represented in the English-speaking world, a fact which, as Perry Anderson highlights, results in discourses which are suffocated by the two chemical elements of this 'blanketing English fog, of traditionalism and empiricism' (Anderson 1964: 9).

It is this commitment to the empirical, or the self-evident, which is embodied in the 'official' view (Bourdieu 1991), which must, when looking at the 'legitimate' definition of 'sectarianism', be taken into account (Bourdieu 1994: 15):

> It should not be forgotten that a primordial political belief, this doxa, is an orthodoxy, a right, a correct, dominant vision which has more often than not been imposed through struggles against competing visions. This means that the 'natural attitude' mentioned by the phenomenologists, i.e. the primary experience of the world of commonsense, is a politically produced relation as are the categories of perception that sustain it. What appears to us today as self-evident, as beneath consciousness and choice, has quite often been the stake of struggles and instituted only as the result of dogged confrontations between dominant and dominated groups.

The stake of these struggles and the creation of a 'commonsense' position is one of the foundation stones for the shift from a politics of redistribution to one which embraces identity politics, a fashion which credits its meteoric rise to the ascendancy of neoliberalism in the latter quarter of the twentieth century (see the work of Nancy Frazer 1987, 1989, 1995 and particularly Frazer and Honneth 2003).

THE CENTAUR STATE

Having mapped out a general analytical model for loosening the intellectual grip of a 'commonsense' or 'mainstream' view, itself woven through the entire fabric of the state, the second broad area of argument, directly related to the hidden power dynamics of language and symbolic power, revolves around the political project of the neoliberal Leviathan.

As Waiton (2011) points out, the collaborative and individual works of Steve Bruce, Tony Glendinning, Iain Paterson and Michael Rosie, among many others, strongly reject the idea that Scotland is a country riven by sectarian division.

Examining statistical data, they show that the Protestant religious identity is on the wane (Raab and Holligan 2011) and that the educational and employment disadvantages faced by Catholics in Scotland have reduced dramatically from the 1960s to the present day (Bruce et al. 2004, 2006). They claim that the incidence of inter-religious marriage is at an all-time high and that Scotland is becoming ever more increasingly secularised (Rosie 2004; Bruce et al. 2004, 2006; Raab and Holligan 2011).

This is not to suggest that religious or anti-Irish discrimination does not exist, but rather, what emerges is an over-emphasis of a particular problem, located at the lower end of the socio-economic spectrum, and in this case, as with many others, one where the solution is increasingly to be found in the 'criminalisation' of more and more aspects of daily life. This process, presented by the media and other mainstream institutions as 'crime fighting', is little more than a convenient pretext for a broader redrawing of the perimeter of responsibility of the state operating simultaneously on economic, social welfare and penal fronts in an era of advanced neoliberalism (Wacquant 2012).

The hidden aspect of criminalising behaviour which is deemed to be 'offensive' is, as Wacquant has suggested (2008, 2009, 2012), an integral part of neoliberalism's pervasive political project, which entails not a dismantling but a re-engineering of the state, through promoting the market as the best mechanism for the allocation of resources, while increasing the levels of conditionality in welfare provision (Wacquant 2012), all nicely framed in the tropes of 'individual responsibility', a term which is almost always preceded, in current rhetorical discourse, by the notion of 'rights'. This re-engineering of the state reforms and refocuses notions of collectivist welfare provision, obliterating the remaining residue from the dismantling of the Fordist–Keynesian compact, leading to a liberalist–paternalist dichotomy which fosters an approach which results in the state using velvet gloves when dealing with those at the top of the social hierarchy and an iron fist for those at the bottom.

This brings us to Wacquant's other point that 'neoliberalism entails a rightward tilting of the space of bureaucratic agencies that define and distribute public goods, and spawns a Centaur state that practices liberalism at the top of the class structure and punitive paternalism at the bottom' (Wacquant 2012: 66).

This Centaur state, realised through doxic notions and euphemised through tropes which seek not to replace one word for another, but to supplant entire discourses, operates to mask the divide-and-rule nature of capitalist society by deploying discourses based on narrow notions of 'respect'. As Bruce et al. (2006: 173) claim, Scotland has a problem with incivility 'in which . . . thugs sometimes use religion and ethnic origin to divide their impoverished world into them and us (quoted in Flint and Powell 2010: 201). This euphemised discourse largely ignores the genesis of the problem of social division which, as Harvey (2011) points out, owes much to the fact that capitalists have long controlled the surplus army of labour through pitting worker against worker, 'to the degree that the potential labour force is gendered, racialised, ethnicised, tribalised or divided by language, political and sexual orientation and religious beliefs' (Harvey 2010: 61).

This contradictory position taken by Bruce et al. (2006) is arguably the product of a system of inculcation tasked with the function of masking the arbitrary nature of a socially constructed reality, and fostered through various institutions, the most dangerous of which always appear independent or neutral (Foucault 1991), including such seemingly innocent organisations as Nil By Mouth or Sense Over Sectarianism, which arguably serve to reproduce 'commonsense', 'mainstream' and therefore highly political notions of what those who dominate the state deem to be offensive or, in the case of Scotland, 'bad for business' (Flint 2008).

Wacquant's notes on social polarisation and the punitive upsurge can be usefully applied to the current problem of anti-sectarianism in Scotland, particularly with regard to the Centaur state and its tightening grip on the lower strata. Wacquant (2008: 10) states that the general overarching theme of neoliberal law-enforcement policies is that they seek to tackle problems 'while deliberately disregarding their causes'. Indeed, Wacquant's six traits of the neoliberal punitive upsurge against those who occupy the lower regions of social space, when read alongside recent legislative measures to address 'sectarianism' and bigotry in Scotland, are uncannily familiar.

Firstly, the heralding of an end to leniency and the adoption of a 'zero-tolerance' position is evident in the very spirit of the discussions leading up to the Bill. The fact that the first reading of the Bill was put back six months to allay fears that it was being fast-tracked through Parliament in order to be in place for the start of the football season (Scottish Government 2012) is evidence that the message that this issue would *no longer be tolerated* was being sent out by those who had won exclusive rights over the definition of the 'problem' itself. Such circumstantial evidence suggests that the Scottish Government was, as mentioned above, anxious to demonstrate that it was not afraid to grasp an issue, previously seen as insoluble, in order to make further political capital at a time when what was needed was a government strong enough to preside over an independent Scotland. Compare this rush to prosecute football fans who behave in ways deemed to be offensive with the UK Government's approach to banking reform, which incidentally will have to wait until 2019 to see the mild measures proposed by John Vickers implemented. As Robert Jenkins, who sits on the Bank of England's financial policy committee, points out, the date is distant enough 'to allow lobbyists to chip away until the proposal becomes both unrecognisable and ineffective' (Monbiot 2012). Opponents of the Offensive Behaviour at Football Act were afforded no such luxury as the Bill was ushered through the Scottish Parliament in a matter of months.

Secondly, Wacquant draws our attention to the proliferation of punitive laws and an insatiable craving for bureaucratic innovations, in this case Football Banning Orders (see Hamilton-Smith et al. 2011; Hamilton-Smith and McArdle in this volume) and the passing of the Offensive Behaviour at Football Matches and Threatening Communications (Scotland) Act 2012. Other such innovations include Anti-social Behaviour Orders, Acceptable Behaviour Contracts, Dispersal Orders (Flint 2008) and Parenting Orders (see Flint and Nixon 2006). The argument here is that these measures serve only to shift the burden onto one section of society by employing strategies which ultimately attempt to wholly attribute one particular aspect of a multi-dimensional problem to the least powerful sections of society.

The third point is that the need for change is conveyed by alarmist, even cata-
strophic discourse on insecurity, broadcast to saturation by the media, major political parties and professionals in the enforcement of order. This is evidenced through
the reaction of various governments to media stories covering sectarianism over the
years. As Flint (2008) points out, despite the fact that these problems are attributed
to a 'bigoted few' or a 'selfish minority', isolated incidents are mostly portrayed in
an alarmist rhetoric, evidenced when the former Deputy First Minister spoke of 'the
ugly spectre of sectarianism', a society over which 'religious hatred frequently casts a
dark shadow' (Scottish Executive 2002, quoted in Flint 2008: 124).

Fourthly, out of a proclaimed concern for 'efficiency' in the war on crime 'and
solicitude towards the deserving citizen' (in this case, the crime victim), 'this discourse openly revalorises repression and stigmatises . . . people from working class
neighbourhoods . . .' (Wacquant 2008: 10). There were, of course, vociferous objections to the passing of this Act. Many of the criticisms focused on the fact that this
was the demonisation of a particular social group (McWhirter 2011):

> This legislation is otiose, contradictory, authoritarian, subjective, illiberal,
> anti-democratic and contrary to internationally accepted definitions of basic
> human rights. It is threatening and offensive to freedom of speech, freedom
> of association, freedom of thought and to personal liberty. It hands discretion-
> ary powers to the police that are wholly inappropriate in any civilised society,
> effectively giving individual officers the power to deprive people of their liberty
> if they don't like the way they are behaving.

The fifth trait is that any notion of rehabilitation has been replaced by a mana-
gerialist approach (see Flint 2008). Finally, these measures invariably involve a
tightening of the police dragnet, accompanied by the hardening and speeding up of
judicial procedures (Wacquant 2008: 10). The passing of the Offensive Behaviour at
Football Matches and Threatening Communications (Scotland) Act 2012, which
criminalises certain behaviours in a sport which, although changing in demographic
support, still has a large number of lower-class males, perhaps provides the best testimony to Wacquant's final 'trait', which exposes many of the hidden facets of the
neoliberal punitive upsurge.

This issue of the Centaur state is supported in the popular account by one of
Britain's most eminent investigative journalists, Tom Bower (2003), whose work
also provides an appropriate backdrop to the demise of Rangers Football Club.
Bower effectively demonstrates how football represents the wider political economy
in microcosm; with wealth redistributed upwards from the many (the fans) to the
few (the chairmen and board members), secondly, that the money is disproportion-
ately concentrated in the hands of a small number of larger clubs, and thirdly, that
the trickle-down aspect which would see smaller clubs benefit is all but a myth. He
shows how paying fans and television subscribers are funding corruption and large-
scale tax evasion by some of the game's most influential and wealthy individuals.
The most relevant aspect of Bower's book is the chapter which describes how the
Labour Government tried and failed to regulate the game. That an attempt was

made to address the issue is encouraging; that this was ultimately doomed to failure in a system which makes any regulation of life for those at the upper end of the social hierarchy almost impossible, provides a sobering reminder of the true nature of the neoliberal state.

CONCLUSIONS

In a critical sense, the problem of 'sectarianism' is not one of criminal justice, but of criminalisation. The critical thinker must firstly ask: who has the monopoly over the legitimate right to define the issue of what might be deemed to be 'offensive behaviour at football matches' as a crime? Only by understanding the political background to the problem can we begin to understand the problem itself. To summarise the points made above, the social world, as apprehended and presented through public institutions as well as the mainstream media, is inextricably linked to an unconscious set of doxic notions prescribed in large part by certain groups who dominate the state (Bourdieu 1991, 1994) and which underpin the struggles over the legitimate monopoly to define 'social reality', in this case, of football bigotry and its solutions.

Strategically deploying its hoard of political capital, the SNP Government emerged victorious in this struggle, and despite a great number of protestations from many quarters, the Offensive Behaviour at Football Matches and Threatening Communications (Scotland) Act 2011, laying out the statutory prescriptions relating to offences for which arguably already existed sufficient criminal legislation, was more about state-crafting than crime-fighting. With its foundations firmly embedded in the necessity of 'growth' and the accumulation of profit, the neoliberal Leviathan has its own internal logic, it being much easier to privatise than nationalise, much easier for inequality to prevail than for the redistribution of material and symbolic goods, and insofar as it is much easier to deregulate conditions for those at the top of the social order, it is much easier to regulate all aspects of life for those at the bottom.

Commentators like Stuart Waiton and other 'libertarian' writers such as Frank Furedi (2012) and Brendan O'Neil (2011), while criticising the workings of the neoliberal state, fail to unmask these otherwise hidden forms of power and domination, resulting in theory-lite critiques of the dominant vision which give some degree of legitimacy to 'commonsense' views because their critical approach falls so short as to leave unquestioned the very definitions of the reality which reproduce and augment the inequalities which already exist between dominant and dominated groups.

This chapter has attempted to show that the 'offendedness' of elites is merely a strategy in the consecration game, where the struggle over the legitimate right to define reality is the ultimate stake. The situation alluded to here, firmly embedded in the neoliberal Leviathan, casts a long shadow over the future of football, a future where the inequality gap will most probably get bigger not smaller, and with all the incumbent social problems this brings (see Wilkinson and Pickett 2009). This chapter has examined the political nature of the sectarian debate, or rather as

Waiton rightly points out, the growing problem of 'anti-sectarianism'. That there are issues of concern, no one is disputing. Perhaps ironically, the precarious situation that Scottish football now finds itself in may yet provide the solution. Fans, who arguably have more in common with each other than the criminogenic economic elites who run their clubs (Bower 2003), may well yet have the opportunity to play a much more active role, through community ownership of their clubs, at some point in the future. If social problems in society are more the result of structural factors than behavioural issues, then the running of football clubs by their fans may well see the formation of some broader alliances, embodied by solidarities which serve the interests of those involved, namely the supporters of football, rather than the narrow and destructive interests of capital accumulation.

For the dominant classes who preside over the financial (mis)management of football clubs, ethical and legal failings may result in civil action being taken through the courts. For the dominated, however, any perceived misdemeanour with regard to behaviour at football matches has now been officially criminalised and could result in up to five years' imprisonment. It remains to be seen (at the time of writing) whether or not those responsible for the demise of Rangers Football Club, through not only financial mismanagement but what may turn out to be wholesale tax evasion, will be brought to justice. What is more likely to follow, however, is that the juridical deficit between the powerful and the powerless will continue to augment, as will the efficacy of the Centaur state. A line from the Bob Dylan song 'Jokerman' provides, perhaps, an appropriate cadence to the argument presented above: 'steal a little and they put you in jail, steal a lot and they make you king' (or at least give you a knighthood).

NOTES

1. Habitus helps to explain why people of different classes behave, think and act in the rather predictable ways that they do. Inextricably linked to Bourdieu's notions of 'field' (where the games are played) and the various forms of 'capital' (the stakes in the game), habitus can be seen as the individual's own style of play, their own dispositions which determine both the strategies employed and the methods of employment. A person's cultural dispositions, from their taste in music, eating habits, political positions, etc., down to the way they walk, talk and dress are determined by habitus, which is most heavily influenced by 'one's sense of place', that is, where one sees oneself in the wider social world.

2. Bourdieu extended economic-based analyses to consider class connections to practices such as eating habits, shopping choices, sporting activities and attitudes towards the body. People belonging to one class seek to show their superiority to their closest neighbouring class by accumulating social, cultural and educational capital (power) over their nearest class rival, thus maintaining their differential status. Accumulating such power (capital) is compounded by having, and being seen to have, good taste that allows one to separate oneself from class rivals, to make gains in distinction.

REFERENCES

Anderson, P. (1964), 'Origins of the present crisis', *New Left Review*, 1: 23, 30–2.

Berger, P. and Luckman, T. (1966), *The Social Construction of Reality*, London: Penguin.

Bourdieu, P. (1984), *Distinction*, Cambridge, MA: Harvard University Press.

Bourdieu, P. (1991), *Language and Symbolic Power*, Cambridge: Polity Press.

Bourdieu, P. (1994), 'Rethinking the State: genesis and structure of the bureaucratic field', *Sociological Theory*, 12: 1, 1–18.

Bourdieu, P. (2003), *Firing Back: Against the Tyranny of the Market*, London: Verso.

Bower, T. (2003), *Broken Dreams: Vanity, Greed and the Souring of British Football*, London: Simon and Schuster.

Bruce, S., Glendinning, T., Paterson, I. and Rosie, M. J. (2004), *Sectarianism in Modern Scotland*, Edinburgh: Edinburgh University Press.

Bruce, S., Glendinning, T., Paterson, I. and Rosie, M. J. (2006), *Religious Discrimination in Scotland: Fact or Myth*, Edinburgh: Edinburgh University Press.

Dubord, G. (1970), *The Society of the Spectacle*, Detroit: Black and Red Translations.

Eagleton, T. (1991), *Ideology*, London: Verso.

Elias, N. (2000), *The Civilising Process*, London: Blackwell.

Finn, G. and Giulianotti, R. (eds) (2000), *Football Culture: Local Contests, Global Visions*, London: Frank Cass Publishers.

Flint, J. (2008), 'Governing Sectarianism in Scotland', *Scottish Affairs*, 63: Spring, 107–24.

Flint, J. and Powell, R. (2011), '"They Sing That Song": Sectarianism and Conduct in the Informalised Spaces of Scottish Football', in D. Burdsey (ed.), *Race, Ethnicity and Football: Persistent Debates and Emerging Issues*, London: Routledge, pp. 191–204.

Foucault, M. (1991), 'Governmentality', in G. Burchell, C. Gordon and P. Miller (eds), *The Foucault Effect: Studies in Governmentality*, Hemel Hempstead: Harvester Wheatsheaf, pp. 87–104.

Fraser, N. (1987), 'Women, Welfare and the Politics of Need Interpretation', *Thesis Eleven*, 17.

Fraser, N. (1989), *Unruly Practices, Discourse, and Gender in Contemporary Social Theory*, Cambridge: Polity.

Frazer, N. (1995), 'From Redistribution to Recognition? Dilemmas of justice in a Post Socialist Age', *New Left Review*, 1: 212, 68–93.

Frazer, N. and Honneth, A. (2003), *Redistribution or Recognition: A Political–Philosophical Exchange*, London: Verso.

Furedi, F. (2012), 'The elites are making a virtue of intolerance', *Spiked Online*, 8 March 2012, http://www.spiked-online.com/site/article/12223/ (last accessed 27 July 2012).

Giroux, H. (2009), 'Tiger Woods' Infidelity to His Responsibilities as a Corporate Brand', *The Network of Spiritual Progressives*, 15 December 2009, http://www.spiritualprogressives.org/article.php/2009121713042487 (last accessed 1 July 2012).

Giulianotti, R. (2004), 'Celtic, Cultural Identities and the Globalisation of Football: Notes from the 2003 UEFA Cup Final in Seville', *Scottish Affairs*, 48: Summer, http://www.scottishaffairs.org/backiss/pdfs/sa48/Sa48_Giulianotti.pdf (last accessed 1 July 2012).

Hall, S., Critcher, C., Jefferson, T., Clarke, J. and Roberts, B. (1978), *Policing the Crisis: mugging, the State and law and order*, London: Macmillan.

Hamilton-Smith, N., Bradford, B., Hopkins, M., Kurland, J., Lightowler, C., McArdle, D. and Tilley, N. (2011), *An Evaluation of Football Banning Orders in Scotland*, Edinburgh: Scottish Government, http://www.scotland.gov.uk/Resource/Doc/354566/0119713.pdf (last accessed 1 July 2012).

Harvey, D. (2010), *The Enigma of Capital and the Crises of Capitalism*, London: Profile Books.

Hayes, M. (2006), 'Glasgow Celtic Fans, Political Culture and the Tiocfaidh Ar La Fanzine: Some Comments and a Content Analysis', *Football Studies*, 9: 1, 5–18.

Houck, D. W. (2006), 'Crouching Tiger; Hidden Blackness: Tiger Woods and the Disappearance of Race', in A. Ranay and J. Bryant (eds), *Handbook of Sports and Media*, Mahwah, NJ: L. Erlbaum Associates, pp. 469–84.

Jones, O. (2011), *Chavs: the demonization of the working class*, London: Verso.

Kellner, D. (2001), 'The sports spectacle, Michael Jordon and Nike: The Unholy Alliance?', in D. L. Andrews (ed.), *Michael Jordan Inc: Corporate Sport, Media Culture and Late Modern America*, New York, NY: State University of New York Press, pp. 37–63.

McWhirter, I. (2011), 'Salmond's First Own Goal. Sectarianism', *Iain McWhirter Now and Then*, 14 December 2011, http://iainmacwhirter2.blogspot.com/2011/12/salmonds-first-own-goal-sectarianism.html (last accessed 1 July 2012).

Mannheim, K. (1954), *Ideology and Utopia*, London: Routledge.

Monbiot, G. (2012), 'Making Democracy Safe for Business', *George Monbiot*, 9 January 2012, http://www.monbiot.com/2012/01/09/making-democracy-safe-for-business/ (last accessed 1 July 2012).

O'Neill, B. (2011), 'Welcome to the era of the post-moral panic', *Spiked Online*, 7 November 2011, http://www.spiked-online.com/site/article/11377/ (last accessed 27 July 2012).

Raab, G. and Holligan, C. (2011), 'Sectarianism: myth or social reality? Inter-sectarian partnerships in Scotland, evidence from the Scottish Longitudinal Study', *Ethnic and Racial Studies*, First Article, 1–21, DOI:10.1080/01419870.2011.607506.

Rosie, M. (2004), *The Sectarian Myth in Scotland*, New York, NY: Palgrave Macmillan.

Savage, M. (1991), 'Making Sense of Middle-Class Politics', *The Sociological Review*, 39: 1, 26–54.

Scottish Executive (2002), *Ministerial statement on sectarianism: News Release 7/10/2002*, Edinburgh: Scottish Executive.

Scottish Government (2012), *Offensive Behaviour at Football and Threatening Communications (Scotland) Act 2012*, http://www.scotland.gov.uk/Topics/Justice/law/sectarianism-action-1/football-violence/bill (last accessed 1 July 2012).

Waiton, S. (2011), 'Stuart Waiton on anti-sectarianism', *Spiked Online*, 5 December 2011, http://www.spiked-online.com/index.php/essays/article/11866 (last accessed 23 June 2012).

Wacquant, L. (2004), 'Critical Thought as Solvent of Doxa', *Constellations*, 11: 1, 97–101.

Wacquant, L. (2008), 'Ordering Insecurity', *Radical Philosophy Review*, 11: 1, 9–27.

Wacquant, L. (2009), *Punishing the Poor: The Neoliberal Government of Social Insecurity*, Durham, NC: Duke University Press.

Wacquant, L. (2012), 'Three steps towards a historical anthropology of actually existing neoliberalism', *Social Anthropology*, 20: 1, 66–79.

Wilkinson, R. G. and Pickett, K. E. (2009), *The Spirit Level: Why equality is better for everyone*, London: Allen Lane.

Williams, J. and Taylor, R. (1994), 'Boys keep swinging: Masculinity and football culture in England', in T. Newburn, and E. Stanko (eds), *Just Boys Doing Business? Men, masculinities and crime*, London: Routledge, pp. 214–33.

Žižek, S. (1989), *The Sublime Object of Ideology*, London: Verso.

Žižek, S. (2011), *Democracy in What State*, New York, NY: Columbia University Press.

13 Sectarianism Sells – or Does It? A Celtic Supporter's View

Patrick McVey

INTRODUCTION

I was flattered to be invited to provide a chapter for this collection of views on football, bigotry and Scotland. I am no academic and my only public literary experience is the occasional article since 2008 on online Celtic fora and blogs (as Auldheid/Auldyin) on issues affecting Celtic FC and Scottish football. However, it is in writing those articles and reading others, coming from what I believe is a well-educated and articulate support base, that I have formed a view of what the relevant issues and concerns around sectarianism and Scottish football are and developed my thoughts on where it might all lead on both the football and social front. I will begin with my conclusions on sectarianism in our game gained through my own eyes and experience of life and of being a Celtic supporter, and I will describe how I reached them. My views on sectarianism are based not so much on my earlier experiences, for reasons that will become obvious, but mainly on what has emerged from the downfall of Glasgow Rangers since 2008 when Lloyds Bank said 'Enough!' and the aftermath. My four key conclusions are:

1. First and foremost in the context of Scottish football, *there is a perception that sectarianism sells, that it makes money*. It sells season books, newspapers and advertising, as well as TV rights globally, to a world that watches for the potential for violence as much as for the quality of football. It therefore has a high commercial value to the many parties involved, not only in partaking of the game but in the administration and reporting of it. For them all – sectarianism sells.
2. At a human level, sectarianism appeals to an individual's sense of needing to belong to something greater, but draws on the inner instinctive response when one's 'sect' feels threatened.
3. It can be subconscious, and those expressing sectarian views or acting out of a sectarian attitude are often unaware of doing so or will deny that they are.
4. Consequently we will never completely eradicate sectarianism in Scotland but we can limit the damage it can cause Scottish society if as a nation, like an

alcoholic taking the first of the twelve steps to recovery, we admit there is a deep-seated problem that measures like the Offensive Behaviour at Football and Threatening Communications (Scotland) Act 2012 will no more heal than will putting an Elastoplast on a broken leg.

A BRIEF PERSONAL HISTORY

You will note that in my conclusions there is no mention of religion, Ireland, Irish history or the Orange Order, and I was conscious when asked to write about sectarianism in football that I had not myself suffered from sectarianism to any marked degree during my childhood years in the early 1950s or in adult life thereafter. My father, a Catholic Calton man, had experience of it, as had his father, but while my father disliked Rangers as a sectarian institution with a vengeance, he went to some lengths to impress on me the difference between the institution and the individuals. One of his favourite boasts was that I played football with the Catholics in the morning (St Mungo's Academy) and the Protestants in the afternoon (St James Calton Boys' Club). My own epiphany, when I realised and internalised my father's message, came on a visit to Ibrox as a teenager. This required a walk to the St Enoch Underground station from Glasgow Cross to wait in a long queue before getting the Underground to Copland Road. Bedecked in our Celtic scarves, my pals and I were ushered into the near-front of the queue by our Rangers-supporting pals whom we played football in Bell Street with under street light most week nights. We played the usual banter games while in the queue and in those days a Rangers victory at Ibrox was an almost certainty, but it was all good-humoured. We separated at the ground, they to the Broomloan Road 'Rangers end', myself and my pals to the Helen Street 'Celtic end'. The singing at first was weak but as the crowd increased so too did the volume and the number of hymns of hate that were being hurled from both sides of the stadium at each other. 'Hang on a minute,' I thought to myself, 'those are my mates over there, not some Orange bastards I want to see die no more than they want to walk knee deep in my Fenian blood', and I stopped joining in. Apart from a Glasgow Cup game in 1967 when Bobby Lennox tore Rangers apart in a 4–0 victory that was to be the shape of things to come, I have never gone back to Ibrox or attended a Celtic v. Rangers game at Celtic Park. That did not mean my passion for supporting Celtic diminished, although like many young men growing up, getting married and having families, the passion did not always manifest itself by attendance at games, although European Cup/Champions League nights always had a magnetic attraction. If anyone ever wishes to experience that deep feeling of 'belonging', one that is the natural and beneficial side of sectarianism, then there is nothing like being at Celtic Park on a Champions League night. The 4–3 game v. Juventus in October 2001 stands out as much as the hairs on the back of my neck stood up in an 'I was there' night.

In my working life too, because I worked in the UK Civil Service administered to UK national standards from London and not Edinburgh, I rarely encountered malevolent sectarianism to further prejudice any views I might have, although I do

recall two instances on which my conclusion of the often subconscious nature of sec-
tarianism is based. It must have been in early 1980 when the Overseas Development
Administration (ODA) as it was then (now the Department for International
Development) was recruiting staff – one of whom incidentally now finds himself as
The Rangers manager in the most turbulent period in their history – that a fellow
recruitment board member from Centre One, who were also recruiting, remarked
to me that he was mildly surprised at the quality of the candidates presenting from
Catholic schools. I was briefly thrown by this indication of Protestant superiority, but I detected there was no malice in the statement, just an observation being
made in an unconscious way. Thus I nodded in agreement but was thinking, 'I'm
not a bad example of a Catholic education myself *pal*' (italics being the only way to
get my annoyance across on paper!). I managed the ODA office football team for
two years and it was a true and full social mix of both sides of the sectarian divide
throughout the office and East Kilbride itself. Indeed, one of the future Rangers
manager's friends was as big a Celtic supporter as you will find. So it is no exaggeration to say we all got along. However, I did find my patience tested over a couple
of days when I was unlucky enough to be in the company of one Rangers man, a
civil soul on a (well-named) Disaster Recovery Course in London after a disastrous
Celtic defeat at Ibrox. No matter how a conversation started he always brought it
around to the game and how bad it must feel to be a Celtic supporter at that time.
He was pleasant about it but so incessant that I concluded after a while he was
simply unaware of the possible impact on his nose had I been a less tolerant human
being. However, both instances, in the context of civil persons in a civil service
in a civil society, serve to reinforce my view that while some folk might be openly
sectarian and malevolent of intent, there are many decent others who are friends
but unaware of the impact of superiority thinking that comes from being part of
the bigger side of the sectarian divide in Scotland, a kind of intellectual superiority
snobbery that I believe a good Catholic education system has neutralised in modern
Scotland.

THE FORCES OF 'SECTARIANISM'

So, given that the vast majority of my personal 'sectarian' experiences or individual
encounters have not been of the malevolent variety, why is it that my perception
of sectarianism in Scotland is that it is more a malevolent than benevolent force?
What takes sectarianism out of the personal arena and into the institutional one
and affects me and fellow Celtic supporters to varying degrees, from annoyance to
anger and possibly in some cases hatred? The answer to that has to be the way that
Glasgow Rangers, before their demise, became the totem around which the most
malevolent attitudes of sectarianism were allowed to gather and flourish, to the bet-
terment of that entity at the expense of the great game of football in Scotland and
to the financial cost of the other professional football clubs in Scotland, including
my beloved Celtic.

However, in the lead-up to 2008 and for a couple of seasons thereafter, it was my own and others' accepted thinking that it was sectarianism based on the religion of the two sides that was the driver of malevolence. It took a while before it became clear to me that it was not sectarianism on religious grounds that was driving Rangers the institution, or the Scottish Football Association, or their institutional 'hear no evil, see no evil, speak no evil' media supporters in press and broadcasting, but rather *the money* that all three parties perceived was being generated by sectarianism. In my view this was, and is, the underlying reason for sectarianism flourishing and corrupting the game.

On 10 May 2008, when Craig Levein, in a famous post-match interview, ranted, 'It's all about Rangers, it's all about Rangers . . . It's important that Rangers do not lose the title', no one in Scottish football could have known at that time *just* how important winning the title and securing Champions League money was to securing the future of Glasgow Rangers. Or perhaps, more accurately, how this postponed their final demise which began when they ironically failed the UEFA footballing qualification test in 2011 against Malmö and Maribor, having originally secured admission under questionable circumstances in relation to the interpretation of unpaid social tax rules set out in UEFA Club Licensing 2010, by a compliant Scottish Football Association. Many thought in May 2008 that it was just a continuation of the days of yore when Jim Farry held up the registration of Jorge Cadette in 1996, apparently (to some at least) to hinder Celtic's chances of winning a title, or when Bobby Tait, a Rangers-supporting referee, was appointed to officiate a crucial title-deciding game against Kilmarnock in 1998, where he allowed six to eight minutes injury time, giving Rangers more opportunity to score to win. Ironically, to many Celtic fans, Kilmarnock ended up scoring the winner in injury time, thus clearing the way for Celtic to stop Rangers winning ten in a row.

In spring 2010, due to a season of 'honest mistakes',[1] an Open Meeting of Celtic supporters took place at St Mary's Calton. They were angered by referee Dougie McDonald's decision to order off Scott Brown and not Kyle Lafferty in a game at Ibrox. These fans blamed the sectarian persuasion of the alleged MIBs (Masons in Black) rather than any monetary reason. It became clear, however, that something was afoot and deeper questions started to be asked when the same referee, Dougie McDonald, and Head of Referee Development and his boss Hugh Dallas, got into a muddle involving Neil Lennon, and Steven Craven, a third match official no longer allowed to referee even at lower levels, in attempting to publicly justify McDonald's decision to change his mind about a decision that McDonald had made to award a penalty to Celtic in a match in October 2010 v. Dundee United at Tannadice (see Rosie in this volume).

Even in this instance, though, the departure of Dallas was coloured more by the religious perception of sectarianism than any financial one, when it was reported by Phil Mac Giolla Bhain, a Scottish freelance journalist residing in Ireland, that Dallas had passed on a tasteless e-mail message about the Pope who had visited Scotland earlier in September. Dallas was removed from his post for that e-mail but no questions were asked about his explanation of events or why McDonald, already with a history of questionable decisions against Celtic, was chosen for that particular match at a venue where Celtic could always expect a hard game. However, even if these questions had been asked, the first impulse would have been that it was purely the sectarian influence from a religious perspective that was behind it.

THE FINANCIAL IMPERATIVES DRIVING 'SECTARIANISM'

That all changed for me in 2010 when Phil Mac Giolla Bhain broke the story that Rangers were being investigated by HMRC in respect of their usage of Employee Benefit Trusts (EBTs) to pay players by a route that avoided the full payment of tax and National Insurance. That really blew away the legend or myth that sectarianism in Scottish football was at heart a religious issue with historical roots. No it wasn't – not any longer. Now it moved from being about religion or religious rivalry to being about the money that 'sectarianism' brought into the game in Scotland, which I would argue has fuelled the Scottish professional football industry to the detriment, indeed corruption, of the sport itself as well as the ethics of mainstream journalism. That this is so can be seen from the response to Rangers' difficulties by both the Scottish Premier League and the Scottish Football Association, who, rather than apply the rules without fear or favour, instead, out of concerns for financial collapse and backed all the way by the mainstream media (some of whom were ex-footballers and alleged EBT beneficiaries, but all of whom were benefiting from reporting on Scottish football), attempted to gerrymander a rescue of Rangers. Not because they were a Protestant club, not because they operated in a deeply sectarian society, but because of the fear of the loss of revenues and jobs all of those in Scottish football thought would happen if Rangers disappeared. 'Scotland needs a strong Rangers' was the mantra of the rescuers, completely ignoring that a truly strong Rangers had never really existed since at least 2000, when they started to indulge in the twin financial steroids of ever-rising debt and ever-increasing use of EBTs until 2007, when with EBTs under question, they reduced their usage and returned to debt as their main stimulant. The myth of a strong Rangers is proving difficult to dispel, even following their administration and liquidation in 2012. However, in spite of the SPL/SFA machinations, the light being shone on dark places by online blogs and fora like The Rangers Tax Case (who had inside information on EBT usage at Ibrox and used it splendidly), Celtic Quick News, Celtic Underground, etc., as well as the ongoing probing by Phil Mac Giolla Bhain and others, had an unanticipated effect. Their sharing of information and ridiculing of some of the outrageous utterances from football authorities via mainstream media, like claims of Armageddon for Scottish football or civil unrest, sufficiently informed and influenced the minds of supporters of other clubs throughout Scotland to exert pressure on SPL club chairmen not to allow a passage back into the top flight for Rangers that sacrificed sporting integrity on the altar of commercialism. It would be remiss at this point not to mention the courageous lead set by Raith Rovers Chairman Turnbull Hutton when the same football authorities tried to browbeat the lower divisions of Scottish football to accept a plan to treat a now-liquidated Rangers differently that undermined the sporting integrity and the merit principles on which the whole game is based. Such courageous leadership and adherence to ethics by Mr Hutton should find its way to the top of the governance of our game, if not in said gentleman's elevation to an influential SFA post, then certainly in the job specification of any future SFA leaders.

One would imagine, or maybe simply just hope, that at this point an awareness would start to emerge among the key stakeholders in Scottish football: the SFA as governors; the mainstream media who depend on the reporting of the game for a living and whom I believe fuel sectarian attitudes as a result; the supporters of Scottish football who, as the game is a key component of the fabric of Scottish society, have to live with sectarianism's effects; and the Scottish Government itself (who have hidden behind the 'FIFA will not allow us to interfere' excuse, despite arguing for an independence vote to enable Scotland to run itself). This would require an understanding that by now, with the old Rangers no longer in existence and with the very integrity of the game in serious question, the perception that sectarianism sells, that sectarianism makes money, is false, even though, as I will argue, such a perception continues to be very influential in decision-making within Scottish football.

Quite the reverse; sectarianism not only does not sell, it eventually destroys all those who promote, allow or enable its use for short-term commercial gain. You would think that now, with the consequences of a false perception staring them in the face, Rangers' demise would be seized on to replace them with something completely different in attitude and approach. However, the message that sectarianism does not sell does not seem yet to have been realised and internalised. Instead, we had the football authorities talking about league reconstruction to try and restore the failed Rangers model back into the top levels of the game as soon as possible. We had the new owner of the new club called The Rangers trying (and succeeding) in selling tickets on the back of maintaining the same truculent traditions that were the underlying cause of Rangers' demise in what appears to be a headlong rush by all stakeholders (bar the supporters of other clubs) to get back to business as usual leading to more failure (as usual).

THE NEED FOR CHANGE

The reality is that there is no quick cure, there are no easy answers and there is much work to be done by all the stakeholders. I believe the following are the issues that need to be addressed or are change-bringing factors that will determine the future role of sectarianism in Scottish football.

To *the SFA as governors* I say, 'Explore and establish what your job is and *do it* or step aside!' Let those who can, undertake the following:

- Recognise that, even without the financial drivers, sectarianism in the sense of wanting to belong to a group is a normal human condition that requires rules and regulations in a transparent and accountable regime that must deter or prevent the creation of bias to a degree that corrupts. Create such a regime based on fair play, financial as in UEFA rules and ethically through the fair running of the game. I would, for example, look at making refereeing a service more responsive to the clubs and supporters who ultimately pay them than the SFA who train and appoint them. However, and most importantly, police the rules and processes for adherence in order to discourage skullduggery.

- Create a proper system of checks and balances between yourselves and the various Leagues (although preferably only one league body), where the SFA makes sure that sporting integrity is not hostage to, or violated by, commercial deals entered by the Leagues, all working to a clear governance structure.
- Establish your purpose through a clear mission statement that separates roles and responsibilities between yourselves and the Leagues, and if a changing football-ing world and markets suggest the purpose of serving the Scottish game requires your absorption into something greater then do so for the good of Scottish football.
- Above all, 'Be Honest' – you have nothing fear.

To *the Leagues as providers of the game* I say, 'Scotland has one of, if not the, highest record of match-day goers in Europe, if not the world – do not forget our love of the game, for love never fails.' The Scots want to watch fair competition, not Goliath slaying David week in, week out. Work on providing a competitive league but in particular look at removing not only what I believe to be one of the biggest 'skew' factors, but one of the reasons why Rangers in 2007–8 took the decision that history will I am sure show, that why they ultimately failed was to pursue UEFA Champions League money. The rewards for qualification are so high and the con-sequences of failure so dire in competitive terms that they not only encourage clubs to act foolishly, but render the league uncompetitive. A more equitable distribution of Champions League earnings (that will not realistically affect the unlikely pros-pect of a Scottish club winning the Champions League) should be looked at. Also remember that the core business of football is sport, and that for a sport to be a sport it must have integrity – supporters must believe it to be fair and that it will obey its own rules. If there is no integrity there is no sport and so no business.

To *the mainstream media* I say in the words of former Celtic Chairman John Reid (in a different context), 'Those days have gone': those days of faithfully regurgitating what has been passed on by a club's Public Relations department have gone. Those days of unthinking acceptance of what appears in print, if it is ill thought out non-sense, particularly carrying bias from one side of the sectarian divide for or against the other, like a big toe being dipped into a pool of piranhas, is immediately savaged by the Twitterati and stripped to the bone. Your audience is smarter, more articulate and educated than days of yore. My advice here is, 'If you cannot beat them, join them, or retire.'

To *the supporters of Scottish football* I say, 'Take a bow – but continue to organise.' It is now a matter of record how supporters throughout Scotland fought to maintain the integrity of Scottish football by refusing to buy season tickets until the SPL reached the right decision on the footballing fate of Glasgow Rangers. That hon-ourable stance was reflected throughout all professional divisions to the credit of all clubs. As a result of their stance, supporters have established themselves as main stakeholders in the game and we are now seeing further initiatives from, for example, FansFirst Scotland (http://fansfirstscotland.com) in the shape of a 49-page FansFirst plan following principles that make footballing and business sense. Separately, Supporters Direct (http://www.supporters-direct.org/homepage/links/euro-groups/), which networks Trusts (provident societies) within a number of professional and semi-professional clubs, has been galvanised by events and is setting up a network of Scottish fans with government money. Through new initiatives like their 'Fans Parliament and Roadshow' they will provide an opportunity for everyday supporters to get involved in the future of Scottish football. Do so.

To *the Scottish Government* I say, 'Stop hiding behind the FIFA rules about governments not interfering in football and find ways to get involved.' The UK Government managed to do it in 2008 in England when they established an All-Party Parliamentary Football group, so why not the Scottish Government? In February 2012 the First Minister, when asked about HMRC and Glasgow Rangers, was reported (BBC News 2012) as saying:

> Equally, they've [the HMRC] got to have cognisance of the fact that we're talking about a huge institution, part of the fabric of the Scottish nation, as well as Scottish football, and everybody realises that.

It almost beggars belief that a Government holding that view refuses (at least in public) to get involved in addressing the issues surrounding Rangers and Scottish football. The First Minister's view also suggests a fear of the unwanted social consequences of what would happen if Rangers folded, certainly one expressed by Stewart Regan, CEO of the SFA (BBC Sport 2012).

That fear depends on the personal perception one holds of Rangers supporters and mine is coloured (as is everyone's, so they will differ) by their life experience. Are the guys who let me skip the long queue back in the fifties going to turn into a mob? Are the many Rangers supporters I have met in my working and social life going to do the same? Are the good Rangers-supporting lads that my boys have played football with and against potential social vandals? Will there be social unrest to a degree that civil authority cannot cope? Not if my experience is an indicator. That there are Rangers supporters who hold narrow intolerant views of Catholics I have no doubt, and the characteristics of such folk are not confined to Rangers supporters. However, what cannot be denied is that Glasgow Rangers before their demise provided a totem around which malevolent sectarianism could gather and give the impression of being many. When in 2007–8 Rangers were under the microscope for their supporters singing 'The Famine Song', it was noticeable that in telling their support to desist they never condemned the song itself, just said the supporters could face arrest and distanced themselves from the police decision to do so. Some might say this was just the club pandering to the extreme sectarian element of their support, but given what we now know of Rangers' precarious financial situation in 2008, there can be no doubt that the loss of the money ('the bigot pound' in Celtic vernacular), even if only from say 10 per cent of their 40,000 regular supporters, at around £2 million a year, is a price they could not afford to pay.

CONCLUSIONS

Roll forward to late summer 2012 and the new owner of The Rangers, phoenixed from the ashes of the old, has had to use the same traditional truculent sectarian mindset in order to finance his plans for the future of the club. It may be a new company and club but its dependence on the bigot pound seems not to have changed. This is where the Scottish Government can play its part in re-weaving the social fabric of Scotland, by recognising, with the rest of Scotland and Rangers, that culturally they have malevolent sectarian issues that they may need financial help to deal with. This would require the Scottish Government to get together with the SFA and the club to set out a plan to remove The Rangers' financial dependence on the more extreme element of their support.

This could be in the form of a guarantee of payment over a limited period, on agreed verifiable evidence of success, to offset any sales lost by any reduction in their support base arising from the kind of culture change that would make crowd reduction a real possibility. I say 'any' sales lost as the removal of undesirables may encourage the return of Rangers supporters presently discouraged by them, thus rendering any financial guarantee payment redundant.

Sectarianism, from the very narrow perspective of Scottish football, appears to sell, but only at a cost to Scottish society; a cost that Scottish society should tell football, in firm but helpful and constructive terms, it is no longer prepared to bear. I can see fellow Celtic supporters and other citizens being unhappy at the suggestion of using public money to help a club whose debt to the public purse will never be paid. However, it is not about the past, it is about the future, and not just the future of Scottish football but the kind of Scotland we want to leave to our children. Even if the price were five times that suggested, if it led to a football and civil environment where we had football rivalry without the poison, where we had benevolent sectarianism because the linkage to commercial gain had been cut, it would, in my view, be worth every penny.

NOTE

1. This term was coined after a statement by referee Craig Thompson when he failed to award what some believed to have been a 'stonewall' penalty to Celtic in a game against Rangers at Ibrox in October 2009.

REFERENCES

BBC News (2012), 'Celtic hits back at Alex Salmond over Rangers comments', 16 February 2012, http://www.bbc.co.uk/news/uk-scotland-glasgow-west-17067135 (last accessed 30 October 2012).
BBC Sport (2012), 'Rangers: SFA Chief Stewart Regan clarifies "social unrest" concerns', 5 July 2012, http://www.bbc.co.uk/sport/0/football/18719894 (last accessed 30 October 2012).

14 Sectarianism and Scottish Football: A Rangers Perspective

Alasdair McKillop

INTRODUCTION

Rangers and Celtic occupy an unenviable position at the centre of most popular and academic considerations of sectarianism in modern Scotland. Although the debate has undergone changes in intensity and prominence – from 'just a boys' game' (Bruce 1985) to 'Scotland's shame' (MacMillan 2000) – the clubs have usually garnered more than their fair share of attention. A survey carried out for Glasgow City Council (NFO Social Research 2003) concluded, 'The rivalry between Rangers and Celtic was most commonly seen as the way in which the sectarian divide in Glasgow is sustained.' In addition, it found 48 per cent of respondents 'strongly agreed' or 'agreed' that sectarianism 'is almost entirely confined to football'. Michael Rosie (2004: 4), on the other hand, consciously chose to exclude the Old Firm from his study of sectarianism because the rivalry 'stands as a distorting mirror to broader Scottish society'.

Steve Bruce (2011) has argued that football-related controversies 'should not be allowed to dominate or distort perceptions of the Scots, or of Scottish culture'. The work of Bruce (1985) and Rosie (2004) has been characterised by their reliance on empirical data. They were correct to warn of the possible distortions created by viewing sectarianism solely through the prism of the Old Firm rivalry but it remains impossible to ignore completely. Recent incidents and crimes, particularly the disgraceful targeting of high-profile figures associated with Celtic, have led to a level of debate that surpasses previous periods in its intensity. This culminated in new legislation designed to tackle offensive behaviour at football and online which became law in March 2012. Despite the title, the legislation's focus was assumed to be sectarianism, which the media often conflated with offensive behaviour (Goodall 2011).

A few 'Rangers-minded' observations might be made about the contours of the general debate. First, the survey of sectarianism in Glasgow (NFO Social Research 2003) found that 147 of the 1,029 respondents had been physically *attacked* in the last five years. Of these, fourteen felt it was because of their football team and seven because of their religion – three were Protestant and three were Catholic. Of the eight respondents who felt they had been *threatened* because of their religion, four were Protestant and two were Catholic. Three-quarters of respondents said sectarianism was aimed equally at both Catholics and Protestants, although more respondents said it was mainly anti-Catholic (8 per cent) than mainly anti-Protestant (3 per cent), and available evidence suggests Catholics are more likely to be victims of religiously aggravated crime. But to maintain that the problem can be distilled to anti-Catholicism speaks of preference for indulging in tribal point-scoring rather than addressing the complex interplay of anxieties and experiences of others (see Walker 2012a).

Second, 65 per cent of respondents felt that the term 'fenian' was unacceptable, probably because it is used as a derogatory word for a Catholic. David Edgar (2010), a former spokesman for the Rangers Supporters Trust, has said it is a 'hateful' word. Interestingly, almost as many respondents (61 per cent) thought the term 'hun' was unacceptable, while the journalist Richard Wilson (2012) has recently observed that hun has become the equivalent of fenian. Many Rangers fans feel the word is used with anti-Protestant intent. Regardless, it is certainly hateful yet there doesn't seem to be a similar consensus on its use as there is with 'fenian'. Third, when discussing the sectarian dynamics of the Old Firm rivalry it is commonly asserted that Celtic have a significant number of Protestant supporters while Rangers can count virtually no Catholics as fans. Referring again to the NFO study, it was found that 4 per cent of those who said they were Celtic fans described themselves as Protestant while 5 per cent of those who said they supported Rangers described themselves as Catholic. Clearly there are limits to the conclusions that can be drawn from a single survey but perhaps this assumption needs to be revisited. Both clubs seemingly continue to draw overwhelmingly from distinct religious groups.

Reflecting the views of a support that is both variegated and notoriously fractious is difficult and attempts have been made to acknowledge areas of dispute. The chapter will strive to be forward-looking and positive but also critical where appropriate. The first section explores Rangers fans' long-standing but complex Protestant identity and suggests this has become increasingly problematic and is likely to remain so unless changes are made. The second section considers the impact of recent developments, including legislation, the financial crisis at Rangers and the role of the internet as a new forum for fighting old battles. The conclusion offers some thoughts on future developments.

A PROTESTANT CLUB IN TWENTY-FIRST-CENTURY SCOTLAND?

Rangers have endured sustained criticism when it comes to the sectarian attitudes of some of their fans. A range of organisations, including newspapers, churches, football bodies and charities, have condemned sectarian behaviour. Responding to this, the club have tried to tackle the problem through initiatives such as Pride Over Prejudice and, more recently, Follow With Pride. The guidelines for the latter ask fans to focus more on the history of the club itself as opposed to wider cultural and political associations. Announcements are made before matches about unacceptable singing and in the last ten years action has been taken against more than 3,000 supporters, with more than 550 banned for sectarianism.[1] The club has also participated in summits on sectarianism, become a stakeholder in initiatives such as *Sense Over Sectarianism*, and the former Rangers player Terry Butcher was appointed a trustee of the anti-sectarianism charity Nil By Mouth. In 2011 the club supported the establishment of a national Football Policing Unit and was a participant in a Joint Action Group. These actions recognise the unacceptable behaviour of certain fan elements and the responsibility the club has to try and improve the situation. In the stands, groups such as the Blue Order have emerged in the last decade in an attempt to revive the atmosphere at Ibrox by singing songs and importing European chants that focus more explicitly on the team.

Protestantism remains an important current within the fan culture. For many it is central rather than peripheral or a staging post for intersecting identities such as unionism. It is vibrant when sometimes it has seemed like little more than a role to be performed as part of a ritualistic rivalry with Celtic. Harry Reid (2012), in an article for *The Rangers Standard*,[2] explored the contrast between the image and values he associated with the club in the past and its contemporary low standing. Rangers, he argued, had once embodied much that was good in Scottish Protestantism. He said, 'Rangers had standards and dignity, a sense of pride and self-belief: they were a decent club representing something resolute – aye ready – in the Scottish character and their supporters were honourable people.' Reid was of the opinion that capable and experienced Rangers individuals had failed to offer their services to the club in its hour of utmost need because of the reputation of the fans. This is a powerful indictment of a support that no longer lives up to the best of its traditions.

A number of those who responded to Reid's article lamented what they saw as the Church of Scotland's retreat from public debate and its perceived concern with promoting a middle-class agenda that meant little to those shaped by a robust, popular working-class variety of Protestantism (see also Walker 2012b). There was also disappointment that the Church of Scotland had not entered into the sectarianism debate to defend Rangers fans in the way that the Catholic Church was seen to have defended Celtic fans. This, however, overlooks the Kirk's seeming inability to articulate a cohesive set of values or ideals never mind defend what is, in effect, a very loosely associated group. It is hard to escape the conclusion that the Kirk has felt marginalised and disorientated since the advent of devolution, while its own history in this area probably induces wariness. It has also been argued that the non-hierarchical organisational structure of Presbyterianism doesn't serve it well in an era when a recognised figurehead is an asset in dealing with the incessant demands of the media (Steven 2007). But it might also be asked if Rangers fans have made it easy for the Kirk to intervene and whether this is something that should be desired in the first place? Is an institution that feels as though it is on the back foot likely to come to the aid of a similarly beleaguered group that regularly attracts controversy and condemnation? To this sense of isolation might be added the impression that the community Rangers fans were traditionally drawn from is not well represented in Scottish culture (McKillop 2012a).

These are not new sources of complaint. Back in the 1970s, some fans considered it a betrayal when the Church of Scotland criticised Rangers for not signing Catholics and even then Rangers supporters were noted for having a long-standing defensive mentality. This needs to be addressed but space does not permit it here. What might be said is that Rangers fans have to be smart about the positions they choose to defend. Too much time, energy and credibility has been wasted in the defence of isolated outposts and supposedly integral traditions. The notion that the club is the last bastion for Protestantism in retreat might also contribute to a tendency towards defensiveness and consideration should be given to ways of extricating the club from the wider narrative of Protestant decline.

No real data exists on how different generations of Rangers fans feel about Protestantism but it might be hypothesised that it has more significance for older fans. They are the ones who are most likely to have an attachment formed by sustained interaction with the Kirk while younger generations have had more exposure to a defensive and caricatured version of Protestantism expressed at Ibrox. The biggest problem, however, is not that fans have lost sight of the best of Protestantism but that it has too often been expressed in negative ways. It is difficult to escape the conclusion that this has done serious damage to the reputation of both club and fans. Graham Walker (1990) traced the origins of cruder, anti-Catholic sentiments on the terraces back to the 1960s. If the generational divide exists then it should be a source of dismay that those with a genuine attachment to the best of Protestantism were also the same generations who watched it sour. It is now twenty-three years since Rangers signed Maurice Johnston and more than just an ever-dwindling minority within the Rangers support would do well to remember that fact.

That a sense of Protestant identity has intersected with support for Ulster unionism also seems to have alienated fans of other teams and none. This perhaps prompted Alan Bairner (2012), writing for *The Rangers Standard*, to ask, 'What did the Battle of the Boyne really matter to those of us brought up in the Kirk?' It might be suggested that some of the iconography and attitudes exhibited at Ibrox would have been anathema to a Kirk which was part of an establishment worried about Scotland catching the Ulster virus. His article prompted the prominent Rangers fan John DC Gow (2012)[3] to argue, 'the truth is that much of the "Protestantism" that many Rangers fans profess, isn't in any way associated with Christianity in any spiritual sense. It's a form of Protestantism that has no real foundation except historical dates and obsessions.' This would seem to be in tune with recorded comments from Rangers fans about the Church of Scotland (Esplin 2000). Reverberations from Northern Irish loyalism might also contribute to the default defensiveness noted above (Giulianotti 2007).

There would appear to be two options. First, Rangers fans take a definitive post-Protestant turn and eradicate any attachment to Protestantism because it has too often been expressed as anti-Catholicism. This would be an extreme course of action and it would be a sad development for many fans – although it should be noted that others would welcome it. The weight of history operating against this outcome is considerable. The second option is that imagination is allied with a greater degree of self-policing to find new ways of positively expressing a sense of Protestant heritage and identity. This is clearly possible: observe the way the 'Billy Boys' song has almost completely disappeared. The characteristics described by Reid seem to have been lost in the reckless pursuit of success and an increasingly damaging rivalry with Celtic. It might be suggested that the writing of some sort of fans' charter, which outlines what is expected of a Ranger in terms of values and behaviour, would be a useful tool for changing attitudes. This could draw on the values often articulated by fans but make them less abstract. Potentially it could help with self-policing and contribute to the club's rebuilding by drawing on the best of the past. A culture of aspiring to be better has been lost and needs to be rediscovered.

OLD BATTLES, NEW TERRAIN

For many people, support for Rangers or Celtic has become a means of expressing deeply held identities and cultural affinities that seem to be discounted in much public discourse. Indeed, there was concern that the SNP Government's recent legislation could complicate the expression of legitimate identities shaped by connections with Ireland, a point made in a number of submissions to the Justice Committee.[4] The next few years, however, contain the potential for the support in general to be cast adrift in cultural and political terms and this might have profound consequences. What has been called a shared 'popular culture of the Irish Question' (Walker 2001) could see the Old Firm's relationship with Scottish society complicated still further in the context of independence. Such a scenario might see older identities and associations framed as problematic and anachronistic, something to be discounted as people are encouraged to celebrate a simplified Scottish identity. The SNP Government's stance on sectarianism has been compared unfavourably to that of its Labour–Liberal Democrat predecessor, with one commentator suggesting that tackling the problem wasn't seen as politically beneficial either in the short term or in relation to the SNP's objective of securing independence (Gallagher 2009). Tom Gallagher (2012) argued the recent financial crisis at Rangers offered the SNP an opportunity to demonstrate that the party was serious about the idea of a 'social union' post-independence by supporting a club that represented 'organized cultural Britishness'. This has largely failed to materialise, although the minority of Scottish nationalists within the Rangers support would surely have welcomed it.[5]

A number of recent incidents have added to a rivalry that already had an abundance of historical grievances. The first significant development was Rangers fans singing the 'Famine Song', which included the line 'the famine is over, why don't you go home?' This was a poorly conceived terrace chant directed at Celtic fans which drew understandable condemnation from a range of sources. Some commentators argued that this was evidence of the acceptability of anti-Irish racism in Scottish society (MacMillan 2011). It is notable that the same commentators had previously stated that Scotland's problem was simply anti-Catholicism (see

MacMillan 2000). Thankfully, the song has been dropped from the repertoire of the Ibrox choir, although it continues to be mentioned frequently in criticism of the fans. Recent events that culminated in Rangers playing in Division Three have heralded a new era in Old Firm relations. The lack of regular encounters for at least three years – barring league reconstruction or meetings in cup competitions – promises to have unpredictable results but has been welcomed by some (Gow 2012). The vocabulary of the rivalry will probably change in the short term but continued triumphalism from Celtic fans and some Scottish nationalists – particularly claims that Rangers are dead (see Small 2012) – will only lead to bitterness and the creation of new fault-lines, and the attitudes of those eager to write the obituary of a popular social institution deserve to be scrutinised. Despite the lack of competitive encounters, the hostilities seem certain to continue online.

The internet has given new life to some old antagonisms and created a space where grievances can be magnified and manufactured: it has arguably been detrimental to the relationship between the two sets of fans. The anonymity and distance afforded by this type of interaction has lent itself to extremism, moral posturing and aggression which contrast with a culture of sociable interaction in other areas of life. A culture of easy offence and tale-telling has been encouraged (see Waiton in this volume), yet it was notable that the communications aspect of the SNP's legislation was more readily accepted than its offensive behaviour counterpart. Twitter, Facebook and message boards such as *Follow Follow* and *Kerrydale Street* allow fans to congregate and discuss their respective clubs. There is a democratic aspect to them and it would be wrong to deny their many positive attributes. Some of the comment is informed, funny and entertaining but some of it is most certainly not. The notion that Rangers fans have a monopoly on hatred can be quickly dispelled by noting the abuse and bigotry aimed in their direction – this is particularly true for prominent fans such as Gow and Chris Graham.[6]

Operating alongside these sites are blogs such as that of the Scottish-born, Irish-based Phil Mac Giolla Bhain (2012). He has cultivated a following among some Celtic fans though his standing among the wider support is difficult to gauge. Although his background as a journalist gives him a veneer of respectability, 'The Incubator' is a particularly crude blog containing references to breeding and genetics suggesting that Rangers fans were the product of a criminally insane murderer and a ten thousand pound gorilla and that 'even police dogs would contract diseases if they got their teeth into them'. In addition, Rangers fans are regularly described as fascists, racists or members of a subculture. Ironically, Mac Giolla Bhain has been one of the most vocal when it comes to denouncing Rangers fans and Scottish society for what he sees as their hatred.

Despite the claims of Mac Giolla Bhain and his adherents that he is excluded from mainstream discussion for challenging the status quo and providing his particular narrative of the Irish experience in Scotland, it is a source of anger and frustration among some Rangers fans that he is occasionally afforded a platform or praised by key commentators (see Hassan 2012; McKenna 2012). The fact that Mac Giolla Bhain continues to be entertained is viewed by some as an indication of the distorted thinking when it comes to bigotry.

CONCLUSIONS

There is a need to acknowledge positive developments rather than focus relentlessly on the actions of small minorities who continue to indulge in bad behaviour. This encourages a sense of defiance that often finds expression in the kind of behaviour that critics claim to want to eradicate. It might be suggested that the focus on the undeniable but often magnified misdemeanours of Rangers fans has conveniently allowed others to escape from serious scrutiny of questionable aspects of their own culture and behaviour. We have reached the point where the facile 'Rangers are the worst offenders' argument is simply an abdication of responsibility on the part of others. Rangers fans didn't create the new 'offensive behaviour' environment but they certainly expect scrutiny to fall on everyone equally – a point made by both the club and the Rangers Supporters Assembly in submissions to the Justice Committee.

Rangers fans should utilise the new sense of collective identification to have wide-ranging and challenging discussions about what it means to support Rangers. What values and identities should be held in common? Are the old anchors such as Protestantism and unionism still relevant? Are there new and positive ways that old traditions can be acknowledged that don't give voice to hatred of others or act to exclude those who don't subscribe to them? These are undeniably challenging questions but the culture isn't static and neither should it be. The popularity of the 'Gallant Pioneers'[7] in recent years testifies that the fans are willing to embrace new themes and use a rich history to back their team in the present day. In future, more might be done to acknowledge the roots of the club and support in industrial Glasgow (see McKillop 2012b; Esplin and Walker 2011). A culture that has the strength to evolve is preferable to one that shuts down debate and sinks under the weight of its own outdated dogma.

Arguably we have reached the limit of the coercive apparatus put in place by the football authorities and the state. This is unlikely to be dismantled in the near future and should continue to have some limited utility when it comes to prosecuting violent offences or cracking down on flagrant bad behaviour. Proscribing forms of behaviour and cultural expression are unlikely to prove enduring because they will not be popularly accepted and further change is only likely to come from the fans through a long-term process of debate. It is hard to identify what else Rangers and Celtic can do to prevent bad behaviour by their fans but facilitating discussions might be one of the options left to those who run the clubs. The political, social and economic dynamics that characterise Scottish society have changed radically since the advent of the Old Firm rivalry. At a time of converging socio-economic profiles and relative peace in Northern Ireland, songs of hate and support for violence are no more than songs of hate and support for violence. The supposed structures of justification have been removed. It's time to move on.

NOTES

1. This information was contained in the Written Submission from Rangers Football Club to the Justice Committee of the Scottish Parliament when it was considering the Offensive

Behaviour at Football and Threatening Communications (Scotland) Bill and can be accessed at: http://www.scottish.parliament.uk/S4_JusticeCommittee/Inquiries/OB59._Rangers_ Football_Club.pdf (last accessed 16 August 2012).
2. Harry Reid is a former editor of *The Herald* and author of books on the Church of Scotland and Scottish Football. *The Rangers Standard* is a website created by a group of supporters which brings together fans, academics and journalists with the objective of encouraging positive and path-breaking thinking about Rangers.
3. John DC Gow is a popular blogger, writer for ESPN and a co-creator of *The Rangers Standard*.
4. Submissions to the Justice Committee can be accessed at: http://www.scottish.parliament.uk/ parliamentarybusiness/CurrentCommittees/31448.aspx (last accessed 16 August 2012).
5. Based on personal conversations.
6. Chris Graham is a blogger and co-creator of *The Rangers Standard* who regularly appears across the media to discuss Rangers.
7. The popular name for those who founded the club in 1872.

REFERENCES

Bairner, A. (2012), 'The Sash we Never Sang', *The Rangers Standard*, 9 July 2012, http://www. therangersstandard.co.uk/index.php/articles/rfc-politics/139-the-sash-we-never-sang (last accessed 15 August 2012).
Bruce, S. (1985), *No Pope of Rome! Anti-Catholicism in Modern Scotland*, Edinburgh: Mainstream.
Bruce, S. (2011), 'Scottish sectarianism? Let's lay this myth to rest', *Comment is Free*, 24 April 2011, http://www.guardian.co.uk/commentisfree/belief/2011/apr/24/scotland-sectarianism-research-data (last accessed 16 August 2012).
Edgar, D. (2010), *21st Century Blue: Being a Bear in the Modern World*, Derby: DB Publishing.
Esplin, R. (2000), *Down the Copland Road*, Glendaruel: Argyll Publishing.
Esplin, R. and Walker, G. (2011), *The Official Biography of Rangers*, London: Hatchette Scotland.
Gallagher, T. (2012), 'Rangers: an Elementary Test of the Social Union', *Scotzine*, 14 February 2012, http://www.scotzine.com/2012/02/rangers-an-elementary-test-of-the-social-union/ (last accessed 16 August 2012).
Gallagher, T. (2009), *The Illusion of Freedom: Scotland Under Nationalism*, London: Hurst & Co.
Giulianotti, R. (2007), 'Popular Culture, Social Identities, and Internal/External Cultural Politics: The Case of Rangers Supporters in Scottish Football', *Identities*, 14: 4, 257–84.
Goodall, K. (September 2011), 'Tackling Sectarianism Through the Criminal Law', *Edinburgh Law Review*, 15: 3, 423–7.
Gow, J. (2012), 'No More Old Firm', *The Rangers Standard*, 23 July 2012, http://www. therangersstandard.co.uk/index.php/articles/current-affairs/145-no-more-old-firm (last accessed 16 August 2012).
Hassan, G. (2012), 'The Wave of Democratic Protest that Changed Scottish Football will Change Society', *The Scotsman*, 4 August 2012, http://www.gerryhassan.com/ uncategorized/2439/ (unedited version), (last accessed 16 August 2012).
Mac Giolla Bhain, P. (2012), 'The Incubator', *Phil Mac Giolla Bhain*, 20 April, http://www. philmacgiollabhain.ie/the-incubator/ (last accessed 16 August).
McKenna, K. (2012), 'Glasgow Rangers FC represented everything that made working-class Protestant Scotland proud to be British. How was the football club reduced to this state?', *New Statesman*, 13 June 2012.
McKillop, A. (2012a), 'The Tribe: Rangers and Scottish Literature', *Scottish Review*, 8 June, http://www.scottishreview.net/AlasdairMcKillop281.shtml (last accessed 16 August 2012).
McKillop, A. (2012b), 'Glasgow Rangers: Clyde Built', *The Rangers Standard*, 30 August 2012,

http://therangersstandard.co.uk/index.php/articles/club-history/159-glasgow-rangers-clyde-built (last accessed 24 January 2013).

MacMillan, J. (2011), 'Is it now officially OK to sing anti-Irish, anti-Catholic hate songs in Scottish football stadiums?', *The Telegraph*, 29 March 2011, http://blogs.telegraph.co.uk/culture/jmacmillan/100052373/is-it-now-officially-ok-to-sing-anti-irish-anti-catholic-hate-songs-in-scottishs-football-stadiums/ (last accessed 27 August 2012).

MacMillan, J. (2000), 'Scotland's Shame', in T. M. Devine (ed.), *Scotland's Shame? Bigotry and Sectarianism in Modern Scotland*, Edinburgh: Mainstream, pp. 13–24.

NFO Social Research (2003), Sectarianism in Glasgow – Final Report, Glasgow: Glasgow City Council.

Reid, H. (2012), 'Rangers, Protestantism and Scottish Society', *The Rangers Standard*, 4 July 2012, http://www.therangersstandard.co.uk/index.php/articles/rfc-politics/136-rangers-protestantism-and-scottish-society (last accessed 16 August 2012).

Rosie, M. (2004), *The Sectarian Myth in Scotland: Of Bitter Memory and Bigotry*, Basingstoke: Palgrave Macmillan.

Small, M. (2012), '"Rangers" starting in the lowest league is a victory for fans over an inept elite', *Comment is Free*, 16 July 2012, http://www.guardian.co.uk/commentisfree/2012/jul/16/rangers-lowest-league-victory-fans (last accessed 2012).

Steven, M. (2007), 'The Place of Religion in Devolved Scottish Politics: An Interest Group Analysis of the Church of Scotland and Scottish Catholic Church', *Scottish Affairs*, 58: Winter, 96–110.

Walker, G. (2001), 'Identity Questions in Contemporary Scotland: Faith, Football and Future Prospects', *Contemporary British History*, 15: 1, 41–60.

Walker, G. (2012a), 'Scotland's Sectarian Problem: Irish Answers?', *The Political Quarterly*, 83: 2, 374–83.

Walker, G. (2012b), 'The Religious Factor', in T. M. Devine and J. Wormald (eds), *The Oxford Handbook of Modern Scottish History*, Oxford: Oxford University Press, pp. 585–601.

Walker, G. (1990), 'There's not a team like the Glasgow Rangers: Football and Religious Identity in Scotland', in G. Walker and T. Gallagher (eds), *Sermons and Battle Hymns: Protestant Popular Culture in Modern Scotland*, Edinburgh: Edinburgh University Press, pp. 137–59.

Wilson, R. (2012), *Inside the Divide: One City, Two Teams, the Old Firm*, Edinburgh: Canongate.

Conclusions

15 Necessary Debates and Future Research and Policy Imperatives

John Flint and John Kelly

ACADEMIC CONTRIBUTION AND CONSTRUCTIVE DIALOGUE

One of the objectives of this book has been to ensure that academics and fans contribute significantly and constructively to debates about bigotry, football and Scotland. We believe that the contributions within this volume demonstrate the value of historically and contextually based academic approaches informed by contemporary evidence. We have sought to nurture some debates (for example, about the prevalence of sectarianism in modern Scottish life) which were at risk of becoming ossified or defined through increasingly entrenched positions. There will always be legitimate disputes about approaches, analytical frameworks and methods used, and although some room for ideological differences inevitably remains, a degree of consensus is essential. As Billig (1996: 53) noted:

> In order for two people to argue a point, they must agree upon far more than they disagree about. For instance, they must agree upon a common language . . . Therefore, an argument, like a game, depends on a wide area of agreement in order for the disagreements to be aired.

Agreement of language is a necessary starting point or else there can be no argument, never mind a positive outcome, but given that universal accord is unlikely, perhaps we can conciliate by adapting a pearl of wisdom from one of sociology's great figures, Erving Goffman: perhaps it is better to clothe the children in an ill-fitting coat that keeps them warm than let them shiver waiting for the perfect fit. We therefore avoid the futile wait for the perfect coat, compromising instead with a plea to all parties to at least be conceptually clear about their analytical definitions.

While some religious-based identities are by their nature sectarian, seeking to solve ethno-religious bigotry by being intolerant of the sectarian identities of others is no solution. Having a sectarian identity is legitimate. The actual problem is expressing intolerance towards an 'other' because of their sectarian identity.

Unfortunately, it is unremarkable for many in Scotland to regard the solution to 'sectarianism' to be further acts of latent intolerance. Isolated acts of terror like those witnessed in 2011 are clearly inexcusable. But equally inexcusable, yet imperceptible, is the sleepwalking prejudices of sections of Scotland's football fans, its media and its governing bodies, who continue trying to solve ethno-religious prejudice by inadvertently engaging in it themselves.

We believe that this book demonstrates the value of inter-disciplinary dialogue, discussing points of significant difference, sometimes with diametrically opposed positions, but with constructive engagement and greater reflexivity about our own standpoint and genuine attempts to better understand the arguments and allegiances of others. At the risk of being overly ambitious, we hope this collection will act as a catalyst for further academic (and hopefully fan) co-operation that can ensure that the contribution of the academy is innovative, relevant and fan-centred in the years ahead. As editors, and active football fans with different club allegiances, we have learnt a lot from each other and from all of the contributors, and we are convinced that this starting position of openness and willingness to engage and be challenged can enable us all to move on from some rather stale, and ultimately futile, pronouncements of superiority or certainty.

RETHINKING GEOGRAPHICAL, HISTORICAL AND SOCIAL CONTEXTS

The contributions compel us to rethink and challenge the geographical, historical and social contexts framing bigotry and football in Scotland. For example, the chapters by Michael Rosie and John Kelly require us to recognise that sectarianism is not exclusive to the west of Scotland, nor that attitudes towards sectarianism can be confined to studies of Celtic and Rangers supporters. Contributors have also illustrated the importance of recognising the historical and political relationship between Ireland and Britain in influencing how sectarianism originated, how it has been constructed and how it is commonly anchored in the collective consciousness of opinion formers in Scotland. There is a need to acknowledge that new spaces for sectarianism, and its regulation, are becoming more prominent, including the use of social media and fora. We should also recognise the increasing use of sport for collective commemorations and remembrance within popular cultural activities like football, and the narratives, counter-narratives and controversies that these engender (Silk and Falcous 2005; Kelly in press). This might involve distinguishing ethno-religious bigotry from political difference and acknowledging everyone's right to object to being incorporated by proxy into endorsing a cause and/or the particular way it is officially framed (as Rio Ferdinand and Jason Roberts did so publicly with the Kick it Out T-shirt campaign in 2012 with regard to anti-racism).

It is also necessary to analyse contemporary events through an historically sensitive lens and to understand the centrality of history and memory to constructions of identity. Andrew Davies powerfully illustrates how contemporary manifestations of sectarian conduct, and the policing and regulation of such conduct, have their precedents in the 1920s and 1930s. John Flint and Ryan Powell argue that a discourse of living in an enlightened modern age and the primacy given to commerce in rejecting archaic 'sectarian' identities are nothing new. John Kelly, Joseph M. Bradley and Alasdair McKillop persuasively demonstrate how historical understandings are inherent to the identities of many football supporters of Scotland's clubs. Acknowledging this, and recognising the legitimacy of these identities, is challenging, necessitating as it does difficult questions about diversity, multiculturalism and the plurality of 'Scottishness' in Scotland. However, it also challenges the belief that such identities could and should simply be 'swept into the dustbin of history' (Scottish Executive 2006: 1), that they are irrelevant stereotypes or that sectarianism is merely or primarily an issue of urban disorder and ninety-minute bigotry.

CONSTRUCTING AND GOVERNING 'SECTARIANISM' AND FOOTBALL

One of the most positive developments in debates about the new legislative framework in Scotland has been a broadening out of discussions about fundamental rights and responsibilities relating to the expression or degradation of identities and allegiances within the spaces of Scottish football. Stuart Waiton and Paul Davis disagree about the moral underpinnings constituting offensiveness and free speech and the consequent legitimacy of regulation. However, they are united in attempting to place these debates within fundamentally important moral, philosophical and political questions.

Similarly, Niall Hamilton-Smith, David McArdle, Irene A. Reid, Kay Goodall and Margaret Malloch contribute to a reinvigorated exploration about definitions and concepts within and beyond legal terminology and the media. As Joe Crawford points out, the ability to name the world is primarily what is at stake in debates about bigotry in Scotland, and this includes Scotland moving out of its comfort zone as a self-perceived tolerant nation.

NEGLECTED PERSPECTIVES

A key objective of this book has been to identify perspectives that have been, to date, neglected in dominant discourses. Kay Goodall and Margaret Malloch emphasise that gender is one such dimension. In the initial aftermath of the 2010–11 season there was a brief flurry of interest in wider issues such as domestic violence and Scotland's relationship with alcohol. Political and media interest in these issues have somewhat receded but Goodall and Malloch powerfully illustrate how sectarianism impacts on women in Scotland and how competing views within debates about bigotry have failed to address issues of power and domination along gender lines when framing ethno-religious bigotry.

Similarly, Joe Crawford and several other contributors seek to highlight the centrality of social class and hegemonic neoliberal rationalities in the construction of sectarianism. In moving beyond defining anti-sectarianism as yet another moral panic, these contributors show how the particular construction of sectarianism and new forms of legal regulation target the allegiances and conduct of working-class football supporters. They challenge the economic rationalities and assumptions that prominent Scottish football clubs and Scottish football institutions have premised their strategies on, as Patrick McVey shows in the case of Rangers FC, and suggest that interests and solidarities should not simply be based on club affiliations.

Finally, we wanted to demonstrate how football supporters themselves could contribute, on an equal basis, to an academic collection like this and how academics, as much as politicians and football authorities, need to learn from supporters' perspectives. In addition to a number of academic contributors being active fans, both Patrick McVey and Alasdair McKillop give fan-centred accounts providing clear evidence of the ability of supporters to develop articulate, nuanced and constructive positions which refute lazy stereotypes of Old Firm football fans and which suggest there is considerable potential for supporters to develop greater understanding of opposing positions and to be more reflective and critical of their own. Both McVey and McKillop are also careful to indicate that neither themselves, nor anyone else, can accurately claim to speak on behalf of all supporters, given the diversity of perspectives on these issues within the supporter base of all clubs in Scotland.

TOWARDS A WAY FORWARD

How then can a positive agenda be taken forward to tackle bigotry in Scottish football, to reinvigorate our national game and to acknowledge, if not resolve, wider issues of conflict and inequality in Scottish society? One key theme to emerge is empowerment. This requires, firstly, a more explicit acknowledgement of continuing forms of inequality in Scotland, in terms of ethno-religious identity, gender and social class. It also includes a recognition that the solutions to bigotry and disorder in Scottish football may, in part, lie with football supporters themselves but that they require radical new models and leadership, whether this be through community ownership of clubs or the genuine willingness of club and fan officials to support those fans attempting to address sectarianism. The present crisis in the Scottish game is both undeniable and an opportunity to link attempts to reduce bigotry with a fundamental rethinking of the role of football in Scottish life and how groups within Scotland wish the national game to reflect their nation and its heterogeneity, exposing prejudice but celebrating rather than blaming difference.

These challenges are dependent on achieving greater conceptual clarity and removing some of the ambiguity in current thinking. For example, and of particular importance in the context of the forthcoming referendum campaign, we need to state categorically that particular religious and political identities – Catholicism, Protestantism, unionism, republicanism and Irish and British allegiances, and their expressions – are not, in themselves, bigoted and should not be conflated as forms of sectarianism as the term is understood in Scotland. As one of us (John Kelly) and Joseph M. Bradley argue, the idea of a multicultural and tolerant modern Scotland has to include these identities and the right of our citizens to celebrate these identities even if others regard them as questionable, inauthentic, anachronistic or even oppositional to some imagined homogeneous 'Scottishness'. Similarly, commentators have to recognise the diversity of opinions among the supporters of each club and avoid seeking to impose one legitimate form of belonging (see Alasdair McKillop's chapter for an exploration of this issue). There is also a need for greater conceptual clarity about the extent to which sectarianism is or is not different from other forms of racism or hate crime and how we can learn from responses to these related definitions, including the recent controversies in England involving John Terry and Luis Suárez and concerns about the efficacy of anti-racism campaigns.

As Irene A. Reid and other contributors state, we need to broaden the scope and definitions of the problems that we seek to address. Rather than closing down sectarianism as a form of temporary and essentially meaningless urban disorder, we should instead open up avenues of exploration about the wider causes and cultural manifestations of this disorder, including poverty, alcohol and domestic violence, and the social dynamics that continue to affect particular groups, including women, which are often neglected in current debates. Niall Hamilton-Smith and David McArdle and Kay Goodall and Margaret Malloch have clearly demonstrated the limitations of legal regulation, epitomised in the uneven development of Football Banning Orders, which have increased by 50 per cent in the last twelve months (Duguid 2012), and the lack of convictions using the new legislation on online sectarian offences (Farrell 2012). This is not to simplistically dismiss the potential role for such legal mechanisms, but rather to argue that there are broader issues that cannot be adequately resolved through the law alone.

These debates and issues are not unique to Scotland. For example, issues about offensive songs have arisen recently in the very different contexts of Tottenham Hotspur Football Club (BBC News 2012) and South Africa (BBC News 2010). In terms of work on racism, we could learn one obvious lesson. Just because 'race' is no longer accepted as legitimate justification for any meaningful difference, does not mean racism no longer exists. To assert such a causal relationship would be ridiculous. Just because religious observance (even labelling) might be reduced or is no longer meaningful, does not mean hatred based on irrational beliefs about religion or the religious person (irrespective of the reality of that person being or not being religious) does not occur. Racism does not disappear because there is no meaningful biological difference between ethnic groups. Ethno-religious bigotry does not disappear because there is less (or little) religious observance or an increase in mixed marriages. The religious badge justification for prejudice, like its racial counterpart, spared people the pains of examining the complex economic, cultural, political, psychological and historical conditions that enter into group relations. The condition does not disappear just because people are less religious in practice.

In American culture the term 'African-American' simultaneously signifies both a racial and national symbol: despite 'black' not being explicitly used and despite the possibility of white Africans living in the USA. Likewise in Scotland, 'Irish-Scot' or the Irish in Scotland simultaneously signify both religious (Catholic) and national (Irish and Scottish) symbols. This, of course, is despite the reality of significant numbers of non-Catholic Irish existing in Scotland. More crucially, when Irish-Scot combines with Celtic – or is perceived to – for many, this additional combination incorporates the problematic or, to some, contemptuous Irish republican identity. Viewed in this context, when Celtic are involved, it is difficult for some to untangle Irish Catholicism from Irish republicanism and this may help us understand the subconscious aversion some still have to Irish-Catholic symbols in a football context.

There has been much debate about whether Scotland is or is not like Northern Ireland, and how the changing processes in Northern Ireland have impacted on sectarianism in the Scottish context. Perhaps what we have not done sufficiently is seek to learn about mechanisms for reconciliation, which are still relevant even if the scale of conflict is different. Again, there is a role for leadership here, for example the new Rangers provides an opportunity for Rangers fans to engage more emphatically with the problems of their past as well as continuing to celebrate and protect Rangers' undoubted achievements. This is actually an opportunity for all fans to embrace a new future and this includes Celtic fans. Singing about the IRA or republicanism may not be anti-Protestant and in many instances may be completely legal and culturally legitimate, but it is undoubtedly offensive to many neutrals. This may be the main challenge (among many) facing the implementation of the new Bill. On the one hand we cannot and should not be arresting people for what some deem to be offensive. On the other hand throngs of young men and women singing about the IRA (or UVF in Rangers' case) cannot ignore the wider ideological baggage the IRA and UVF have for many people in Scotland. There should be no surprise among them that others within Scotland tar their fans with the terrorist-supporting label, nor should Celtic fans be surprised when others mistakenly perceive Irish and Catholic signifiers within a Celtic context as 'sectarian'. Celtic and its fans have legitimate and proud reasons for expressing elements of Irish and Catholic identities. Their fans are entitled to hold republican views and there should be no laws outlawing political expression at football matches. But nobody should be surprised when others mistakenly and seamlessly connect Celtic's Irishness, its links with Catholicism and its supporters' Irish republican sympathies with sectarianism.

Those in Scotland who view Irish symbolism pejoratively are often not anti-Irish/Ulster bigots even though their attitudes can occasionally coincide with intolerant attitudes around difference. They simply attach alternative ideological baggage to these symbols. There is a difficult balance to achieve, however. To what extent should diasporic groups abandon their cultural songs and symbols to appease wider sections of the community who often remain ignorant of some of the deeper meanings and traditions, and to what extent should the diaspora groups adapt to ensure they do not offend? This is one of the key questions and should rely more on decency, sensitivity and respect than legal obligations.

As Paul Davies argues, concepts of tolerance and civility are universal and should apply to football supporters as much as any other group of citizens. As Stuart Waiton also suggests, a focus on being offended and a desperate attempt to exaggerate difference and claim moral superiority risks masking other forms of solidarities and shared interests that Joe Crawford and Patrick McVey identify. While a large degree of leeway must be given all groups to interpret meanings for themselves, this is not the same as allowing all groups free rein to simply lay claim to defining terms in some post-modern free-for-all where multiple meanings coexist. Rather, context is everything. As Kennedy (2003: 56) illustrates to those who view the derogatory insult of 'asshole' as the equivalent of the culturally loaded 'nigger'; 'But *asshole* does not carry the ideological baggage that burdens the term *nigger*' (original emphasis). While we cannot discuss this further here, it is worth noting because it shows us that wider contexts ('ideological baggage') shape and determine the meanings of words and insults as opposed to it being the exclusive preserve of the offended to cry wolf. Moreover, it helps us remind ourselves that contextual relations work two ways. First, the historical contexts are required when judging whether or not terms have been used as religious insults or not (such as in debates around the use of 'fenian' and 'hun'). Second, the wider Scottish communities view Irish-Catholic and Ulster-Protestant identities and signifiers as disdainfully 'sectarian' in large part *because* of the context of their respective public demonstrations, which often involve boorish, alcohol-fuelled groups of young males visiting Scotland's towns and cities singing about the IRA or the UVF in the company of bewildered members of the public going about their everyday business.

We also need a new research agenda to improve our understanding. This includes a much more comprehensive and sophisticated understanding of the actual social dynamics within Scottish communities and how football and related allegiances actually play out in relations between groups, including continuing to investigate the question raised by Andrew Davies about the extent to which football is actually a catalyst for greater social division. There is a need to examine how identities develop in the context of Scotland currently grappling with its own sense of identity and political destiny and to ensure that new mechanisms such as the internet and social media are subject to academic scrutiny. We must monitor the impact of the new legislation. Finally, as demonstrated by Michael Rosie, we need to ensure that academics and other stakeholders, including football fans, value the particularities of each other's contributions within a dialogue which is as diverse, challenging and vibrant as the social world of Scotland which it seeks to understand. We hope Allport's (1979: xvii) fear is wrong and that it is not 'easier to smash an atom than a prejudice'.

REFERENCES

Allport, G. (1979), *The Nature of Prejudice*, London: Addison-Wesley.
BBC News (2010), 'South Africa's ANC stops singing "Shoot the Boer"', BBC News, 7 April 2010, http://news.bbc.co.uk/1/hi/world/africa/8607452.stm (last accessed 25 November 2012).
BBC News (2012), 'Tottenham fans continue controversial chanting', BBC News, 9 November 2012, http://www.bbc.co.uk/sport/0/football/20262698 (last accessed 25 November 2012).
Billig, M. (1996), *Arguing and Thinking. A Rhetorical Approach to Social Psychology*, Cambridge: Cambridge University Press.
Duguid, D. (2012), 'Rise of the brawl boys in Scottish football', *The Sun*, 25 November 2012, http://www.thesun.co.uk/sol/homepage/news/scottishnews/4663902/Rise-of-the-brawl-boys-in-Scottish-football.html (last accessed 25 November 2012).

Farrell, M. (2012), 'No convictions secured under law targeting sectarian hatred online', STV News, 5 November 2012, http://news.stv.tv/scotland/198491-no-convictions-secured-under-law-targeting-sectarian-hatred-online/ (last accessed 25 November 2012).

Kelly, J. (in press), 'Popular Culture, Sport and the "Hero"-fication of British Militarism', *Sociology*.

Kennedy, R. (2003), *Nigger: The Strange Career of a Troublesome Word*, New York, NY: First Vintage Books.

Scottish Executive (2006), *Action Plan on Tackling Sectarianism in Scotland*, Edinburgh: Scottish Executive.

Silk, M. and Falcous, M. (2005), 'One day in September/A week in February: Mobilizing American (sporting) nationalism', *Sociology of Sport Journal*, 22: 4, 447–71.

Index

Note: page numbers in italics denote tables or figures